Australian Catholic Histor·

Contacts

General Correspondence, including membership ..... .na renewals, and Journal submissions should be ...ur essed to

The Secretary

ACHS

PO Box A621

Sydney South, NSW, 1235

Enquiries may also be directed to:

secretaryachs@gmail.com

http://australiancatholichistoricalsociety.com.au/

Cover image:
Saint Michael the Archangel Church, Wollombi, photograph John Harrison.
See article page 62.

JOURNAL OF THE AUSTRALIAN CATHOLIC HISTORICAL SOCIETY

JACHS ISSN: 0084-7259

JACHS 40 2019 soft cover ISBN: 978-1-925612-11-0
JACHS 40 2019 hard cover ISBN: 978-1-925612-12-7
JACHS 40 2019 epub ISBN: 978-1-925612-13-4
JACHS 40 2019 pdf ISBN: 978-1-925612-14-1

Editor: James Franklin

**Published by ATF Press Publishing Group under its ATF
Theology imprint
PO Box 234
Brompton
SA 5007
www.atfpress.com**

**Editorial control and subscriptions remain with the Australian
Catholic Historical Society**

www.atfpress.com

Journal of the Australian Catholic Historical Society vol 40 2019

CONTENTS

FATHER ANGELO CONFALONIERI AND THE VIEW FROM PORT ESSINGTON, 1838–1849

Mark McKenna*

At Port Essington, 4000 km from Sydney, between 1838, when Captain Gordon Bremer and second in command, Captain John McArthur, established Victoria Settlement and 1849, when the colony was finally abandoned, the British government conducted a relatively short-lived attempt to settle Australia's tropical north. The naval garrison, which consisted initially of over 200 Royal Marines, was named after the young Queen Victoria.

Predating the settlement of Darwin by three decades, Victoria Settlement was actually the third attempt to secure British settlement in Australia's north. Fort Dundas (1824–9) and Fort Wellington, in Raffles Bay (1827–9) had already failed, when the British government finally decided to take the advice of Phillip Parker King, who, in 1818, had first identified Port Essington as the perfect site for British settlement in northern Australia.

Why Port Essington was established

The British rationale in establishing Victoria Settlement was three-fold. Although Captain Bremer had formally claimed British sovereignty over northern Australia in 1824, throughout the 1820s and 1830s, there was considerable discussion in both London and Sydney as to whether foreign powers were entitled to take possession of points on the north coast of Australia. Henry Ennis described the fragility of Bremer's 1824 claim of sovereignty wonderfully. 'Transported by the feelings associated with Bremer taking possession', Ennis reflected on how this was achieved. Imagine, he said, a small party of Englishmen 'placed at a distance of nearly nineteen thousand miles from home, in a part of the world which had hitherto never been visited by civilized man, and turned, *as it were by magic,* into a British settlement.' It was precisely this *magic*—the raising of the British flag, the reading of an incantation, the toast to the King—which left Bremer's claim to sovereignty exposed.

Without the existence of British marines and officials on the ground, that is without permanent British settlement, British sovereignty in the north was

*   Mark McKenna is Professor of History at the University of Sydney. His books include *From the Edge: Australia's Lost Histories* (2016), ch. 2 of which contains a footnoted version of similar material to the present article. This is the edited text of his talk to the ACHS on 15 Sept 2019.

General view of Port Essington, N.T., Australia, 1839, John McArthur
Source: the National Library of Australia

vulnerable. From a great distance, sovereignty could be asserted, but it could not be easily enforced. As a result, partly to thwart any chance of the Dutch or French settling in the north of Australia, it was decided to establish the naval garrison at Port Essington, which, it was imagined, would soon be followed by waves of settlers taking up land as the settlement expanded.

To bolster arguments for planting out the Dutch and the French, Victoria Settlement was imagined as Australia's new Singapore. These dreams of a settlement that would be a hub for British trade in South-East Asia, would later be transferred to Darwin and they have more recent echoes in the many wild and preposterous schemes to develop Australia's north. As early as the 1820s one Dutch naval officer had argued that any British settlement on the north-coast of Australia would become 'the emporium of the Archipelago of [the] Arafura [Sea]'. The eyes of this British settlement would be focused not on Sydney but on the far more immediate environment of Singapore, China, India and of course, London.

Captain John McArthur, commandant at Port Essington from 1839, after Bremer's departure, perceptively observed that the settlement was established partly to take advantage of the many 'busy pushing capitalists, who are searching every quarter of the globe'.

Given that more than half the ships leaving Sydney in the first four decades of settlement were destined for Asian ports, the idea of a large British trading port thousands of kilometres closer to those trade networks made perfect sense at the time. The execution of this idea, however, was another matter.

From the outset, the settlement was plagued by a number of challenges, poor planning and inadequate support, isolation reinforced by a poorly chosen site for the settlement that was more than 20 kilometres along the harbour from the open sea, rampant disease and the travails of a tropical climate, a hurricane that flattened the settlement only one year after it began, and any number of visitors who wasted no time in spreading their damning and negative conclusions about the settlement. One such visitor was the scientist Thomas Huxley, who arrived onboard Owen Stanley's *Rattlesnake* in 1848, already bored with his voyage at sea. Victoria Settlement, Huxley proclaimed, is

> the most useless, miserable, ill-managed hole in Her Majesty's dominions, it deserves all the abuse that has ever been heaped upon it. It is fit for neither man nor beast. Day and night there is the same fearful damp depressing heat, producing an inconquerable languor and rendering the unhappy resident a prey to ennui and cold brandy-and-water… I can't say more for Port Essington than that it is worse than a ship, and it is no small comfort to know that this is possible.

During its short ten year existence, an impressive cast of visitors passed through, some even taking up residence—shipwrecked priests, artists, scientists, surgeons, naturalists, adventurers and explorers—all of whom kept extensive journals. Despite the settlement's failure, it constitutes one of the most thoroughly documented and neatly encapsulated experiments in the history of British colonization. It reveals much about the attitudes of the British government towards the occupation and settlement of the Australian continent in the mid nineteenth century and their interaction with its indigenous inhabitants – the Iwaidja.

Victoria Settlement was highly unusual in many respects. Because the settlement's numbers never increased to the point where settlers sought to occupy the areas inland from the coast, it represented an unusually peaceful colonial encounter, with only one documented indigenous death due to conflict in the eleven years of settlement. Cultural interaction was therefore largely free of the frontier warfare experienced in other areas of the continent. If there was a perceived threat to the settlement it was not from the Aborigines. The settlement's canons were pointed out to sea. In addition the Aborigines were already accustomed to outsiders, as Makassan fishermen, mostly from Sulawesi, had been fishing for trepang and trading on the north coast of Australia for at least two centuries. There were Makassan words in Indigenous languages, Makassan goods around their campfires, and Makassan blood in their veins. The British were the *second* wave of arrivals, even less permanent a fixture, as it turned out, than the Makassans.

So far as Port Essington's physical environment was concerned, it was a highly contained and unusually fertile field of scientific observation and collection. As the only settlement in northern Australia at the time, it was visited by several naturalists and held a strong attraction for those such as John Gilbert, who lived there in 1840–1 and collected for John Gould, 'while the survey ships *Beagle, Fly* and *Rattlesnake,* all had naturalists on board'. Ludwig Leichhardt was another visitor, arriving in 1845 after an overland journey of 5000 miles that took him almost 16 months to complete, and brought him to tears as he entered the tiny settlement after such a long period of isolation in the bush,

> [We passed through] an open forest [until]… some white houses and the row of snug thatched cottages burst suddenly upon us. I was deeply moved in finding myself again in civilized society, I could scarcely speak, the words growing big with tears and emotion.

During his short time there Leichhardt busied himself collecting.

Indeed, some of the earliest and largest collections of flora and fauna specimens from Australia's north came from Port Essington. The settlement was effectively Britain's window into Australia's tropical environment, one that Charles Firth argues was also of 'outstanding importance in Australian systematic biology'. The journals of the naturalists who visited, and many others including that of the commandant, McArthur, contain valuable lists of bird life in particular, often with detailed descriptions of wing-span, plumage and eye colour. Recording the features of the natural environment was both a scientific obligation and a welcome distraction from the oppressive climate.

As was so often the case throughout the British Empire, preconceived ideas of place were *imposed* on chosen sites of settlement. As in the West Indies, Africa and other parts of the Empire, the first ships to arrive carried pre-fabricated buildings, in this case 'a two-roomed, wooden framed weather board house for the Commandant; a three roomed officers quarters… two men's barracks, a kitchen, storehouse and a utility building to be used as a hospital'. Also on board was a pre-fabricated Church, of which it was claimed, that by merely erecting it, Port Essington would become the epicentre of Christianity for the Arafura Sea. Ominously, before the first ships left Sydney, a large punt that contained the timber and materials to be used for the Church sank before it could be loaded.

The portability and relatively quick erection of pre-fabricated buildings was a testament to the extraordinary mobility and resourcefulness that characterized British imperial expansion. Initially at least, it also revealed a cavalier indifference to the site-specific requirements of design and construction. The British arrived immediately dismissive of the lightweight shade and shelter structures of both Indigenous people and the Makassans. They proceeded to erect their pre-fabricated timber buildings with small windows, poor ventilation and narrow eaves. They laid out a village square and placed thatched cottages around it. Eventually, Cornish stonemasons erected cottages for the settlement's officers and their wives that were perfect for their native land but nothing more than furnaces in the tropical north. Women cooked over open fireplaces in these hothouses during the height of the wet season. One can only imagine the dignified perspiration that daily poured from their bodies.

Commandant McArthur's observation in 1842 regarding gardening at Port Essington held for almost every aspect of this venture in colonization; It was a constant challenge, he noted, to 'abandon preconceived notions and prejudices'. This process was greatly encouraged by the cyclone that swept away nearly all the prefabricated structures after only one year, including the Church. Yet there were aspects of the environment to which they struggled to adapt—stultifying heat, the torrential downpours that destroyed their roofs, the swarms of mosquitoes and sandflies, the crocodiles that lurked in the surf, the noxious and offensive odours that emerged from the mangrove swamps, bodily complaints such as ulcers, eye diseases and fevers, particularly the ever-present threat of malaria (at a time before it was understood) and finally the voracious and unstoppable brigades of white ants which consumed every timber structure in sight (there is a wonderful story of Bremer, in 1839, moving his sofa every day in a vain effort to thwart their advances). One of the most amusing yet telling commentaries on these travails of climate and environment can be found in McArthur's notebook, in which he wrote sarcastic verse which ended with the following damning lines,

To the shape of a rat had this world been subjected,
At the tip of its tail Victoria's erected.

The process of adaptation was painful and slow. By the early 1840s Macarthur had learnt to use the local ironwood, which although harder to work, was more resistant to white ants. Buildings were raised off the ground on eight feet piles to allow for easier inspection, as in colonial Asia and Africa. The hospital was built from brick and stone. Bark cladding proved far cheaper and easier to use than weatherboards, while steep pitched roofs were far more effective against the tropical downfalls.

These were important but relatively small advances. But there was a larger problem posed by the environment that continued to undermine the settlement's sense of security—the ever-present sensation of *impermanence*. It was not only the sheer force of nature that seemed to tear down their attempts to eke out an existence, it was also the unsettling images of decay that appeared so swiftly. The artist Oswald Brierly, who visited the settlement on his way back to England after six years in Australia, remarked on a curious phenomenon: the white ants' activities he said, lent the '*appearance of Antiquity* in a settlement of so few years standing'. In the cemetery, Brierly saw one wooden cross, with only its outer shell remaining after the white ants had finished their work. Later that day, walking into McArthur's private residence, he found a 'large gloomy apartment lined with cedar and many squares of... [faded] calico which 'hung down in shreds'. This 'theatrical melancholy' he realized was in keeping with the air of deterioration in the settlement generally.

For the nineteenth century British imagination, which longed for deeply embedded settlement and at least the outward appearance of permanence in a colonial setting, there was something decidedly unnerving and unnatural about these images of decay. The environment appeared to deny them grand statements of imperial presence. It constantly reminded them that they were interlopers, not so much colonizers as disappointed speculators. Observing the sight of the Aborigines burning country every dry season, the man who eventually came to inform McArthur that the settlement was to be abandoned, Henry Keppel, reflected on the destruction wreaked by the fires,

> The conflagration spreads with fearful rapidity and violence, consuming everything in its way, creeping up the dry bark of the trees, running along the branches to the withered leaves, and involving everything dead or alive in one common ruin, until the whole country, as far as the eye can reach, is in a grand and brilliant illumination, which, to be fully appreciated, should be seen. It is accompanied by

a low murmuring sound, interrupted now and then by the loud report of the fall or bursting of some large tree, well calculated to increase the melancholy of poor wretches worn out with sickness, and without hope of relief.

Watching these fires, Keppel imagined 'the final destruction of our world'. Unlike Indigenous people, for whom the fire represented the promise of renewal of country, Keppel saw Armageddon. It was not only nature that reminded the European of the transient nature of their endeavours, but also Indigenous cultural practice, which appeared at face value to exist without any concept of a past or future. The apparent present-centredness of Indigenous cultures threatened European pretensions to permanence and destabilized their eye to posterity. While they might comfort themselves, as they often did, with the belief that tropical climates were unsuited to their constitutions, there was also evidence to suggest that a much deeper level, the failure of Victoria Settlement pointed to a moral, logistical and intellectual failure on the part of the British that no dreams of rescue by imported labour could ever disguise. Only a few years after the settlement was established, ideas of a new Singapore on the north coast of Australia were already exposed as fantasy. For the men and few women who remained there throughout the late 1840s, even after the settlement was briefly rejuvenated by the arrival of 50 more marines in 1845, there was a never-ending struggle to overcome isolation, homesickness and the very real threat of an early death.

McArthur's correspondence, with its frequent mention of the 'great suffering' at the settlement sometimes makes for difficult reading. While his commitment to the settlement never faltered, his frustration could not be disguised. Because of the isolated nature of the settlement and the time taken for his letters to arrive in London and for replies to return from the Colonial Office, it could often take well over twelve months before he had a response. It was impossible to make swift decisions. And in the corridors of the Colonial Office, thousands of miles removed from McArthur's reality, Port Essington was not so much a *place* as a point on a map, a military outpost that was either to be funded and supported, or to be abandoned. In August 1843, after losing many men to malaria, McArthur's numbers were reduced to 46. He wrote requesting that a relief party be sent immediately. Seventeen months later, the party arrived. Nothing could stem the high attrition rate. As John Mulvaney has pointed out, the stark fact is that 'more than 40 per cent of persons stationed [at Port Essington] either died or were invalided out'.

For those who managed to escape death and disease, the psychological pressures of living there were considerable. Those who attended the regular burial services wondered if they would be next. Walking to the cemetery early one morning, Oswald Brierly was disturbed by what he saw there, "its very records all decaying", "I felt the most nervous I have felt anywhere," he wrote, "and I was glad to hurry away". Brierly also captured the lethargic feeling induced by the climate, there was, he observed, this "pent up close feeling that [I] could not escape". McArthur felt something similar, writing that he was living as if 'from the world shut out', a feeling best captured in his wonderful inscription on the first page of the notebook he kept, 'John McArthur, Victoria, North Australia Worlds End'.

Because the settlement had its back to the inland of the continent, it was effectively an island. The sea was the only promise of rescue and relief. John Lort Stokes, who visited the settlement in the early 1840s, described how the mere 'sight of a vessel is ever cheering to the hearts of those who have been... cut off from the world'. Yet with the ship's arrival and the promise of communication, Stokes also reflected on the feelings of apprehension at news from home. 'The receipt of a letter,' he said, 'perhaps bearing an ill omen in the very colour of its wax, is very far from generating unmixed emotions of pleasure... a seal must ever be broken with feelings of great anxiety.'

Dreaming and fantasy were one way to cope with the exile from home. McArthur dreamt of the "fields and woods" of his childhood home, "the haunts of [his] youth", mixing his account keeping duties with maudlin poems, many of them devoted to his former lover, and he wrote longingly of his desire to once again "'tread on English ground," a country that he feared he might never see again. Ludwig Leichhardt also recorded his dreams at Port Essington. [I dreamt of my] "love of a girl", he wrote, "which occupied my imagination the whole morning". While Leichhardt and McArthur were dreaming of their love for women, the officers' wives, few in number, were no doubt dreaming of escape, many of them returning to Sydney or in some cases dying at the settlement together with their young children. The settlement was a place largely defined by men and military discipline. The extreme gender imbalance would prove to be consistent with the settlement of the Northern Territory in the future. Even in the early 20th century there were barely more than a thousand Europeans in the Territory, an overwhelming majority of them men. Physical prowess, strength and survival skills were the most prized qualities an individual could possess in such an environment.

To lighten his men's boredom and the almost prison-like claustrophobia induced by the climate, McArthur organized games with bat and ball, 'stone gathering competitions', wrestling matches and sprinting races, sometimes between different ships' crews such as the *Beagle* and the *Britomart*.

Perhaps the most celebrated example of entertainment Port Essington style took place in 1843, when four ships happened to be in the port, and Captain Owen Stanley staged a play, the farce entitled 'Cheap Living' [written by Frederic Reynolds and first performed at Drury Lane in 1797]. The prologue to the published version of 'Cheap Living a comedy' alerts the reader to the fact that in the play 'you must fancy a female is really a man; Not merely conceal'd in the manly array, But a man, bona-fide, throughout the whole play.' Stanley had found an ingenious way of bringing more women into the settlement, even if only for one evening. To stage the production he painted his scenery using what he called 'the earths of the country'. The play was staged in a workshop converted for the purpose and named Victoria Theatre. It was a riotous success.

Fr Angelo Confalonieri at Port Essington, 1846–1848

At the age of thirty-three, Father Angelo was Australia's first Catholic missionary in northern Australia. Given the august title 'Vicar Apostolic of Port Essington' by his superiors in Rome, he arrived at Victoria dressed in rags and clutching his crucifix after his ship, the *Heroine,* was wrecked on a reef in Torres Strait. His journey had been long and arduous. After leaving his home near Lake Garda and studying to be a missionary at Propaganda Fide, the Vatican institute for evangelisation in Rome, he travelled via Lyon, Paris and London in 1845 in an effort to recruit more priests to his mission and secure financial support. In September that year he sailed from London with more than twenty Irish, French and Italian missionaries bound for Perth, Sydney and Port Essington. Their mission was to realise Pope Gregory XVI's intention to evangelise the Australian continent. Like his counterparts in the Colonial Office in London, Pope Gregory ruled a vast empire. From his Vatican office he carved the map of Australia into spheres of Catholic influence and filed the documents relating to Australia under 'Oceania'. Bishop Brady was to preside over the 'diocese' of Perth, Angelo

Confalonieri, Port Essington and Northern Australia, while another priest was appointed 'Vicar of King George Sound' in south-west Australia. It was another form of magical possession, assumed rather than negotiated and blissfully ignorant of the practical difficulties of placing territories ten times the size of Italy in the hands of one man.

By all accounts Father Angelo fervently believed that he would convert the Aboriginal people of Port Essington to Christianity. Tossed into the sea when the *Heroine* struck the reef and dragged to safety by Nelson, the captain's 'great Newfoundland dog', then picked up by another ship and brought to Port Essington, he lost his two Irish assistants, James Fagan and Nicholas Hogan, and all of his worldly possessions. God, he believed, had saved him for one reason: so that he might carry out his mission to save the souls of the 'poor and naked savages' in the 'forests' of northern Australia before 'a Protestant mission' could establish itself there.

Writing to church authorities in Sydney only three days after he arrived, Angelo told the story of his shipwreck and miraculous survival, pleading for a pair of spectacles—'my short sightedness is so great that I can hardly perceive objects until I touch them'—a 'breviary, some books of devotion', an altar-stone and the 'necessary sacred vestments' that would allow him to say Mass. Desperate for funds and material support, he was also adept at dramatising his plight: 'alone, abandoned upon these inhospitable shores —without money, without aid, without clothes, without hopes, pale and emaciated, almost torn to pieces by the breakers—the poor Don Angelo lives as it were by miracle.'

As a young priest (if his hagiographer can be believed) he had spent months walking alone in the Italian and Swiss Alps with little protective clothing and few provisions. In order to pass the test of physical and mental endurance to prepare for his life as a missionary, he attempted to emulate his Saviour's ordeal of forty days and nights in the desert. Trekking in the Alps, where village inns were usually within reach, would prove almost luxurious compared to the travails of life at Port Essington.

Because Angelo had lost all his papers in the shipwreck, McArthur had to take him on trust. Heartened by the priest's enthusiasm, he provided labourers—both his own tradesmen and Aboriginal men—to build him a small house at 'Black Rock near the entrance of the harbour', 25 kilometres removed from the settlement. Angelo referred to it as his 'little shack'.

This situation would allow Angelo to be undisturbed in his effort to 'live among the savages, and thus learn their language, and observe their customs and manners'. To walk along the low-lying, red-rock shoreline at the harbour's entrance today is to understand something of the isolation Angelo experienced. Writing to Propaganda Fide at the Vatican from the almost preposterous address 'North Australia, Port Essington', he complained regularly of *'immensa distanza, e difficile communicazione'*. Rome was an eternity away. McArthur kept Angelo supplied with 'food and clothing' from the 'Government stores', although by all accounts, self-sufficiency was not his forte. Years of having had his meals placed in front of him had left Angelo unprepared for life alone. John Sweatman was amused: 'in all worldly matters he was ... ignorant & helpless', especially in 'domestic matters ... when he had his flour, he did not know how to mix or cook it! He was a terrible beggar too, and pestered us without ceasing, though always in the most polite language and with a thousand apologies'.

To gain the trust of Aboriginal people, Angelo 'lived wholly in their manner', including eating 'roots' and 'half-cooked possums with entrails'. He was often seen with Aboriginal people wandering through the bush, sometimes far inland, 'notebook in hand', aided in his efforts by a young Aboriginal boy, 'Jim Crow', who served as his 'interpreter' and occasionally waited on his table. Once he had the confidence of Aboriginal people, he offered to take 'care of their children', teaching them to 'repeat prayers in Latin'. He saw immediately that he had more chance of indoctrinating them than he had of converting their parents. An outstanding linguist, Angelo 'mastered their language', boasting to his superiors that 'after having spent a year of almost continuous, hard, miserable life in the forests together with these poor savages, I can now speak their language perfectly'.

He reckoned rightly that 'almost all speak nearly the same language ... but with different dialects that are easy to understand'. Everything, however, was more complicated than it seemed.

He produced a map of the 'Aboriginal Tribes of the Cobourg Peninsula', although as linguist Bruce Birch has shown, despite the map's value, the 'tribal' names Angelo recorded were actually Malay names for locations rather than Aboriginal names for groups of people. Where Angelo did succeed was in his beautifully written 'Specimen of the Aboriginal Language or Short Conversation with the Natives of North Australia Port Essington'.

When I held this document in my hands in the Vatican archives in late 2014, I was immediately struck by the enormous care and pride Angelo had taken in its compilation and presentation. This was truly a work of devotion. Angelo had sent the manuscript, which he described as a 'little essay on the language of this poor family of human beings', from Port Essington to Propaganda Fide not only because he knew that it would be a permanent record of his work there, but because it embodied his mission and calling.

The title page was painstakingly inscribed in black, blue and red ink while the fragile manuscript, bound carefully with string, was barely more than eight centimetres wide and 16 centimetres long. Inside, every entry was immaculately written, with subheadings brilliantly coloured in red. After listing phrases which reveal something of Angelo's everyday transactions—'give to me your spear and your pearls, your turtle shell, basket and I will give to you tobacco, rice and other', 'make fire', 'bring small wood', 'little boy come here be not afraid', 'I must return to my house but tomorrow morning I will return and see you'—the manuscript ends with Angelo's *raison d'être*: 'Religious Questions and Answers'.

> Who made the Sun, the Moon, the earth?
> I do not know.
> My dear child, I will tell you. God made the sun ...
> Did die your Soul?
> Never
> Where will go your Soul, when your body die?
> Before God
> What for before God?
> To receive reward if it was good; and to have punishment, if it was bad. The reward will have in heaven with God, forever, and the punishment in Hell with the Devil forever.

Reading his exquisitely compiled manuscript and hearing of the 'love, attachment and affection' he was shown by Aboriginal people, Angelo's former teachers at Propaganda Fide could be forgiven for thinking that he had succeeded in converting 'the natives' to Christianity. But the truth was otherwise. Aboriginal people had actually succeeded in forcing Angelo to question the purpose and effectiveness of his mission. John Sweatman described how they would trick 'the poor padre' when he asked them for translations of the liturgy. Instead of giving him the correct word in their language they would offer him obscenities. When Angelo came to say Mass he could not understand why they 'laughed at his sermons'. Others told of Aboriginal men and women repeating their prayers in the main square of the settlement 'with many gestures as rather a good joke than otherwise'.

Parroting prayers was not evidence of conversion. More often than not it was a way of securing 'a bag of rice'. Indeed, John Sweatman claimed that Angelo 'despaired' of ever succeeding. 'Had they had any idolatry of their own, [Angelo] said, he might have rooted it out and taught them Christianity instead, but having no idea of religion whatever, he feared it would be impossible to make them understand anything about it.' Although he had lived with them (or at least near them) and learnt some of their language, Angelo had still not grasped the importance of their Dreaming and creation stories— an oral gospel that bound the people of the past, present and future to the land and all that inhabited it.

In 1847, by which time his initial enthusiasm had worn thin, Angelo told McArthur that he was not making sufficient progress. His only hope, he said, 'was to maintain and teach the children', ideally after they were taken away from their parents. In his correspondence with church authorities in Sydney, he came close to admitting defeat: 'their poverty and misery is so very deep, their condition is so degraded, their debasement is so terrible that it presents the hardest difficulties for the Mission'. The man who had learnt more of the closely related local Aboriginal languages (Garig and Iwaidja) than any other European at Port Essington and earnt the admiration of the majority of Aboriginal people he lived with, so much so that he was given a 'skin name' ('Nagojo') and thus adopted into their kinship system, nonetheless saw them as 'people altogether brutal' with 'no understanding but for their belly'. He gave others the impression that he wanted to leave the settlement and even doubted his mission. The surgeon Crawford, who had many long conversations with Angelo, claimed that he found him 'wholly without religious feeling', 'well acquainted with theology and a strong stickler for the doctrine of his church, but more like an advocate than a believer. Indeed he frequently gave occasion to doubt whether he himself gave credence to what he thought'. The longer Angelo lived with Aboriginal people at Port Essington the more his piety dissolved. It was he who was being converted.

In early June 1848, Lieutenant Dunbar, McArthur's boatman, who normally delivered supplies to Angelo, 'went down in [the] deck boat ... not having heard that he was ill'. On landing at Black Rock he found him lying in his house 'complaining of want of sleep' and 'headache'. Concerned, Dunbar persuaded Angelo to come back with him to the settlement hospital. Within less than a week Angelo had died, yet another victim of malaria. Secondhand accounts claimed that his last moments were 'fearful'. He allegedly 'denied that there was a God'. Far more likely is that the thought of dying in such a godless place as Port Essington terrified him. On 11 June, McArthur and all the officers and soldiers at the garrison attended his funeral and burial 'with the respect due to a highly esteemed man'. McArthur, who over the previous two years had supplied him with provisions and occasionally taken his boat out to Angelo's and dined with him, was deeply saddened by his passing. Perhaps also because his death was yet another reminder of how the climate and isolation at Victoria had claimed the lives of so many of those who originally arrived full of hope. At the time of Angelo's death the cemetery contained nearly fifty graves. Soon the number of dead would outnumber the number of residents.

Departure

In 1849 when Henry Keppel communicated to Captain McArthur and the party of Marines 'the unexpected' news that he had come to remove the settlement, the garrison rejoiced. It was if a war had ended. At the same time as the British rejoiced, Keppel watched as Aboriginal women showed their grief by cutting their heads and faces with sharp flints'. The marines then carried out their orders to destroy what remained of the settlement to ensure that 'other parties' would not seek to settle there. Thus, the first attempt to turn the settlement into ruins was made by the very same people who struggled for more than a decade to build the settlement. What the Iwaidja must have made of this almost gleeful act of destruction is difficult to know. Keppel noted that,

> We left behind at Port Essington a number of cattle [and horses]; there were already many quite wild in the bush ... the [sight of the] garrison marching down to embark, with the band at their head, did not excite sufficient interest to draw the natives from their search for what they could find among the ruins of the buildings.

They appeared uninterested. As his ship sailed away from Port Essington, Keppel described how his crew held 'corobories' [sic] and dances so often, that frequently afterwards the kangaroo dance was as well performed on the main deck of the *Meander*, many thousand miles from the place where it originated, as we had seen it on the spot.

Postscript

In the early 1980s, after the ravages of a smallpox epidemic in the late nineteenth century and the removal of Aboriginal people to Croker Island in the 1950s and 60s, a small number of Aboriginal communities returned to live on the Coburg Peninsula. Today there are probably less than 40 to 50 individuals residing there. Aside from the National Parks Office, which resides 20 kilometres up harbor from the ruins of Victoria Settlement, no Europeans live at Port Essington and only a handful of cattle farmers and pearlers did so in the intervening years. Even 165 years after the British settlement was abandoned, Europeans remain, at best, occasional visitors to Indigenous Country.

2017

The Consulate of Italy for Queensland and the Northern Territory and the Diocese of Darwin hosted a symposium on 12 July to commemorate John McArthur's life, and, at the same time publicise a plan to build a memorial to mark his legacy.

John McArthur, a sketcher and naval officer, was born on 16 March 1791, third son of James McArthur and Catherine, nee Hawkins, and a younger brother of the pioneer New South Wales pastoralist Hannibal Macarthur (the family spelt the surname both ways). A captain in the Royal Marines, John was officially appointed commandant of the naval garrison and settlement at Port Essington (Northern Territory) when its founding commandant Sir Gordon Bremer left in June 1839, although he was unofficially in charge from the first, having helped establish it in 1838. He remained at Port Essington for the whole of the settlement's existence, under miserable conditions, and seems to have been the major force which ensured its survival. T H Huxley called him ('with all reverence') 'a pragmatical old fogey.'

FATHER JULIAN TENISON WOODS, 130 YEARS ON…

Janice Tranter*

On 7 October 2019, 130 years after Fr Woods' death, we seek to see him newly through a series of glimpses. Starting when he was fourteen, we see him in several Octobers and sometimes 7 Octobers till his death on this day in 1889. This way of seeing, one could say, a CT scan way, might open new perception of his life in particular times and in its totality.

In October 1847 fourteen-year old Julian was living on the island of Jersey with his parents and younger family members. They had gone there from their home in London, hoping his mother's health would improve. For Julian, Jersey was a wonderworld with free rein for his eagerness to study, and, with his younger brothers, search the island, climb, swim, dive and join the fishermen in open sea boating. In October, the world was turned on its head by grief, with his mother's rapid decline then death on 5 November. He could never speak of it.

Four years later, in October 1851, eighteen-year old Julian was a Passionist novice in Aston Hall, where he was sent from the Broadway Novitiate to benefit his health. His health did not respond, but he gained helpful guidance in his studies from Fr Ignatius Spencer. There was another gain with lifelong impact. When the life of St Teresa of Avila was being read her words on St Joseph, whom he always loved, 'so took possession of him' that he resolved from that day to 'take him as my special patron and protector'. From then, he said, he cast a glance to Joseph every day.[1]

Two years later, October 1853, twenty-year old Julian was a Marist novice at the college at Montbel, a place of great beauty near the Riviera. After his poor health ended his life as a Passionist after two years, he was embracing a second road towards ordination as a Marist. He came to Montbel after spending the students' holidays with a young Marist priest's family in the Auvergne[2] where the spectacular volcanic formations whetted his taste for

---

1 *Memoirs of Reverend J E Tenison Woods,* dictated, 1887. Archives, Sisters of St Joseph, Lochinvar. The *Memoirs* state it was Autumn, 1851. 'Being read' refers to the custom of reading religious books aloud, for example, at meals, while the community ate in silence.

2 The young priest was J C Foucheyrand. Fr Gaston Lessard sm Rome wrote 'I note with interest that Foucheyrand was appointed to London in the fall of 1853'. Pers.

* Janice Tranter rsj is a member of the Sisters of St Joseph, Lochinvar. She has a number of articles published on Father Woods and Josephite history. The article is based on a talk in St Joseph's Chapel, Lochinvar, 7 October 2019.

geology and he met local French Sisters, the Sisters of St Joseph, who were to him a 'revelation', a radically new idea of religious life for women.

He arrived in Montbel in time for a retreat with the novices and the dedication of the College to St Joseph on 7 October. The fifteen novices (Julian, the only one from England) and five Marist priests processed around the College carrying a statue of St Joseph and singing hymns to Mary and to Joseph. Julian composed the tune for a new hymn to St Joseph sung that day and, as the only organist there, played the organ. At the conclusion of the procession they installed the statue at the gate.[3] The 7 October was a grand occasion and for the English novice a fullhearted new beginning: he pursued his studies, shared long mountain walks with his fellow students and enjoyed trout fishing in the Var. By the end of the first examinations, which he passed, his hopes were dashed. His health had failed, bringing 'greatest anxiety and distress' about his longed-for ordination. He felt, he said, 'as if there was some fatality which ruthlessly destroyed my prospects... To encourage myself I used mark down the days and cross off each one as it concluded with the delight of a poor prisoner who counts with joy the hours as they go by.'[4] When an English teaching vacancy came at the Marist La Seyne-sur-Mer College, Toulon, Father Peter Julian Eymard, rector and superior of the College invited Julian to continue his studies there, where the study programme would be less taxing.

The next October, 1854, twenty-one-year old Julian was back in London. His one desire, to be a priest in a missionary order, had seemingly led to nothing for a second time. His period at La Seyne was 'among the happiest of his life', but ill health dogged him. He revered Eymard, who 'left a deeper impression on him than anyone else in his life'. He clung to Eymard's encouragement 'not to be uneasy about my bad state of health, for I would find that it was some special design of God connected with my vocation'.[5] At La Seyne, Julian had continued his priestly studies under a tutor, enrolled in art and science courses and taught English. When the College holiday came, Eymard advised a journey with a young Marist priest, the itinerary planned by Eymard to include meeting the Curé of Ars. The journey was

communication with writer. 13 April 1995.

3   A Marist priest wrote a new hymn to Mary and one to Joseph. G. Lessard, Rome, from Fr Mayet's Memoirs.

4   *Memoirs* 1, 92.

5   *Memoirs*, 2, 94

doomed before it began when a loved Marist companion fell in a faint beside Julian as they were walking, and died. Julian was ill with shock, 'nervous excitement' and 'cardiac irritation'. After severe leeching (the medical 'cure') and a degree of recovery, the weakened Julian and his companion set out for what was a miserable journey. As well, his meagre travel funds from his small teaching fee meant using rigid economy and were insufficient to include Rome as desired. 'The only gleam of comfort... was a few words of advice and consolation from the Curé. He was allowed by our Lord to understand many things that were sealed ... to me'.[6] On his return, La Seyne college was closed by the threat of cholera in the nearby ports. Not knowing what to do, he returned to London.

In London, with no idea of how he would reach ordination, he attended medical lectures, thinking this would be useful as a priest. On 1 October at Vespers at St George's Cathedral, Southwark, he met Bishop Robert Willson from Tasmania. The next day Willson consulted Julian's long-time mentor, Canon Oakeley, and invited Julian to Tasmania as assistant convict chaplain and teacher while continuing study for ordination.[7] Julian accepted and in a fortnight was on board with Willson and his small party, sailing to Australia. The 7 October 1854 was between two worlds: the one he knew and the unknown on the other side of the world. He later said he had 'reached as a state of complete apathy'. There was no sense of 'heroic devotion': Australia was the only door opening to him and priesthood. 'Thus my field of labours appeared to be chosen and my vocation decided... What I consider one of the great turning points in my life was arranged and decided'.[8] He felt 'the wound of breaking up all ties with my own country.' Once on the journey, despite the sense of loss, he wasted no time planning and beginning a study programme which he followed diligently. It was 'a method... which he adhered to more or less regularly during the rest of his life', pursuing many subjects at the same time, varying the subject regularly, learning a great deal, his active mind engaged to the full.[9]

---

6   *Memoirs* 1, 95.

7   Margaret Press, Julian Tenison Woods, 'Father Founder' (North Blackburn Vic: Collins Dove, 1994), 1, 48–9, 249 n.1.

8   *Memoirs*, 1, 97

9   *Memoirs* 11, 10. He describes the time given for each subject, the way he varied them, the subjects he studied and the degree to which they were undertaken. His organised and disciplined approach gives a key to his many achievements. It is a method for an able student of any era.

In October 1856, twenty-three-year old Julian was at Sevenhill, South Australia, living with the Jesuit community in their spartan pioneering establishment. Bishop Murphy of Adelaide had invited him there to complete his study for ordination, with the understanding that he could return to England when the Bishop had more priests. Julian accepted the offer and set out with 'alacrity and delight'. From the day of the death beside him of his young Marist priest friend at La Seyne, a nervousness distressing to himself had clung to him. The day he set out for Sevenhill, it disappeared. As well, at Sevenhill a 'complete change' came over him. Till then, his heart was in Europe, to be a missionary priest there. At Sevenhill his one desire became 'to give his life entirely for the Australian missions'. 'He felt that nothing could move him from his desire to be a missionary priest in Australia'.[10] He pursued his priestly as well as geological studies, gathering a growing rock collection from the local area.

The Octobers of the next ten years saw him as the dedicated, energetic pastor of Penola, loved by all and recognised for his science. Bouts of illness didn't stop his zeal. He jokingly wrote to a friend that if he doubted the amount of his parish work, 'I wish you were my horse for a month'.[11] His greatest concern was the lack of religious education for the scattered bush children. By October 1862 he had written to Mary MacKillop, met a year or two before, of 'our prospects'. He had spoken with Mary of his longing to do something for the children, growing up with no word of religious instruction. Mary said later that *all my desires seemed to centre in a wish to devote myself to poor children and the afflicted poor, in some very poor Order... The way in which he [Father Woods] described their wants so completely agreed with all my previous desires, that when he asked me whether (provided he got the Bishop's consent to commence an Institute to meet these wants) I would remain and become one of his first children in the flock, I joyfully consented.*[12]

By October 1866, aged thirty-three, Julian had been appointed Director General of Education and Bishop's Secretary. Soon the Penola people farewelled, in their words, the 'gentle minister of our loving God'.

10 *Memoirs*, 11, 7–8.
11 28 November 1863, to W H Archer in Anne Player, (ed), *The Archer Letters*, 1983, reprinted 2016.
12 Mary MacKillop to Bishop Shiel, 10 October 1871, *Life of Mother Mary of the Cross MacKillop, Foundress of the Sisterhood of St Joseph of the Sacred Heart*, (Westmead, Sydney, 1916), 50.

The Octobers of 1867–1870 saw Julian utterly spent in Adelaide: pastoral work, single-handedly setting up a school system, establishing the new sisterhood and forming the hearts of the Sisters in the spirit of Joseph. Already in mid-1867, he asked Mary to 'pray earnestly to St Joseph for my health... I find myself failing'. He had written the Rule and sent it to her. By October three years later, he was near breaking point. The Vicar General, his firm supporter, had died of a stroke in June, possibly brought on by the revelation of and dealing with a priest's sexual abuse of children that Julian had reported to him.

On 1 October 1871 thirty-eight-year old Julian was in Newcastle, New South Wales with Archbishop Polding. Having come to visit Bathurst diocese, as arranged by Bishop Shiel of Adelaide and Bishop Quinn of Bathurst to give missions and find a location for a Josephite foundation, Julian and Quinn had hurried to Sydney at word of the threatened closing of the Josephite convent in Adelaide. In Sydney Julian received word of Mary MacKillop's excommunication. Going to Archbishop Polding to consult with him on the Adelaide crisis, he was taken by Polding to Newcastle, and at Polding's direction, was preaching a mission in St Mary's Newcastle. On 2 October he went with Polding to Maitland to confer with Bishop Murray. Returning to Sydney the next day, he was directed to preach retreats to the Sisters and children at the Benedictine convent and school at Subiaco, then lecture on Education in Sydney, then preach at Wollongong. On 18 October, he went to Bathurst to meet the Bishops of Bathurst and Maitland. On 20 October he was back at Hunters Hill. He was like a puppet, ordered to work and move from place to place while his heart was with the suffering Sisters in Adelaide. By the end of the month, at Subiaco, in Margaret Press's words, 'his health buckled under the strain, and he became so ill, haemorrhaging and paralysed with migraine' that the Marist Superior, Fr Joly, and the Benedictine chaplain, Fr Ambrosoli, believed he was dying.

The next October, said Mary MacKillop, 'now began his real mission life', starting in Raymond Terrace in the lower Hunter Valley.[13] On 6 October 1872, at the end of the week's mission, thirty-nine-year-old Julian came through Maitland and Lochinvar to Branxton for the next mission, beginning

---

13 Mother Mary of the Cross MacKillop, *Julian Tenison Woods: A Life* (Strathfield: St Paul's: 2010), 191. On 3 October during the mission he preached at the laying of a foundation stone.

the same day.[14] On 7 October he returned through Lochinvar to Maitland for a Dominican Profession,[15] returning that day to Branxton.[16] Next came a week's mission in Muswellbrook, a trying mission when he was not well. Next followed the Clergy retreat at Maitland.[17] The last three days of the month he preached at Camden and Narellan before setting out for Perthville.[18] October 1872 began eleven years of missioning from North Queensland to Tasmania. Here, from 1874, along with missioning, he resumed the scientific work of the Penola years. These years also saw his founding of the Perpetual Adoration Sisters in Brisbane and the virtual re-founding of the Josephite group at Perthville.

October 1883, 1884 and 1885 saw Julian in Asia. With no more invitations to mission in Australia – missionary orders had come – he accepted a request to undertake mineral surveys in present Malaysia. In August the discarded missioner made his way, taken from all he knew, looking with longing to his return.[19] In October he reached Singapore.[20] The next October he was in Malacca, the next in Arima, Japan.[21]

October 1886 saw fifty-three-year old Julian preaching in Darwin

---

14 The journey from Maitland to Branxton was by train or by the road past the site where the Sisters of St Joseph made their foundation from Perthville, Bathurst diocese, in 1883. While the Sisters continue to reside here, the dominant buildings are now St Joseph's College and St Patrick's Primary School.

15 Two Irish Sisters were professed. He had preached at the Dominican chapel opening, 30 April 1872.

16 Here he learned his friend, Fr Hinteroecker SJ, aged 52 died on 6 October, missioning in Tasmania.

17 Woods wrote to Mary MacKillop from each of these four missions.

18 Woods' mission dates are from 'Woods' Movements: 1871–1889' in Anne Player,' Julian Tenison Woods: the interaction of Science and Religion' (unpublished, available in Josephite archives and some libraries 1990). Woods came to Raymond Terrace from Perthville via Sydney, c.350 km. Maitland to Camden is c.220 km., Camden to Perthville, c. 200 km. The only Sydney-Newcastle transport was by boat.

19 For further on Woods see Mary Cresp and Janice Tranter, 'Julian Tenison Woods, Itinerant Missioner', *Journal of the Australian Catholic Historical Society* 37/1 (2016), 1–9; Mary Cresp and Janice Tranter, 'Julian Tenison Woods: From Entangled Histories to History Shaper', *Australasian Catholic Record* 95 (2018), 286–303.

20 Awaiting him was a letter from Sister Joseph at Lochinvar, who had written on arriving at Lochinvar in September. Woods to Sr Joseph, 6 October 1883, J Tranter and M Hughes, ed., *Letters from Father Founder to Sr M Joseph (Ambrose) and Sisters at Lochinvar, 1883–1887* (2012), 15–16.

21 Anne Player, ed, *'Yrs Most Affily', Letters from Father Julian Tenison Woods to Terry and Sarah Tenison Woods 1878–1887* (Brisbane: *Sisters of Perpetual Adoration*: 2008), 101–4.

after taxing expeditions in the Northern Territory. Hurrying to Sydney in December to his dangerously ill brother, there was no time to call at Lochinvar.[22]

October 1887, 1888 and 1889 saw Julian in Sydney in increasing, painful, radical debility and cared for by the semi-religious community of women led by Gertrude Abbott in Elizabeth Street. In early 1889 he said, 'though severely ill, somehow or other it is with hopeful confidence that I say *Resurgam* [I will rise up]. I am cheerful and happy and am sure I shall be so to the end.'[23] In September 1889, at his request he was invested again in the Passionist habit.

On Sunday evening, 6 October, someone brought into his room a small statue of Our Lady of Victories. He said, 'I expected her long before'.[24] On Monday morning 7 October, holding a blessed candle in his right hand and the statue of Mary in the other, he died at 11.25, in the presence of the Passionist Superior, Fr Marcellus, Fr Ambrosoli, confessor in his illness and friend since 1871, and the Elizabeth St Community. Two more priests arrived as he died.[25] Mary MacKillop came a quarter hour later. He was fifty-six.

Mary tells us that the year after Fr Woods' death, a Marist Father visiting the Sisters at North Sydney recognised Julian from a portrait there. He had studied with Julian at St Joseph's, Montbel.[26]

May Julian recognise in us today the sentiments he strove to make his own, the sentiments of the Heart of Jesus.

---

22 Tranter and Hughes, ed., *Letters from Father Founder*, 33.

23 13 March 1889, to W H Archer, *Archer Letters*.

24 Sr M Columcille (ie Sr M John Dowling), *Memoirs of our Founder* (Dunedin: 1892), 42.

25 Fathers McCarthy and E M O'Brien, Rector of St John's College. Elizabeth O'Brien to Mr and Mrs Woods, 561 Elizabeth St Sydney, 10 October 1889; M John Dowling to My dearest Sisters (Wilcannia diocese), Sisters of St Joseph of the Sacred Heart Archives, North Sydney (11 October 1889).

26 Mary MacKillop, *Julian Tenison Woods; A Life*, (Strathfield, St Pauls Publications: 2010), 11.

DISENTANGLING THE MCGIRRS OF COLONIAL NEW SOUTH WALES

Colin Fowler*

The author's interest in the McGirrs arose from curiosity about a conversation that took place on a voyage to Australia in 1855–1856. The Irish-born and English-educated Myles Athy, aspirant to a monastic vocation at Sydney's Benedictine monastery, kept a diary during this voyage to Australia in 1855.[1] Well into the journey he recorded a conversation with one of the three Irish secular priests on board, in which the 'Paddy' clergyman expressed his support for the Russians in the Crimean war, then into its final stages:

> There is one priest here who is such an Irishman that you cannot say the slightest thing in disparagement of them but he has his horns out at once. I am one. I thought that I was Irish enough, but because I do not turn every thing they do into virtues we do not agree … He is all on the Russian side, hoping that they may win.[2]

Downside-educated Myles, was appalled at such disloyalty to the Empire. Such opposition to the British Empire was a not an unfamiliar Irish nationalist attitude—'England's difficulty is Ireland's opportunity'.[3] Athy, to whom a Paddy might have applied the derogatory term 'West Briton', did not name the priest. However, the three secular priests were named by the Dublin newspaper, The Nation, in describing the entourage of Archbishop Polding leaving Liverpool aboard the Phoenix on 26 October 1855: the Rev. J. Keating, 'a gentleman who has already resided in Australia as a missionary priest for some years', the Rev. P Newman and the Rev. J McGirr, 'recently a missionary in Southwark'.[4] Initial research suggested that the most likely Russian supporter was John McGirr, who was a native of County Mayo within the Archdiocese of Tuam, over which the combative patriot archbishop, John McHale, 'the Lion of the West', presided from 1834 to 1881.[5]

---

1   Anne Wark, *Journal of a Voyage to Australia 1855–56 by Myles Athy, a recruit for St Mary's Monastery, Sydney: a transcription* (Adelaide: ATF Press: 2017).

2   Wark, *Journal of a Voyage*, 139.

3   American Fenians were active in soliciting support from the Russian Consul in Washington. See Joseph Denieffe, *A Personal Narrative of the Irish Revolutionary Brotherhood* (New York, 1906), vi–viii.

4   *The Nation*, 24 November.

5   See Hilary Andrews, *The Lion of the West: a biography of John McHale*

*   Colin Fowler was parish priest of Pyrmont. His book *150 Years on Pyrmont Peninsula: The Catholic Community of Saint Bede 1867–2017*, was reviewed in *JACHS* 37/2. A longer version of this article appeared in the 2019 edition of the County Mayo journal *An Choinneal*.

Three priests bearing the name 'J. McGirr' ministered in colonial NSW between 1855 and 1874; one was John, two were James. Contemporary newspapers conflated the details of their lives, and secondary sources compounded the confusion.[6]

All three McGirrs were schooled at St Jarlath's College in Tuam, County Galway. The College, bearing the name of the patron saint of the archdiocese, had been founded in 1800 by the then Archbishop, with the initial aim of preparing young boys for entry into the National Seminary, the Royal College of St. Patrick at Maynooth, outside Dublin. St Jarlath's evolved into a college both for seminarians and lay students.[7] During the long reign of John McHale, his keen interest in Irish history and language fostered the beginnings of a tradition of Irish nationalism in the College and throughout the Archdiocese.

The results of the annual June examinations were regularly published

(Dublin: Veritas, 2001).

6   There is a single file on 'Father J McGirr' in the Sydney Archdiocesan Archives, in which are contained photocopies of pages of the 1861 Catholic Directory referring to the older James McGirr, and photcopies of two newspaper articles of 1869 referring to the younger James McGirr.
    The manuscript of T J Linane, *From Abel to Zundolovich. Biographies of priests on the Australian scene up to 1900* (Sydney Archdiocesan Archives) notes two only Reverends McGirr, John and James, and calls them brothers; the published volume, *Byrne to Dixon*, Armadale (1979) includes 'names for future biographies', among which are found the three McGirrs, but there is no comment on their relationships.
    In the index of the two-volume collection of Polding-related documents and resource material, *Adjutor Deus*, the 'Fr J McGirr', to whom several letters are addressed in 1857, is identified confusedly as: 'McGirr, Rev. James. Born Ireland, ordained Tuam 1846; teacher at Lyndhurst, St. John's College, St Stanislaus' College Bathurst, died in Orange' (M Xavier Compton et al [eds], *Adjutor Deus: Documents and resource material relating to the episcopacy of Archbishop John Bede Polding OSB*, 2 vols, Sydney 2000, II.xvii).
    The official necrology of the priests of the Bathurst diocese conflates details of the two Reverend James McGirr, see 'Rev. Father James Joseph McGirr' in L Grant, *Salt of the Earth: a Bathurst Necrology*, Bathurst (2005), 185.
7   An unflattering comparison was made between the 'gentlemen' of Maynooth and graduates of St. Jarlath's by Polding's cousin and English agent, Dom Paulinus Hepstonstall, in a letter of 1839 from Somerset to Sydney: 'As yet I have not been able to obtain six Clergymen expected to arrive out in the course of the present year. Of the three Irish gentlemen Messrs. Ryan, Keaveny and Walsh, I have yet only seen the first … They are from the College of St. Jarlath at Tuam. As compared with the gentlemen from Maynooth, I fear you may not be quite so well satisfied with their exterior qualifications; at least Mr. R. appears to me to have an awkward and uncouth accent.', Heptonstall to Ullathorne, 19 November 1839, Brian Condon: *Letters and Documents in 19th Century Australian Catholic History*: http://www.library.unisa.edu.au/condon/CatholicLetters/18391119.htm

by county and national newspapers. The name M'Girr is prominent in these reports in the 1840s and 1850s. Only twice in the results perused is a Christian name provided. The June 1843 results recorded John McGirr as gaining a mark styled 'next in merit' in Sacred Scripture. 'Next in merit', following 1st premium, 2nd and 3rd, seems to have been a polite designation for a simple pass. John McGirr was ordained for Calcutta in July. Also reported was a 2nd in Natural Philosophy awarded to James McGirr.[8] James left for India in 1846. The 1851 McGirr results were outstanding: nine 1st premium and six 2nd places.[9] In none of these instances is the Christian name of the student given, however, it is tempting to assign a share in these excellent results to the younger Rev. James McGirrs and Michael McGirr, his cousin, who both became celebrated teachers in Bathurst.

The relationships between three of the colonial McGirrs is clearly stated in two obituaries in Sydney's *Freeman's Journal*: that of a 'fine old Irishwoman' in October 1887 and of Michael McGirr in February 1890. The 'old Irishwoman' was the centenarian Mrs. Margaret McGirr of the Westport district of County Mayo. As well as celebrating how 'in hard famine days of forty-seven 'tis well remembered how she was wont to feed the starving and dying poor, and to coffin, with her own hands, the friendless dead', the obituary, reprinted from the *Mayo Examiner*, recorded family details:

> She had six sons and three daughters – the second eldest son, the late Rev. James M'Girr, CC Moylough, for some time in India and Australia, and whom she had for long the happiness to see minister at the altar. Her fourth son, Mr. Michael M'Girr, still lives, and is in Australia, proprietor of the Sydney *Freeman's Journal*, and while he is an honour to the new land of his adoption, he is still true unto the old land of his birth.[10]

The obituary of her son Michael confirmed him as a sibling of Reverend James and added the information that the brothers were cousins to the younger Reverend James: 'The deceased had one brother a priest (the late Rev. James McGirr), and two cousins, the late Rev. James McGirr, of Bathurst, and Father Peter McGirr, now of Cong, Ireland'.[11]

---

8   *Freemans Journal*, 8 July 1843.
9   *Freemans Journal*, 5 July 1851.
10 *Freemans Journal*, 22 October 1887. Father Peter J McGirr, a great-nephew of Mrs Margaret McGirr, was ordained in 1882 and served all his life in the Tuam Archdiocese, dying at Balindine, Co Mayo, in 1908, aged 51. I am grateful to Fr. Kieran Waldron, archivist of Tuam Archdiocese, for this information and other assistance.
11 *Freemans Journal*, 8 February 1890.

It is to be noted that the Reverend John McGirr was not mentioned in either obituary. This evidence convincingly contradicts sources that claim him as a brother of James. A 1947 reminiscence in the Melbourne Catholic newspaper, the *Advocate*, described Rev. John McGirr as a grand-uncle of the Honourable James McGirr, premier of NSW.[12] The same relationship is elsewhere claimed for the two other reverends, which makes John a cousin to them. These are the family relationships assumed in this article. Their estimated dates of birth were: John 1818; James 1822; James Joseph 1829; Michael 1833.[13]

The McGirr clan was originally from County Armagh, but following the 1795 'Battle of the Diamond', a deadly attack by the Protestant population on Catholic neighbours, there was a mass migration of Catholics to the Province of Connaught, where members of the McGirr family settled in Culleen and afterwards in Louisburgh, a new 'planned town' built by the Earl of Altamont on his West Mayo estate in 1795.[14]

Having established the relationships between the colonial McGirrs, it will be of interest to review their careers in order of arrival in New South Wales: John 1856, Michael 1857, James 1860, James Joseph 1864.

Eleven years before John McGirr's 1855 departure for Australia on the *Phoenix*, he was reported as being among a party of Irish missionaries embarking on the iron steamer *Fire Queen* setting out on her maiden voyage from Kingstown for Calcutta in April 1844.[15]

After ecclesiastical studies at St Jarlath's College, John McGirr had been ordained for Calcutta in July 1843 by Archbishop McHale. His recruitment for the Bengal mission would have happened during the time spent in Ireland during 1843 by Thomas Olliffe, apostolic missionary, who had been chosen as co-adjutor to Bishop Patrick Carew, Vicar Apostolic of Bengal. Both before and after his episcopal consecration in October 1843, he toured

---

12 *Advocate*, 26 February 1947.
13 The absence of early 19th century birth/baptismal records in Mayo parishes makes it impossible to exactly date years of birth.
14 See Patrick Hogan, 'The Migration of Ulster Catholics to Connaught, 1795–96', *Seanchas Ardmhacha: Journal of the Armagh Diocesan Historical Society*, 9 (1979), 286–301. I am grateful to John Lyons, editor of the Louisburgh parish magazine, for alerting me to the Catholic migrations from Armagh.
15 *The Tablet*, 13 April 1844 (reprinted in the *Bengal Catholic Herald*, 29 June 1844). The *BCH* added at the end of the extract that the *Fire Queen* had suffered piston damage before reaching Cork. The delayed party of missionaries finally arrived at Calcutta in September (*Bengal Catholic Herald*, 7 September 1844).

Ireland seeking volunteers among priests, seminarians and nuns. Olliffe, a member of a prominent Cork family, was 'not fully thirty years of age' when consecrated in his home city.[16] He had joined the new Bengal Vicariate Apostolic in 1838 immediately after studies at Propaganda Fide and ordination in Rome. In 1850 he became the first Vicar Apostolic of Eastern Bengal, based at Dacca, while remaining coadjutor to Archbishop Carew. He succeeded Carew in 1855. He died at the age of 45 in March 1859 at Naples, while returning to Ireland for his health's sake. The appointment of English-speaking bishops, many Irish, to Indian sees was part of Propaganda's effort to wrest control of the dioceses of the subcontinent from the Portuguese crown.[17]

John McGirr's ministry in Bengal was principally in education at St John's in Calcutta. In a notice in the *Bengal Catholic Herald* of December 1848 concerning the college, the rector was named as 'Rev J. McGirr'; among the 'gentlemen' assisting him in 'conducting the several classes' was 'Rev. Mr. McGirr Junr', in charge of 'Greek, French and the Use of Globes'.[18] James McGirr, John's young cousin, had arrived in Bengal as a seminarian in August 1846.[19]

In a letter written from Dublin on 9 September 1851 to the *Tablet*, John McGirr appealed for funds and personnel for the new Vicariate of East Bengal, to where he had moved with Bishop Olliffe following the establishment of the Dacca diocese in 1850.[20] In November the *Tablet* reported that two 'exemplary ladies' from the Loreto convent at Navan were setting out for Dacca, 'their remote destination, under the protection of the Rev. Mr. McGirr'.[21] This is the last reference found connecting John McGirr to India. The next reference to him is as 'recently a missionary in Southwark'

---

16 'Consecration of the Right Reverend Dr Oliffe', *Cork Examiner*, 9 October 1843. New South Wales was to receive a branch of the Cork family in 1836; like the NSW McGirrs, the Olliffes showed a distinct preference for the legal profession in later generations.

17 John Bede Polding had been appointed to Madras in July 1832, but after much hesitation, he declined and Rome accepted. He remained Vicar-Apostolic-elect until June 1833; the Papal brief for his episcopal ordination as bishop of the Titular See of Hierocaesarea remained valid until applied to his appointment as V-A of New Holland in June 1834.

18 *Bengal Catholic Herald*, 30 December 1848.

19 '*Per W. S. Hamilton from Liverpool* – James McGirr and William Grogan, Catholic Students' (*Friend of India*, 13 August 1846).

20 *Tablet*, 13 September 1851 (reprinted in *Bengal Catholic Herald*, 22 November 1851).

21 *Tablet*, 15 November 1851 (reprinted in *Bengal Catholic Herald*, 17 January 1852).

setting out for Australia in October 1855.[22]

Archbishop John Bede Polding, during his sixteen-month stay in Europe from May 1854, had been recruiting with a special focus on the educational needs of his Archdiocese. On board the *Phoenix* with the Archbishop were three Benedictine nuns destined for Subiaco Convent School and two Irish priests for St Mary's College, Lyndhurst. As Polding explained to Cardinal Barnabò of Propaganda Fide in Rome some years later:

> On my return to the Colony in 1856, I wished the Benedictine Community to limit itself to the education of its own members, and the secular clergy to attend to the education of the secular clergy at the college of Lyndhurst. A secular priest was constituted President, another, Vice-President each with a salary of £100, besides board and lodging; and everything necessary was provided for them. I engaged also some assistant teachers.[23]

The appointment of John McGirr and Patrick Newman to the college soon after their arrival in February 1856 was recorded in the Benedictine Journal: 'Great changes at Lyndhurst college ... The Revd J McGirr has been appointed 'Principal'; Revd Paul [Roche OSB] 'Prefect'; Rev Newman and Mr P O'Dee Subprefects.'[24]

However, as Polding went on to explain bitterly to Barnabò, things did not work out as he had hoped: 'But the president grew discontented, considering his salary too low.'[25] In a subsequent letter to Propaganda, Polding enclosed a chronological list of priests who had abandoned or had been dismissed from the mission since 1840. Last of the 31 names was John McGirr: 'Quarrelsome. Disappointed at not having a profitable mission, according to his tastes, he asked to be allowed to retire. This permission was freely given'. Most of the listed dismissals were for drunkenness or immorality.[26]

McGirr was replaced as President of Lyndhurst at the beginning of 1857. He continued briefly in Sydney in charge of the Petersham mission, but in November it was announced that 'the Rev. Mr. McGirr, formerly of

---

22 *The Nation*, 24 November. Information from the Southwark Archdiocesan Archives has not been forthcoming.

23 Polding to Barnabò, 13 May 1859 [Letters II.285].

24 *Benedictine Journal*, 4 February 1856, Sydney Archdiocesan Archives. The *Catholic Almanac* for 1857 lists Rev. W[illiam] McGirr as President. Mr. O'Dee was another Polding recruit aboard the *Phoenix*.

25 Polding to Propaganda Fide, 13 May 1859 (Polding Letters II.285).

26 Polding to Propaganda Fide, mid-May 1859 (Polding Letters II.294).

Lyndhurst College, is now attached to St. Francis', Melbourne'.[27] His first assignment was to the mission at Creswick in central Victoria. As a former missionary in Bengal, he was appointed to a committee to collect funds for the relief of victims of the Indian Mutiny of 1857.[28]

In 1859 he took charge of the Gippsland mission in eastern Victoria. His ministry was summarised in 1948 by the Vicar-General of the Sale Diocese, Tipperary-born Patrick Mary O'Donnell, later archbishop of Brisbane from 1965 to 1973, the last of Australia's Irish-born archbishops:

> During the four years of his pastorate Father McGirr proved himself a master of organization at a time when conditions of living and primitive methods of transport might have daunted a less able man. From Tarraville he ranged the vast expanse of his parish, riding northwards and to the east ... He was a familiar figure in mining camp and squatter's homestead, his evident zeal and ready wit gaining him the friendship and esteem of men of every creed ... A member of a scholarly family and great-uncle of the present Premier of New South Wales, much could be written of his work in Gippsland.[29]

However, his time in Gippsland was not without controversy. In September 1861 the Melbourne *Age* carried the headline: 'Clerical Interference in Elections: an extraordinary sermon'.[30] The article reported on a 300-strong public meeting held at Sale on polling day to protest against the 'conduct of the Rev. Mr M'Girr, the Roman Catholic priest, for having from the altar, on the Sunday previous, thought proper to address the members of his congregation as to the manner in which they should vote'. One of McGirr's congregation, a Mr. McGhee, addressed the meeting:

> The Catholics in this country were quite intelligent enough to think for themselves upon the respective merits of candidates before them, and he hoped that they would make this election a lesson to others that in matters of politics they would not be dictated to by religious advisers ... And as they only had the benefit of Mr M'Girr's services once a month for an hour and a quarter, he thought that his congregation should have the benefit of all he could give them in that time. They

---

27 *Freeman's Journal*, 7 November 1857.
28 'INDIAN RELIEF FUND AT CRESWICK', *The Star* (Ballarat), 17 February 1858.
29 *Advocate*, 23 December 1948.
30 *Age*, 5 September 1861.

ought to have as much of religion as he could cram into them in that short interval.[31]

When, four weeks later, Father McGirr was again in the Sale pulpit, it was not religion he crammed into his congregation, but a verbal attack on Mr. McGhee. The *Age*, under the heading, 'The Rev. Mr. McGirr Again', commented that 'the reverend gentleman has been delivering another edifying "pastoral" to his benighted flock', and published a letter from McGhee expressing his outrage:

> Mr M'Girr favored us yesterday, Sunday, in church with a few amusing ebullitions of temper, displayed against myself. His brilliant declamation and withering sarcasm failed to produce its intended purpose. He made a few complimentary comparisons between Judas and myself, the point of which I could not discover ... As I go to church to hear a sermon - not a mass of scandalous language - I must unwillingly exclude myself from the benefits of his ministrations, as I strongly object to the house of God being converted into a beer-garden.[32]

McGirr did not mollify his 'ebullitions of temper' when he crossed the Tasman in October 1864 to take up a mission in the newly discovered gold fields on the west coast of New Zealand's South Island. In June 1867, the Melbourne *Age* and several Victorian provincial newspapers carried a story, which began: 'A fracas has occurred at Hokitika that has caused much scandal among the Roman Catholic residents there'. The incident involved a public dispute after Sunday Mass between McGirr and the local Catholic school teacher over some books, which the priest demanded be returned and the teacher claimed to have been given to him in consideration of work carried out. 'Both complainant and defendant called one another liars, which resulted, as the complainant alleged, in Father M'Girr striking him on the face.' The case went before the magistrate and 'the information was dismissed'.[33] Other cases involving McGirr found their way to the magistrate's court: McGirr v. Hardcastle (November 1867); McGirr v. Smith and Co. (February 1868); Hardcastle v. McGirr (March 1868).[34]

When the litigious priest finally took his leave 'for the far distant shores

---

31 *The Age*, 5 September 1861.
32 *The Age*, 1 October 1861.
33 *The Age*, 7 June 1867.
34 *West Coast Times*, 9 November 1867, 14 February 1868, 14 March 1868.

of the mother country', he was afforded a fond farewell and parting gifts. In his speech of thanks he made some remarkable claims: 'During my life I have ever been a man of peace (Cheers) … I have been for five-and-twenty years a Clergyman, and never during that long-period have I had a contention with a single person (Great applause).' He went on to make comments about Irish loyalty, which might seem to contradict the very basis of this article—the identification of John McGirr as a supporter of the Russians in the Crimean War:

> I can safely affirm, no one more loyal than an Irishman (Hear, hear and cheers). It is true that Ireland has her grievances, but I confidently expect that those grievances will soon be redressed, and that we shall once more live in love and peace, and become one united dominant nation (Loud applause). Speaking of the Irish, where is there a more loyal or braver Regiment than the 18th Royal Irish, to which I was chaplain in India (Cheers). They were at Inkermann—the Irish took the Redan. They never found an Irishman leave his post. They were always first in attack and last in retreat. Of those Irishmen none were ever disloyal to his Queen or country.[35]

The context of this expressed pride in Irish participation in the Crimean War needs to be considered: in March 1868 the West Coast's Catholic community heard that three Fenians had been hanged in Manchester for killing a police sergeant. Catholics in Hokitika organised a huge funeral procession in honour of the Fenians. When it reached the local cemetery, the priest, Father William Larkin, conducted a burial service and a memorial Celtic cross was erected in honour of 'the Manchester martyrs'. Larkin was arrested, charged, convicted of riot and seditious libel, fined £20 and imprisoned for two months.[36] Perhaps McGirr was taking the opportunity offered by his farewell to safely distance himself from the local disturbances, as well as from the much-reported attempted assassination of Prince Alfred, Duke of Edinburgh, at Sydney later in March by the Fenian Henry O'Farrell, which resulted in anti-Irish hysteria throughout the Antipodes.

In October 1869 his death notice appeared in the Melbourne *Age*, which had assiduously followed his controversial ministry near and far: 'The mail which has just arrived has brought the intelligence of the death, at Southend,

---

35 *West Coast Times*, 7 April 1868.
36 See Neil Vaney. 'Larkin, William John', *Dictionary of New Zealand Biography*, first published in 1990. Te Ara – the Encyclopedia of New Zealand: https://teara.govt.nz/en/biographies/113/larkin-william-john

England, on the 8th of August, of the Rev. John McGirr, C.C., late of Gipps Land'.[37]

The 'Rev Mr McGirr Junr', who joined his cousin John in Bengal in 1846, was back in Ireland in 1852. He had completed his ecclesiastical studies and been ordained during his time in India.[38] The archives of the Tuam Archdiocese provide the following list of James McGirr's appointments: he served on Achill Island from 1852–53 and then moved to Clare Island until 1859. There is then a gap and his next appointment was in Milltown Co Galway from 1866 to 1872. Thereafter he was appointed to Moylough/ Mountbellew County Galway, where he died on 11 Dec 1881, aged 63.[39] The gap, from 1860 to 1866, was filled by his presence and ministry in NSW.

James' ministry on the Mayo islands was not without controversy. In January 1853, the Dublin *Freeman's Journal* published a letter from 'James M'Girr, C. C., Achill' under the heading: 'Downfall of Jumperism in Achill – Extraordinary Scene in a Catholic Graveyard'.[40] The letter unfolded the unseemly struggle between the Catholic priest and a Protestant minister over the body of a supposedly repentant 'Jumper' – a convert from Catholicism to Protestantism. The conflict culminated at the Catholic cemetery where the '*pseudo* minister', protected by four police officers 'with screwed bayonets', was attempting to read the Protestant burial service 'where no Jumper, since the time that Jumperism first began, or heretic since the days of Luther had been buried'. McGirr praised the attending magistrate for his intervention in calling aside the Rev. Mr. Barker, telling him to close his book and sending him home 'with his pack of ranting illiterate Jumpers'. In a lengthy response, the Reverend Joseph Barker gave a different version, complaining that he had been assailed by 'a number of ruffians, who shoved me about and made several attempts to snatch the book out of my hand'. He claimed a 'perfect right' to be conducting the burial service in the Catholic cemetery because 'every grave-yard in the parish is *de jure* the freehold property of the rector'.[41]

James added a post-script to his letter with an appeal for donations towards the repair of 'our little chapel' and for the 'founding of a little

---

37 *The Age*, 2 October 1869.
38 Lack of response from archivist of Calcutta Archdiocese makes certainty about his ordination difficult.
39 Email from archivist to author, 24 November 2017.
40 *Freeman's Journal*, 28 January 1853.
41 *The Achill Missionary Herald*, February 1853.

library of religious works in the chapel, which might serve, in some manner, to counteract the evil tendency of Jumperism'. From his new mission on neighbouring Clare Island, James wrote to the *Freeman's Journal* expressing gratitude for donations received—ten pounds from a Wexford benefactor and 'a sum collected in halfpence' by the 'generous poor of Manchester'. He concluded 'hoping that some of those wealthy and charitable persons upon whom an all wise and merciful Providence, in its own inscrutable designs, has bestowed prosperity, ease and affluence in this world will imitate the generous example of the poor of Manchester, by remitting us something for the chapel'.[42]

James arrived in Australia during 1860 for the good of his health, as stated in the *Freeman's* 'notes from our files of 1882', the year of his death in Ireland: 'A well-known priest, Rev. Father McGirr, of Sydney, Bathurst, Petersham, Five Dock, Concord, died in April. He was for seven years a professor at St. John's College, Calcutta, and came to Sydney for the good of his health. He regained it but again became ill, and his medical advisers told him that he must return to Europe.'[43] He was initially assigned to Bathurst, where his brother Michael had been conducting the local Catholic school since 1857.

The *Freeman's* Bathurst correspondent submitted a fulsome account of the town's celebration of St Patrick's day in 1861. McHale-inspired Irish patriotism was on full display as James responded to Dean Grant's toast, 'The Irish Patriots', which 'was drunk with enthusiastic cheers, the band playing *Mourir pour la patrie'*,

> The Rev. J. McGirr, on rising to respond to the toast, said that the very word patriotism expressed that innate and natural tone of one's country which was implanted by the hand of nature in every human breast. Every Nation could point to some eminent individuals in whose soul the holy flame burned more vividly, and with deeper intensity than in others ... But it is needless to multiply instances of Irish patriotism, he would tire their patience ('No, no') by dwelling longer upon a theme which every Irishman was conversant with, and he would now conclude by hoping that the dawn of day was fast breaking, when, from the concentration of public opinion on the many grievances of Ireland, the consummation for which the patriots lived and died, would take place, viz., complete religious and civil liberty, such as God had

---

42 *Freeman's Journal* (Dublin), 29 September 1853; 29 December 1853.
43 *Freeman's Journal*, 27 March 1930.

blessed this happy land with. He would conclude by hoping that the day was drawing near, when the words of Moore would receive their realization, in the fact that Ireland could at length have it predicted of her that she was – 'Great, glorious, and free ... First flower of the earth, and First gem of the sea.' ... The toast was drunk with cordiality. Air by the Band–'Rory O'Moore'.[44]

Michael M'Girr, in rising to propose the next toast, said that it was fortunate for him that the 'lily needed no painting'. Without further preface, he begged to propose 'the ladies'. The toast was drunk with all honours, the band playing 'Here's a health to all good lasses'.[45]

Later in the year James was in Sydney taking up appointments at Burwood and then Petersham. With his health declining he planned his return to Ireland, leaving Sydney in September 1864. In February 1866, the *Tuam Herald* announced that 'the Rev. James M'Girr, a subject of this diocese, and but recently returned to his native country, after many years of a zealous and toilsome missionary career in the far-distant land of Australia, has been appointed by His Grace to the curacy of Milltown in this neighbourhood'.[46]

In 1872 his eloquent patriotism was again to the fore at a meeting of the people of Milltown in support of the candidacy of Captain Nolan, 'the man for Galway'. He reminisced about his attendance at his first political meeting in 1844 at Castlebar, where Daniel O'Connell held one of his great rallies for Repeal. He then spoke of witnessing in 1854 the eviction of a poor tenant fallen into arrears: 'I went myself and offered to go security for the payment of the amount due, but the agent was unmoved and he brought his "brigade" on the spot. The poor man's house was levelled and his family, thirteen in number, were forced to quit their home on a bleak and frosty morning (groans)'. He concluded by calling on the townsmen to return to Parliament 'the man who will do away with these things forever'.[47]

Captain John Philip Nolan was duly elected, soundly defeating Captain William Le Poer Trench. Trench appealed the result on the grounds of intimidation during the campaign, chiefly on the part of clergy. The trial

---

44 Rory O'Moore (c. 1600–1655), was a leader of the 1641 rebellion, commemorated in a rebel song.

45 *Freeman's Journal*, 27 March 1861

46 *Tuam Herald*, 24 February 1866.

47 *Tuam Herald*, 27 January 1872.

judge found 36 persons guilty of undue influence and intimidation, including the Archbishop of Tuam, the Bishops of Clonfert and Galway, and 29 priests, the majority of the parish priests in the constituency. Captain Nolan was unseated and Captain Trench returned to the House of Commons.[48] This case of clerical election interference made the John McGirr affair in faraway Gippsland look insignificant indeed.

In October 1873, James added his signature to a petition from the Archbishop of Tuam and his clergy calling for the repeal of the Act of Union between Ireland and Great Britain:

> Resolved: 'That, impressed with a deep sense of the social and moral evils of which the legislative Union has for more than seventy years been productive to our country, we deem it a duty to lend every legitimate aid towards their abatement, and for that purpose, towards the total or qualified repeal of the disastrous union from which they continue to flow.[49]

Father James McGirr's death on 18 December 1881 was announced in the Dublin *Freeman's Journal.*[50] The Sydney *Freeman's* carried the article the following April:

> The deceased clergyman, who was in his 59th year was only one short month ago in apparently excellent health ... but alas, after a short illness of five days, he succumbed to a fatal attack of gout in the stomach. He had been the beloved C.C. of Moylough for the past nine years and his zeal in the discharge of his duties, his pious and unassuming manner and his great anxiety for the spiritual and temporal welfare of his flock, will not soon be forgotten ... His missionary career in India and in Sydney, Australia, was characterised by unceasing devotion to the interests of religion.[51]

His young cousin, Father James Joseph McGirr, had died at Orange in New South Wales in 1874 at the age of 45.[52] He had arrived in Sydney in June 1864, and began ecclesiastical studies at Lyndhurst College, where his cousin had

---

48 'JUDGMENT OF MR. JUSTICE KEOGH', House of Commons Debate, 13 June 1872, vol 211 cc1669–76: https://api.parliament.uk/historic-hansard/commons/1872/jun/13/ judgment-of-mr-justice-keogh See J H Whyte, 'The Influence of the Catholic Clergy on Elections in Nineteenth-Century Ireland', *The English Historical Review*, 75 (1960), 239–259.

49 *Mayo Examiner*, 6 October 1873.

50 *Freeman's Journal* (Dublin), 23 December 1881.

51 *Freeman's Journal*, 29 April 1882.

52 *Freeman's Journal*, 27 April 1867.

been President.[53] He was ordained at Bathurst on Palm Sunday in 1867. His was the first ordination by Matthew Quinn, the newly installed first bishop of Bathurst.

James was immediately appointed as Rector of St. Stanislaus College, newly founded high school for boys in Bathurst. His cousin Michael and his wife, teachers in the parochial school, provided accommodation for St. Stanislaus scholars in their home. An advertisement for the college was carried in the *Freeman's Journal* in January 1868, placing it in competition with Sydney's Lyndhurst College:

> COLLEGE OF ST STANISLAUS, BATHURST. Under the patronage and immediate superintendence of His Lordship the Bishop of. Bathurst. The studies of the College will be resumed Monday, JANUARY 20th, and will comprise besides the usual branches of a sound English commercial education, all that may be obtained in the first class Catholic Colleges of Great Britain and Ireland ...
>
> The Mathematical department is conducted by P. M'Hale, Esq. of the College of St. Jarlath, Tuam, and the English department is under the superintendence of Mr. Michael M. M'Girr ...
>
> For further particulars application may be made to His Lordship the Bishop of Bathurst; to the Rev. J. M'Girr, Prefect of Studies ...

Three members of the college staff were cousins: James and Michael McGirr and P. McHale. More relatives were to arrive from County Mayo within a few years. Soon after James' transfer in 1872 from Bathurst to the township of Bushman's, in the Lachlan gold fields, two of his nephews, James and John McGirr, joined him from Ireland. In 1873 the township was renamed Parkes, in honour of a visit by Henry Parkes, Premier of the Colony.

After his transfer to Orange in 1874 for health reasons, Father McGirr was honoured in Parkes by the naming of the new parish church:

> His Lordship Bishop Quinn solemnly blessed and dedicated our church under the name and invocation of' St. Jarlath, the patron Saint of the Archdiocese of Tuam, over which the illustrious Dr. M'Hale, the 'Lion of the fold of Judah', as O'Connell designated him, has so

---

53 His negative experiences of the monks at Lyndhurst were incorporated into the devastating report on the Sydney Benedictines written by W A Duncan at the request of Archbishop Vaughan in 1877, see T Kavenagh, 'Vaughan and the monks of Sydney', *Tjurunga* 25 (1983), 185.

nobly ruled for a full half century ... Father M'Girr who drew the first of his ecclesiastical aspirations at the shrine of St. Jarlath ... chose the patron of his youthful studies to be the heavenly guardian of his missionary labours, and so, for all future time, our church will be known as St. Jarlath's.[54]

The name of St Jarlath did not survive 'for all future time' in Parkes. In 1942 the patronage of the parish was changed to the Holy Family. The *Catholic Weekly*, the successor to Sydney's *Freeman's Journal*, reported: '[The Anglican minister] did not know who was responsible for changing the name of the new church from St. Jarlath's to the Church of the Holy Family, but as a humble leader of another Church, he congratulated Dr. Fox [bishop of Wilcannia-Forbes] on the change.'[55]

In May 1874 the Reverend James, in the McGirr litigious tradition, brought a charge against his own nephews:

Mr. F. Dalton, the gold-commissioner ... has been engaged two days this week hearing a charge which has been preferred against two brothers, viz. James and John M'Girr, and the wife of John, Mary M'Girr, by the Rev. James M'Girr, their uncle, for selling sixty-seven head of cattle, which had been let to James on terms from week to week. The only plea they have put in as yet is, that he had given them the cattle, and they thought they were at liberty to do as they chose with them. But prosecutor produced an agreement, showing that he had only let them from week to week. Mrs. M'Girr has been discharged, but the two men have been remanded for further evidence.[56]

In November the case was resolved in favour of the nephews: 'On the charge of stealing 67 head of cattle, the property of James Joseph M'Girr, in the W. district, Jas. and John M'Girr have been acquitted.'[57]

In the meantime, James Joseph had died at Orange. The *Freeman's Journal* coverage of the death and obsequies was reprinted in the *Mayo Examiner*: 'The death of Rev. Father M'Girr has cast a gloom over the Catholic people here, with whom he was a great favourite. He died at Orange on the 8th instant ... As soon as it was known through the town, the good people of Orange testified their grief and respect by every means in their power.'[58] The

---

54 *Freeman's Journal*, 28 March 1874.
55 *Catholic Weekly*, 26 November 1942.
56 *Australian Town and Country Journal*, 9 May 1874.
57 *Armidale Express and New England General Advertiser*, 6 November 1874
58 *Freeman's Journal*, 13 June 1874; *Mayo Examiner*, 7 September 1874.

death certificate stated that the cause of death was disease of the liver; the informant was his cousin Michael Mullins McGirr of Sydney and former colleague at St. Stanislaus College. The deceased was said to have been 45 years of age and 11 years resident in the Australasian colonies.

On 4 February 1890 the last of the first generation of Australian McGirrs died in Sydney - Michael Mullins McGirr, brother of Father James and cousin of Fathers John and James Joseph. The ten-column obituary in his *Freeman's Journal* spoke of his Irish patriotism:

> In patriotism… the deceased was intensely enthusiastic–a nationalist to the core, and an ardent Home Ruler. He never under any circumstances forgot 'the old folks at home,' and his purse was always out when any appeal came across the water from Ireland. In almost all the Irish movements in the colony for the past 30 years or more, he took a practical and earnest, if not always a prominent part, and for several years he was one of the hon. treasurers of the Irish National League of New South Wales. During the visit of the Messrs. Redmond, he was instrumental in raising the large sum which was sent home, and during the Irish Famine Relief Fund movement in the colony he was very active.[59]

Sympathetic notices were published in Sydney's leading newspapers.[60] The Bathurst papers printed extensive obituaries.

In 1948, more than 150 years after the County Armagh McGirrs fled to County Mayo, 92 years after Father John McGirr arrived in Sydney, 88 years after Father James McGirr and his brother Michael arrived in Bathurst, 84 years after Father James Joseph McGirr arrived in Sydney and 75 years after his nephews John and James McGirr arrived at Parkes, a McGirr returned to Culleen from Australia, as reported in the *Mayo News*:

> From a large, streamlined limousine, which came to a halt on the narrow road to Culleen village, on the southwestern slopes of Croagh Patrick, stepped the Prime Minister of New South Wales, Australia. He [Jim McGirr] was on the very spot where his father [John McGirr] had bid farewell to his family, 73 years previously, and set sail for distant Australia.[61]

---

59 *Freeman's Journal*, 8 February 1890.

60 The *Australian Town and Country Journal* referred to M M McGirr's *Freeman's Journal* as 'an eminently liberal Catholic newspaper', *ATCJ*, 8 February 1890.

61 Mayo News, November 1948 (reprinted: '30 Years Ago', *Mayo News*, 2 December 1978).

James Franklin*

On St Patrick's Day 1943, Éamon de Valera, Taoiseach of Ireland, broadcast on Raidió Éireann a remarkable speech on 'The Ireland that we dreamed of'. It begins:

> The ideal Ireland that we would have, the Ireland that we dreamed of, would be the home of a people who valued material wealth only as a basis for right living, of a people who, satisfied with frugal comfort, devoted their leisure to the things of the spirit – a land whose countryside would be bright with cosy homesteads, whose fields and villages would be joyous with the sounds of industry, with the romping of sturdy children, the contest of athletic youths and the laughter of happy maidens, whose firesides would be forums for the wisdom of serene old age. The home, in short, of a people living the life that God desires that men should live.[1]

In 1921, 'John O'Brien' (Father Patrick Hartigan) published his book of poems on rural Australian Catholic life, *Around the Boree Log*. A verse from 'The Little Irish Mother':

> *There's a Little Irish Mother that a lonely vigil keeps*
> *In the settler's hut where seldom stranger comes,*
> *Watching by the home-made cradle where one more Australian sleeps*
> *While the breezes whisper weird things to the gums,*
> *Where the settlers battle gamely, beaten down to rise again,*
> *And the brave bush wives the toil and silence share,*
> *Where the nation is a-building in the hearts of splendid men –*
> *There's a Little Irish Mother always there.*[2]

---

1   Audio in RTE Archives: https://www.rte.ie/archives/exhibitions/eamon-de-valera/719124-address-by-mr-de-valera/, text at https://en.wikipedia.org/wiki/The_Ireland_That_We_Dreamed_Of; discussed in Michele Dowling, 'The Ireland that I would have': de Valera and the creation of an Irish national image', *History Ireland* 5/2 (Summer 1997): 37–41; Tricia Cusack, 'A 'countryside bright with cosy homesteads': Irish nationalism and the cottage landscape', *National Identities* 3 (2001): 221–238; earlier expressions in Patrick Maume, 'A pastoral vision: the novels of Canon Joseph Guinan', *New Hibernia Review* 9/4 (Winter 2005): 79–98; Catherine Candy, *Popular Irish Novelists of the Early 20th Century: Patrick A. Sheehan, Joseph Guinan, Gerald O'Donovan* (Dublin: Wolfhound Press, 1996).

2   John O'Brien, *Around the Boree Log* (London: Angus & Robertson, 1978): http://www.middlemiss.org/lit/authors/obrienj/poetry/littleirishmother.html; discussion in Jeff

*   James Franklin is editor of the *JACHS*. This is the edited text of a talk to the ACHS on 16 February 2020.

That too is the 'life that God desires that men should live.' Both visions are rural, Catholic, Irish, virtuous, poor (actually, virtuous *because* poor) (and somewhat gendered, but not grossly: men are supposed to be virtuous as well as women).

The world context of the rural ideal

There is a very long back-story in Western civilization to the idea that the old virtues are preserved among simple rural people, in contrast to the many vices indulged in by rootless cosmopolitans and cynical city intellectuals. We will treat it very lightly here by way of background.

Les Murray recalls the ancient Greek contrast between rural Boeotia and urban Athens. Fashion-conscious and frenetic Athens is contemptuous of Boeotia as slow-moving and old-fashioned, but poetry, Murray says, does not work so well in the Athenian mode: 'Conflict and resolution take the place, in a crowded urban milieu, of the Boeotian interest in celebration and commemoration, modes that perennially appear in spacious, dignified cultures.'[3]

Probably the most admired hero of ancient Rome was the farmer Cincinnatus. With the early Republic in grave danger, the envoys of the Senate find him at his plough. They give him absolute power as dictator. He saves the state and immediately relinquishes power and returns to his farm. Such classical ideals were revived in the eighteenth century. Thomas Jefferson wrote (in a passage quoted by B.A. Santamaria):

> Those who labor in the earth are the chosen people of God, if He ever had a chosen people, whose breasts He has made His peculiar deposit for substantial and genuine virtue ... Corruption of morals in the mass of cultivators is a phenomenon of which no age or nation has furnished an example.[4]

Robert Burns' poem 'The Cotter's Saturday night' (praised in Robert

---

Brownrigg, 'Irish mothers and Mother Ireland in the verses of "John O'Brien" and other poetical priests', in J Brownrigg, C Mongan and R Reid, eds, *Echoes of Irish Australia: Rebellion to Republic* (Galong: St Clement's Retreat and Conference Centre, 2007), 167–181.

3   Les Murray, 'On sitting back and thinking about Porter's Boeotia', in *The Peasant Mandarin* (St Lucia: University of Queensland Press, 1978): 172–184, at 173.

4   Thomas Jefferson, *Notes on the State of Virginia*, quoted in B A Santamaria, *The Earth Our Mother* (Melbourne: Araluen Publishing, 1945), 30; later developments in Kevin M Lowe, *Baptized with the Soil: Christian Agrarians and the Crusade for Rural America* (New York: Oxford University Press, 2015).

Menzies' 'Forgotten people' speech of 1942[5]) includes the lines:

Long may thy hardy sons of rustic toil
Be blest with health, and peace, and sweet content!
And O! may Heaven their simple lives prevent
From luxury's contagion, weak and vile![6]

The political tone of rural virtue tends to the conservative. It is a familiar fact that rural political parties are generally conservative.[7] The British Marxist Raymond Williams, in his *The Country and the City* (1973), remarks acidly that every writer praising the unchanging tradition of rural virtue seems to agree that that timeless order broke down under the stress of imported city vices and radical ideas at just the same moment, namely, when the writer was a child.[8]

Rurality as a political ideal can also be expensive. The Common Agricultural Policy that at one stage soaked up 73 per cent of the European Union's budget, producing wine lakes and butter mountains, was premised on a 'rural fundamentalism',[9] especially French. The 1958 Stresa conference founding the Policy 'expressed their unanimous wish to preserve the character of European farming, which was predominately based on small-size, family holdings'.[10]

The rural ideal played well in Australia too, though here it competed with a more left-wing rural narrative of the 'Australian bushman' and noble shearers founding the Labor Party. The idea that small landholders would find frugal prosperity and simple happiness working their land was behind

---

5   http://www.liberals.net/theforgottenpeople.htm
6   http://www.robertburns.org/works/82.shtml
7   E.g. in Australia, Marc Brodie, 'The politics of rural nostalgia between the wars', in *Struggle Country: The rural ideal in twentieth century Australia,* ed. Graeme Davison and Marc Brodie (Clayton: Monash University Publishing, 2015), ch. 9; Elizabeth Kenworthy Teather, 'The Country Women's Association of New South Wales in the 1920s and 1930s as a counter-revolutionary organisation', *Journal of Australian Studies* 18 (1994): 67–78.
8   Raymond Williams, *The Country and the City* (London: Chatto and Windus, 1973), ch. 2.
9   Ian R Bowler, *Agriculture Under the Common Agricultural Policy: A Geography* (Manchester: Manchester University Press, 1985), 16
10 Rosemary Fennell, *The Common Agricultural Policy: Continuity and Change* (Oxford: Oxford University Press, 1997), 20–21; John Gray, 'The Common Agricultural Policy and the re-invention of the rural in the European Community', *Sociologia Ruralis* 40 (2000): 30–52.

early government visions for convicts, propaganda encouraging emigrants, and legislation allowing selection.[11] Albert Facey's *A Fortunate Life* portrays the result – a hard life but one many were grateful for.

The European Catholic ideal of rural virtue and piety

The Catholic version of the rural ideal was somewhat different from the classical one, naturally emphasising the piety as well as virtue of rural people, and connecting with older medieval and early modern 'ages of faith' when the population of Europe was mainly rural. As the Church in countries such as France failed to retain the allegiance of the new industrial working classes, popular Catholicism in Europe came to be increasingly

Jean-François Millet, *The Angelus* (1857–9)
Musée d'Orsay, Wikipedia commons

---

11 James Franklin, *Corrupting the Youth: A history of philosophy in Australia* (Sydney: Macleay Press, 2003), 238–244; Coral Lansbury, *Arcady in Australia* (Carlton: Melbourne University Press, 1970).

rural. Millet's painting of peasants praying *The Angelus* captures the image nineteenth-century Parisians had of simple rural piety.[12,13]

In film, the classic version is the Italian movie *The Tree of Wooden Clogs*.[14]

In the mid-twentieth century, the ideal of Catholic rural virtue was particularly associated with two regimes in Europe, those of Salazar and De Valera. B A Santamaria spoke in 1940 of

> the great inspiration which Salazar in Portugal and de Valera in Ireland have drawn from the social doctrines of the Church ... [in] two countries, at least, a determined effort is being made to reorganise the national economy on Christian lines, to break the shackles of anarchic and irresponsible capitalism, and to make economics subordinate to human happiness.[15]

Salazar was especially articulate about his model of Catholic rural virtue,[16] so it is worth quoting him at some length as an example of the international nature of the Catholic rural ideal.

In contrast to contemporary assumptions that a main business of governments is economic development, Salazar took at least some degree of rural poverty to be not a bug but a feature. That is because 'material life, economic development, and the unceasing rise in living standards' would 'leave in darkness all that is spiritual in man'.[17] (De Valera too preferred frugal comfort.[18]) Technological improvement is not wrong, but needs to be done in ways not destructive of traditional society:

---

12 Wikipedia commons, https://en.wikipedia.org/wiki/The_Angelus_(painting)#/media/
   File:JEAN-FRAN%C3%87OIS_MILLET_-_El_%C3%81ngelus_(Museo_de_
   Orsay,_1857-1859._%C3%93leo_sobre_lienzo,_55.5_x_66_cm).jpg

13 Similar in Jules Breton's 'Song of the Lark and Blessing the Wheat'; see Maureen
   Ryan, 'The peasant's bonds to Gaul, God, land and nature: The myth of the rural and
   Jules Breton's Le Chant de l'alouette', *RACAR (Revue d'Art Canadienne/Canadian Art
   Review)*: 19 (1/2) (1992): 79–96.

14 https://www.filmcomment.com/article/on-earth-as-it-is-in-heaven-ermanno-olmi/

15 B A Santamaria, 'What the Church Has Done for the Worker', pamphlet, 1940, quoted
   in Gerard Henderson, *Santamaria, A most unusual man* (Melbourne: Miegunyah Press,
   2015).

16 Felipe Ribeiro de Meneses, *Salazar: A political biography* (New York: Enigma Books,
   2009), 339, 623.

17 AO de Salazar, *Discursos e notas politicas* (Coimbra: Coimbra Editora, 1965), vol. 6,
   quoted in Michael Sanfey, 'Salazar and Salazarism', *Studies: An Irish Quarterly Review*
   92 (2003): 405–411.

18 Mary E Daly, 'The economic ideals of Irish nationalism: frugal comfort or lavish
   austerity?', *Eire-Ireland* 29/4 (Winter 1994): 77–100.

Neither by wealth nor by the luxury of technology are we satisfied ... Without distracting ourselves from the activity that gives everyone a greater share of goods and with these, more material comfort, the ideal is to flee from the materialism of our time: make the field more fecund, without silencing the songs of the girls; weave cotton or wool on the most modern loom, without weaving class hatred into the threads and without expelling from the workshop of the factory our old patriarchal spirit.[19]

Governments should instead be encouraging traditional rural culture:

The Casa de Povo [House of the People] should be major centres for a corporative education of the people, and a home or hearth for the village or the town. There the country people should meet after their daily toil, in innocent games, for simple plays, theatre or choirs.[20]

Salazar explains what is wrong with city life:

Misery seems a secretion of progress, civilization. It is not in the countryside (even in full crisis) where life is simple and without ambition, that misery turns afflictive, dramatic. Its great tragedy without remedy first develops in the cities, the big capitals, as insensitive and tough as they are civilized. Mechanization, automatization of progress which turns men into machines, isolates them brutally substituting their desires and affective impulses with complicated and cold interactions.[21]

That does not just apply to factory workers, but to white-collar workers, the habitués of city cafés:

Men who have been brought up and who live exclusively between the school, the government office, and the café—and it is from among them that most of our public men have been recruited—must not take umbrage if we believe that their education has been defective. I do not say, as many do, that city life is a false type of life: it is what it is, vigorous and real despite its artificiality and its defects. I say that it is incomplete, especially if we would judge the life of the nation by it, and if we assume that the life of one class in a city is the genuine life

---

19 A O Salazar, *Discursos e notas politicas* (Vol. 2 1935–1937) (Coimbra, 1945): 276. (Thanks to Robert Stove for translation)

20 *Entrevistas de Antonio Ferreira a Salazar* (2 edition, Lisboa: Parceira A.M. Pereira, 2003, with introduction by Fernando Rosas), interview of 1938, 153. (Thanks to Jean Page for translation.)

21 Salazar, *Entrevistas,* 171.

of the city itself. When we go from the capital to the provinces, from the town to the village, from the club, the newspaper office or the drawing-room to the countryside, the workshop and the factory, the horizon of social realities widens before our eyes and we form quite a different opinion of what constitutes a nation. The distance which separates us who haunt the cafés, who frequent public offices, who have become Ministers and have a share in what may be called the omnipotence of power, drawing up ideal schemes of reform, tracing the lines of important schemes, almost deciding the fate of the world – the distance which separates us from the real nation is immense. The sense of unlimited power which the town gives us because it is dealing with abstract ideas, can find no sustenance in Nature, itself so calm and so retiring, challenging with a smile our impatience and our pride in our creative power.[22]

Naturally, rural smallholders will be politically conservative and reject Communism:

See how the self-interest of States, overall the so-called capitalist States, is to create the greatest number of small property-holders who, far from favouring Communism or Socialism, tend to constitute the conservative reserve of the Nation, that which most opposes the development of libertarian ideas.[23]

Unlike Europe, colonial lands such as the United States and Australia had no peasantry with roots stretching back to the Middle Ages. Attempts were made to create a Catholic rural America, with a small degree of success.[24] These efforts too were admired by Santamaria.[25]

---

22 FCC Egerton, *Salazar: Rebuilder of Portugal* (London: Hodder & Stoughton, 1943), 151–2.

23 Salazar, *Entrevistas*, 41 (interview of 1932).

24 David S Bovée, *The Church and the Land: The National Catholic Rural Life Conference and American Society, 1923–2007* (Washington DC: Catholic University of America Press, 2010); Christopher Hamlin and John T McGreevy, 'The greening of America, Catholic style, 1930–1950', *Environmental History* 11 (2006): 464–499; Michael J Woods, *Cultivating Soil and Soul: Twentieth-century Catholic agrarians embrace the liturgical movement* (Collegeville MN: Liturgical Press, 2009); Allan C Carlson, '"Flee to the fields": Midwestern Catholicism and the last agrarian crusade, 1920–1941', *Chesterton Review* 33 (2018): 53–75.

25 Richard Doig, 'A "New Deal" for Australia: The National Catholic Rural Movement and American agrarianism, 1931–49', *Rural Society* 10 (2000): 139–152.

Santamaria and the National Catholic Rural Movement

In his early working life, Santamaria was not the head of a vast and multifaceted anti-communist 'Movement' but Secretary of the National Catholic Rural Movement, which he described as 'the most personally rewarding work in which I have ever engaged'.[26]

As with many of Santamaria's projects, it was a development of Archbishop Mannix's ideas. A sermon of Mannix's on a visit to the country in 1940 summarises his and Catholic views on the positives of rural life:

STAY IN THE COUNTRY: ARCHBISHOP MANNIX'S ADVICE

A plea for the welfare and development of country life which is vital to Australia was made by the Archbishop of Melbourne (Most Rev. D. Mannix, D.D.) in addressing a large country gathering in Victoria. His Grace said it was consoling to know that all the Catholic people were not confined to the city, but that a considerable sprinkling of them was to be found in the country. Families in the city after two or three generations seemed to die out; they did not seem to last long for one reason or another. He hoped none of those residing in the district to which he was talking would think of going to the city. People should remain in the country as long as they could make a living ... those who were now there should stick to their holdings. Large tracts of land were not vitally necessary; the main thing was to have a sufficiency to make a decent living. Those who got a decent living should not be anxious to turn their backs on the country for the lights, cinemas and other so-called attractions of city life.[27]

Mannix was right about city families having fewer children. A study found that rural Catholic married women had one and a half times as many children as city Catholic married women.[28] So differences between urban and rural behaviours are not purely a matter of perception.

We now know the NCRM mostly through the perspective of later years,

---

26 Bruce Duncan, *Crusade or Conspiracy? Catholics and the anti-Communist struggle in Australia* (Sydney: UNSW Press, 2001), 30–32, 86–89, 154–5.

27 'Stay in the country: Archbishop Mannix's advice', *Bunyip* (Gawler), 24/5/1940: http://trove.nla.gov.au/ndp/del/article/96698982, in James Franklin, Gerald O Nolan and Michael Gilchrist, *The Real Archbishop Mannix: From the sources* (Ballarat: Connor Court, 2015), ch. 10; Mannix perhaps understates the problem described in the American song of 1919 about soldiers returning from WWI: 'How Ya Gonna Keep 'em Down on the Farm (After They've Seen Paree)?'.

28 Lincoln H Day, 'Fertility differentials among Catholics in Australia', *Milbank Quarterly* 42 (2) (1964): 57–83.

when it became another branch of Santamaria's suite of anti-Communist front organisations funding his crusade in the unions.[29] Our view may also be obscured by later leftist caricature of it as about settling peasants with three acres and a cow, a picture specifically disavowed by the movement itself.[30] But in its heyday in the 1940s, when membership grew to 6000, it was neither of those things but a serious movement with economic and philosophical arguments in favour of encouraging self-owned rural smallholdings.[31] It did have a specifically Catholic vision:

> The life on the land is one which is most suited to the practice of the Christian virtues. Therefore, to defend and propagate the life on the land is a definite work of Catholic Action. As Catholic citizens, we have a vital interest in this matter, since the Catholic Church alone possesses the principles which will place rural life on a solid basis.[32]

Santamaria's 1945 manifesto, *The Earth Our Mother*, despite the romantic title, is a work of serious economic reasoning on how rural smallholdings can be made a success in the face of capitalist pressures to consolidate land in large estates.[33]

As it turned out, economic forces proved hostile. The model of small owner-operated businesses has continued to be viable in the suburbs but in the country has been mostly driven out by industrial-scale highly-capitalised enterprises. As Santamaria put it, 'If the agrobiologists were to make their fantasies come true, we might have almost no farmers.'[34] So it is. Australia could have had a version of the Common Agricultural Policy but chose not

---

29 Kevin Peoples, *Santamaria's Salesman: Working for the National Catholic Rural Movement, 1959–1961* (Mulgrave Vic: John Garratt Publishing, 2012); Race Mathews, *Of Labour and Liberty: Distributism in Victoria 1891–1966* (Clayton: Monash University Publishing, 2017), 224–6; Duncan, *Crusade or Conspiracy?*, 155.

30 Tony Ayers, 'Cottage Catholicism: Young Santamaria and the lure of the pastoral', *Arena Magazine* 34 (Apr/May 1998): 20–23.

31 Kathy Madden, 'Dreams and Realities: Some insights into the National Catholic Rural Movement', Master of Humanities thesis, University of Tasmania, 1994: https://eprints. utas.edu.au/20338/1/whole_MaddenKathy1995_thesis.pdf

32 'Catholic Rural Movement', *Catholic Freeman's Journal*, 23/1 (1941): https://trove.nla. gov.au/newspaper/article/146374103. Attempts to found rural Catholic communities described in David De Carvalho, 'Whitlands 1941–1951: An Australian experiment in utopian Catholicism', *Australasian Catholic Record* 80 (2003): 145–163; Gael Smith, *Maryknoll: History of a Catholic rural settlement* (Maryknoll: Artistic Wombat, 2002); a utopian vision in Denys Jackson, *Australian Dream: a journey to Merrion* (pamphlets, Melbourne: Australian Catholic Truth Society, 1947–8).

33 Discussion in Duncan, *Crusade or Conspiracy?*, 87–88.

34 Santamaria, *The Earth Our Mother*, 23.

to. 'O'Brien's' Hanrahan had the last word—'we'll all be rooned', and not by floods and drought but by economic forces unopposed by government intervention.

Irish settlement of rural Australia

Santamaria and Mannix were city theorists with a vision, which may or may not have coincided with or influenced reality. We now turn to the reality itself, the real Catholic rural communities of Australia.

Fr Therry's and Bishop Polding's long days on horseback are well-remembered features of early Australian Catholic history. The communities they visited had grown up through a process of settlement described in a neglected classic of Australian Catholic history, James Waldersee's *Catholic Society in New South Wales, 1788–1860*. Through the efforts of James Meehan, the most active surveyor in the colony in Macquarie's time, many of his fellow transportees from the revolution of 1798 and other Catholics received land grants in the Camden and Campbelltown areas and beyond.[35] Favourable reports sent back to Ireland resulted in chain migration and a swathe of Catholic settlers in the Goulburn, Yass and Boorowa areas and along the Murrumbidgee.[36] Caroline Chisholm helped supply Irish women to marry the Irishmen in those regions. According to her evidence,

> There is a very great demand for them as wives there. An Irishman likes to marry his own countrywoman; and there are a great number of Irish there who are doing extremely well, who formerly got into what is called a little bit of trouble; and they think that their own countrywomen will understanding [sic] them best.[37]

Boorowa was known as the most obviously Catholic region in New South Wales. The Protestant John Dunmore Lang, visiting the town in 1862, wrote,

> Burrowa is one of the most thoroughly Roman Catholic districts in New South Wales. As everybody in the Duke of Argyle's county

---

35 Bernard Dowd, 'James Meehan', *Journal of the Australian Catholic Historical Society* 3/2 (1970): 8–12.

36 James Waldersee, *Catholic Society in New South Wales, 1788–1850* (Sydney: University of Sydney Press, 1974), chs 4–5; Brian Maher, 'The Catholic communities of southern New South Wales', *Journal of the Australian Catholic Historical Society* 11 (1989): 18–32; Brian Maher, *Planting the Celtic Cross: Foundations of the Catholic Archdiocese of Canberra and Goulburn* (Canberra: Brian Maher, 1997).

37 Report of Select Committee of the House of Lords on Colonization from Ireland (1848): quoted in James Waldersee, 'Pre-famine Irish emigration to Australia', *Journal of the Australian Catholic Historical Society* 4/2, (1973): 23–35.

at home is called Campbell, so everybody in and around Burrowa is called Ryan. This, at least, is the general rule, although there are particular exceptions. Burrowa, in short, is the head-quarters and paradise of the Ryans, and might almost be supposed to be a veritable slice of the county Tipperary.[38]

Galong even had Ryans as grandee squattocrats.[39] (By and large the squattocracy were Protestants to a man.[40]) Bathurst and the Lachlan also had high proportions of Catholic settlers,[41] while the Hunter Valley in NSW was home to a significant number of Catholics, who often settled 'beyond the established villages and towns.[42] Other areas of strong Catholic rural settlement were found in southwest and northeast Victoria[43] (sometimes speaking Gaelic[44]).

One aspect of rural Catholicism noted by several observers was its generally anti-sectarian character. Fenian scares, Orangeism and conflicts about jobs and education were largely city phenomena and in the country a spirit of tolerance and cooperation between different denominations was regarded as normal.[45]

---

38 John Dunmore Lang, *Notes of a Trip to the Westward and Southward, in the Colony of New South Wales; in the months of March and April, 1862* (Sydney: Hanson and Bennett, 1862), 27; full story in Malcolm Campbell, *The Kingdom of the Ryans: The Irish in Southwest New South Wales, 1816–1890* (Sydney: UNSW Press, 1997); Waldersee, *Catholic Society,* 120–1; Brian Maher, *A Slice of Tipperary: A story of Boorowa N.S.W. Catholic community* (Bruce ACT: Brian Maher, 2016).

39 Max Barrett, *King of Galong Castle: The story of Ned Ryan, 1786–1871* (Weston Creek ACT: Genie Publishing, 2000).

40 Don Aitkin, *The County Party in New South Wales* (Canberra: Australian National University Press, 1972), 103, 140.

41 Malcolm Campbell and Robert Tierney, 'The missing Catholics: Religion and population decline in the Lachlan district, 1870–1890', *Journal of Australian Colonial History* 18 (2016): 115–138; a detailed local history in Gavin Cashman, *Avoca: The faith of the pioneers* (Black Springs NSW: The Centenary Committee of the Church of St Vincent de Paul, 1988).

42 Beverley Zimmerman, *The Making of a Diocese: Maitland, its Bishop, Priests and People, 1866–1909* (Carlton South, Vic: Melbourne University Press, 2000), 44–45; earlier Michael Belcher, 'The Catholics of Wallis Plains 1820-1835: Catholics in a pre-institutional environment', *Journal of the Australian Catholic Historical Society* 34 (2013): 2–17.

43 Terry G Jordan and Alyson L Greiner, 'Irish migration to rural Eastern Australia: a preliminary investigation', *Irish Geography* 27 (1994): 135–142; Regina Lane, *Saving St Brigid's* (Carlton South: Bridin Books, 2014), ch. 2.

44 Val Noone, *Hidden Ireland in Victoria* (Ballarat: Ballarat Heritage Services, 2012), 43–48.

45 Confirmed by James Logan, 'Sectarianism in Ganmain: a local study, 1912–1921', *Rural*

The *Yass Courier* reported:

On Saint Patrick's Day 1859 the Yass solicitor George C Allman addressed a banquet of the town's most prominent men and women. In his address, Allman, the son of a Protestant Irish settler, Captain Francis Allman, praised his town as a 'successful experiment', a place where people 'of all opinions, grades and religions may meet and remember that they belong to a common country'. His sentiments were echoed by the Reverend Patrick Bermingham, one of the town's two Roman Catholic priests, who described the evening's celebration as one 'calculated to make the inhabitants of the southern districts appreciate the sterling good qualities of each other without reference to race or creed'.[46]

Fr Hartigan ('John O'Brien') was a strong supporter of good relations among Christians, both in words and actions.[47]

The mixing of populations and the low density that meant everyone needed to help one another in hard times encouraged a lack of sectarianism. Everyone had to attend everyone else's ball or bazaar or there wouldn't have been enough people to go round. Father Carragher, parish priest at Ungarie in the 1930s and certainly well imbued with Catholic culture after studying philosophy and theology at Valladolid, said 'If we didn't support one another out here, we'd all have to close our doors.'[48] Sparse populations also encouraged the evil (from the clerical point of view) of mixed marriages.[49]

Catholic education and culture in the bush

It was one thing to settle remote regions with people nominally Catholic, another to develop Catholic devotion, education and culture in those areas with so little contact with the 'outside world'. For all the days spent on horseback by pioneer priests, bush people's contact with formal religion was

---

Society 10 (2000), 121–138.

46 *Yass Courier,* 19/3/1859, in Malcolm Campbell, 'A 'successful experiment' no more: the intensification of religious bigotry in Eastern Australia, 1865–1885', *Humanities Research* 12/1 (2005): 67–78.

47 Frank Mecham, *"John O'Brien" and the Boree Log* (Sydney: Angus & Robertson, 1981), 72, 161, 171, 187, 269.

48 Fergus Cloran, *I Saw the Bay First* (Glebe: Fast Books, 1993), 79; also in Jack Waterford, 'On being rural, Irish and Catholic', *Canberra Times* 10/9 (1983): 13: https://trove.nla.gov.au/newspaper/article/116405831

49 PM Lynch, 'The apostolate of the back-blocks: how to advance the interests of religion in remote country districts', *Proceedings of the Third Australasian Catholic Congress,* 1909 (Sydney: St Mary's Cathedral Book Depot, 1910): 89–102, at 92.

inevitably spasmodic. A letter home to Ireland in 1862 says

> I know some people living (what we call the bush) in the Interiour far in the country. They might be catholics if they hapen to have a family they cant run to a Priest to get them christened they come down here some times with as many as half a Dozen at a time and get them Baptized and the whole of them well able to talk to the Priest. Catholics has the worst chance for anny such thing in the bush.[50]

A similar theme (with some stereotyping of the Irish) is the point of Banjo Paterson's poem 'A Bush Christening' (1893) which gives an outsider's view of the Irish community. It sets the scene with the tenuous hold of religion in the outback:

> *On the outer Barcoo where the churches are few,*
> *And men of religion are scanty,*
> *On a road never cross'd 'cept by folk that are lost,*
> *One Michael Magee had a shanty.*

A priest finally arrives to baptise Magee's son but by then he's aged 10. He concludes that christening must be something like branding horses so he heads off for the bush. The priest has to baptise him by throwing a bottle of whisky after him. By then he's forgotten what name he's supposed to christen him with so he takes the one on the whisky bottle and it's 'Maginnis Magee.'[51]

Waldersee suggests that the first generation of rural Catholics were often not very devoted to their faith. But there are plenty of recollections in later times of major efforts by rural families to reach what masses were available. Kathleen Fitzpatrick recalls the world of her grandparents in rural Gippsland around the 1850s:

> One of the deprivations the Irish colonists felt most was that of the familiar offices of the Catholic Church. A priest came to Nar Nar Goon every six months, arriving on Saturday and staying until Monday morning. When it was known that he was coming Irishmen from miles around bundled their families into buggies and saddled their own horses and converged on Nar Nar Goon on Saturday, when

---

50 Michael Normile (NSW) to his father Michael Normile (Clare), 18 Apr 1862, in David Fitzpatrick, '"That beloved country, that no place else resembles": connotations of Irishness in Irish-Australasian letters, 1841–1915', *Irish Historical Studies* 27 (1991): 324–351, at 337.

51 *The Bulletin*, 6 Dec 1893: http://www.middlemiss.org/lit/authors/patersonab/poetry/christen.html

they all went to confession and spent the night at the Limerick Arms or with friends or just camping. On Sunday morning there was Mass, held alternately at the Limerick Arms and the farm of Mr John Dore, a shipmate of Daniel O'Brien's in the olden days; and after mass there were weddings and baptisms. When these were over there was a splendid banquet for everyone at the Limerick Arms. A great day for the Irish, from which they returned to their farms nourished spiritually and physically, socially and, no doubt, alcoholically.

Nothing astonishes me more, in the history of Daniel and Brigid O'Brien, than the tenacious campaign they waged to bring their children up as civilised people ...[52]

Of course a certain amount of self-help is possible in religion, as in 'John O'Brien's' poem in which the little Irish mother in her slab hut expands more and more the 'trimmin's on the rosary'.[53]

It was difficult to project Catholic education into remote communities. The woeful standard of knowledge is a theme of 'John O'Brien's' poem 'Tangmalangalloo':

There everything is big and grand, and men are giants too –
But Christian Knowledge wilts, alas, at Tangmalangaloo.

The imposing bishop visits the bush school. He asks the unfortunate pupil 'Why is Christmas day the greatest of the year?' and gets the answer 'It's the day before the races out at Tangmalangaloo.'[54]

The tendency of the first post-Irish generation in remote regions to lose its religion is lamented in an address to the Australasian Catholic Congress of 1909:

In the Australian bush how rarely is the Catechism completely mastered, simply because a priest is rarely seen ... The youth of Ireland have the Martyrs of Faith as the heroes of their dreams ... On the other hand, the youth of the Australian bush, when seeking for some hero, must select from his scanty acquaintanceship either some silent, uneducated bushman, ignorant of many things, but particularly

---

52 Kathleen Fitzpatrick, *Solid Bluestone Foundations: Memories of an Australian girlhood* (Ringwood: Penguin, 1986), 36–37.

53 http://www.middlemiss.org/lit/authors/obrienj/poetry/trimminsonrosary.html

54 http://www.middlemiss.org/lit/authors/obrienj/poetry/tangmalangaloo.html ; a true story: JA Mecham, 'The biography of "John O'Brien": Father Patrick Hartigan', *Journal of the Australian Catholic Historical Society* 7/1 (1981): 24–27; Mecham, *"John O'Brien"* ... 143.

of religion ... This portrayal of the bushman's unfavourable religious environment is strongly expressed, for if it is not wholly true of the first generation of Irish Australians, it becomes increasingly true of each succeeding generation. In the former it is largely corrected by the Irish tradition imbibed from the Irish father, thanks to the God-given ability for picturesque narrative and vivid explanation that is the birthright of every son of Erin. On the other hand, the Australian bushman is a silent man, like the children of all the lonely places of the earth ... Moreover, many of our Catholic women are ignorant of their Faith and totally incapable of either influencing a careless husband or instructing their sturdy children.[55]

(At least Protestantism in the bush is not much of a contender, he says, as out there they don't know whether Luther was born before Christ or not.)

The task of basic religious instruction in the bush fell mainly to the nuns. Mary McKillop began her work in Penola, a typical tiny bush community far from anywhere. She said 'We are for the back-blocks ... it is our business to gather in poor children abandoned in out-of-the-way places; when that is over, we ought to make way for others.'[56] The rural dioceses usually had convents even in the smallest towns.[57] When cars became available, some roving nuns like the 'caravan sisters' were able to move beyond the constraints of convent life and meet people where they were.[58]

Courtesy of the massive subsidy to rural postal services that kept rural postage as cheap as in the cities, written material could nourish remote faith. The tens of thousands of subscribers of magazines like the Jesuit *Messenger* and Missionaries of the Sacred Heart *Annals* included many in rural areas.

---

55 T Maguire, 'The soul of the pioneer', *Proceedings of the Third Australasian Catholic Congress,* 1909 (Sydney: St Mary's Cathedral Book Depot, 1910): 103–111, at 105–6.

56 George O'Neill, *Life of Mother Mary of the Cross (MacKillop) 1842–1909: Foundress of the (Australian) Sisters of Saint Joseph* (Sydney: Pellegrini, 1931), 394.

57 Marie Crowley, 'The contribution of women religious in rural Australia', *Australasian Catholic Record,* 87 (2010): 20–29; Marie Crowley, *Women of The Vale: Perthville Josephites 1872–1972* (Richmond Vic: Spectrum Publications, 2002); Mary Ryan, *For Whom Alone We Go Forward or Stay Back: A History of the Sisters of Mercy Wilcannia-Forbes Congregation 1884–1959* (Allawah, NSW: Sisters of Mercy Wilcannia-Forbes, 2004); M Assumpta O'Hanlon, *Dominican Pioneers in New South Wales* (Sydney: Australasian Publishing, 1949), ch.7; a biography in Margaret M Press, 'Leehy, Mary Agnes (1873–1960)', *Australian Dictionary of Biography*: http://adb.anu.edu.au/biography/leehy-mary-agnes-7153/text12351

58 Edmund Campion, *Australian Catholics* (Ringwood Vic: Penguin, 1987), 192–4; Penelope Edman, *Around the Kitchen Table with the Missionary Sisters of Service* (Rangeview Vic: Missionary Sisters of Service, 2008).

In 1914 a distributor of *The Messenger* wrote, 'In some of our Catholic homes in the bush *The Messenger* is the only thing that keeps the Faith alive. The people live in the mountains and cannot come to Mass.'[59] Correspondence courses for the bush were also developed to substitute for the school and adult education available in cities.[60]

Catholic culture in a more general sense included guilds, friendly societies and social events like race meetings. They needed the support of towns, but not big ones:

> In January 1875 the general meeting of the Boorowa Holy Catholic Guild met and heard reports of a most successful first year of operation in which membership, attendances, and the financial position of the Guild had all been strong. The Chairman, the Reverend J Dunne outlined plans to strengthen the Guild's library in the following year. The Guild was instrumental in the organization of the Saint Patrick's Day celebrations in Boorowa the same year. The proceedings commenced with a procession from the town to John Nagle Ryan's neighbouring paddock, where 600 people gathered to attend a race meeting and games.[61]

Not many of the leading figures of the Australian church came from truly rural backgrounds. Two of the conservative intellectuals of the Australian church did so. The Thomist philosopher and anti-communist crusader Dr P J (Paddy) Ryan came from a farm near Albury.[62] Sydney's other celebrated Thomist philosopher, the founder of the Aquinas Academy for laity, Dr Austin Woodbury, came from the Hawkesbury.[63]

Eileen O'Connor's two main associates came from poor rural backgrounds. Her co-founder of Our Lady's Nurses for the Poor was Fr Edward McGrath, from a difficult childhood in Kelly country in Victoria,[64] while her first

---

59 Campion, *Australian Catholics,* 131.

60 Campion, *Australian Catholics,* 192; John T McMahon, *College, Campus, Cloister* (Nedlands: University of Western Australia Press, 1969), ch. 7; Janice Garaty, *Providence Provides: Brigidine Sisters in the New South Wales Province* (Sydney: NewSouth Publishing, 2013), 169.

61 Campbell, *Kingdom of the Ryans,* 158; more on Boorowa's Catholic culture in 'James McDonald, Henry Curran, bushrangers and a Boorowa dream', *Journal of the Australian Catholic Historical Society* 38 (2017): 20–33.

62 James Franklin, 'Ryan, Patrick Joseph, 1904–1969', *Australian Dictionary of Biography,* 16 (2002): http://adb.anu.edu.au/biography/ryan-patrick-joseph-11591

63 Julie Thorpe, *Aquinas Academy 1945–2015: A very personal story* (Adelaide: ATF Theology, 2016), 2.

64 John Hosie, *A Lonely Road: Fr Ted McGrath, a great Australian* (Hindmarsh: ATF

Cover of the 1968 edition of Around the Boree Log

recruit and successor, Theresa McLaughlin, came from an equally poor farm near Lithgow.[65]

Tim Fischer, Deputy Prime Minister and Ambassador to the Vatican, played up his origins as the 'boy from Boree Creek', which is in the Narrandera area, 'John O'Brien' country.[66]

Around the Boree Log[67]

'John O'Brien's' picture of a 'simple folk and hearty', happy and devout rural people is dismissed as 'glutinous sentiment' by some supercilious modern intellectuals. City folk.[68] That is surely too dismissive of the report of someone who was on the spot and recorded in fine detail what he saw. It is perhaps not all that was happening, but certainly part of it. His picture of life 'At Casey's after mass' is straightforwardly based on the observation of someone who was there:

Past the kitchen door they rattled and they took the horses out;
While the women went inside at once, the menfolk hung about
Round the stable down at Casey's, waiting dinner down at Casey's;
And they talked about the Government, and blamed it for the drought,
Sitting where the sunlight lingers, picking splinters from their fingers,

Press, 2010), ch. 4.

65 Jocelyn Hedley, *Hidden in the Shadow of Love: The story of Theresa McLaughlin and Our Lady's Nurses for the Poor* (Strathfield: St Paul's, 2009), 12–18.

66 Peter Rees, *The Boy from Boree Creek: The Tim Fischer story* (Crows Nest: Allen and Unwin, 2001), ch. 2.

67 Cover image of *Boree Log*: https://en.wikipedia.org/wiki/John_O%27Brien_(poet)#/media/File:Aroundtheborelog.jpg

68 Fitzpatrick, 'That beloved country', at 330; even Patrick O'Farrell speaks of 'O'Brien's' 'cloying' and 'nostalgic sentimentality': *The Irish in Australia* (rev. ed, Kensington: University of New South Wales Press, 1993): 149, 192.

Settling all the problems of the world beyond a chance of doubt.
From inside there came the bustle of the cheerful wholesome hustle,
As dear old Mrs. Casey tried all records to surpass;
Oh, there's many a memory blesses her sweet silver-braided tresses;
They were "lovely" down at Casey's – always joking down at Casey's–
Spending Sunday down at Casey's after Mass.[69]

'O'Brien's' most famous creation, Hanrahan whose catchphrase is 'We'll all be rooned', is depressive, but his pessimism is mocked in the poem.[70] Everyone else is positive.

Cullenbenbong

'John O'Brien' was not an insider of his community and was producing poetry, not memoir. It could be suspected that his somewhat rose-coloured picture has some degree of propagandist purpose. So it is valuable to read a straightforward memoir that in effect says the same thing as he does. This is *Cullenbenbong,* by Bernard O'Reilly, who later became an authentic Australian hero by leading a difficult expedition that saved victims of a plane crash.[71] The tiny farming community of Cullenbenbong lay in a valley at the western edge of the Blue Mountains. His picture matches 'John O'Brien's' exactly:

> When the riding party reached the top of Tinkers Hill, where it joined the Ganbenang road they came up with other families on horseback, for it wasn't merely the baby's christening day, it was the one Sunday of the month when Father Hogan drove out from Hartley to the little wooden church at Lowther.[72]

> On went the cavalcade. Yarning comfortably they splashed through the gravelly shallows of Marsden's Creek, while the horses kicked spray high in the air and the warm sun slanted down through a fairyland of willows in their tender spring dress. Then the climb up to the Divide amongst the new-blooming black-thorn, with other families joining in until the party was at full strength—the various Cullen and O'Reilly

69 http://www.middlemiss.org/lit/authors/obrienj/poetry/atcaseys.html
70 "John O'Brien", 'Said Hanrahan', *Catholic Press,* 31 July 1919, https://trove.nla.gov.au/newspaper/article/106072280
71 David Stove, 'A hero not of our time', in D Stove, *Cricket Versus Republicanism* (Sydney: Quakers Hill Press, 1995), 4–13.
72 Bernard O'Reilly, *Cullenbenbong* (Brisbane: WB Smith & Paterson, 1944), 25–6.

families, the McAvineys and McAuleys, the Flanagans, Ryans and Kellys—all ages, on all types of horses, sometimes double and treble banked, yarning and smoking and singing and acting the goat, drinking in the spring sunshine, the breath of clematis and the songs of the birds—lovely old people, lovely old days.[73]

He recalls his father's prayers when by himself:

Presently with the help of the family Dad would be ready, and we would all trail out to where the horses were tied under the acacias and see him off ... Then would come the patting of the pockets: 'Matches, tobacco, knife, glasses, rosary beads.' The beads were always in his pocket, even if he were only going up the hill for a hearth log; not for the sake of displaying his religion, but for company he'd tell you; like the glasses he was forever breaking and mending them with bits of fine wire. It was Dad's practice if riding at night to say his prayers as he rode, and then he'd be all ready for tea and bed when the destination was reached. It wasn't a bad idea, and we still keep it up.[74]

O'Reilly even has a spontaneous touch of De Valera and Salazar's view that prosperity can be a bad thing:

Too soon a little prosperity came to the valley and the sulkies which were the first expression of it hastened the destruction of one of the happiest features of the valley life. So it was in many other quiet valleys. Later still came the motor car, a cold nasty thing which took all the comradeship from the road, and made every fellow traveller a nuisance or a potential enemy.[75]

Kelly Country

While 'John O'Brien' and Bernard O'Reilly were telling the truth, it was not the whole truth. They weren't all saints out there. Original sin was not absent in rural parts, nor subsequent sins.

The low density of population in rural areas could mean a distance from civilising influences, including the rule of law, which the less saintly might take advantage of. According to an opinion piece in the Catholic press of 1859, it was well-known that rural morals were terrible, and the clergy were not on top of the problem.[76]

---

73 O'Reilly, *Cullenbenbong*, 29
74 O'Reilly, *Cullenbenbong*, 136–7.
75 O'Reilly, *Cullenbenbong*, 29
76 'Rural morals', *Freeman's Journal* 10/12 (1859): https://trove.nla.gov.au/newspaper/

Take the case of Ellen Quinn. Born in County Antrim about 1832, she was something of a truant at school. The family arrived in Port Phillip as assisted migrants in 1841 and moved to a farm outside Melbourne. She became pregnant to and married John ('Red') Kelly, an Irishman who had been transported to Van Diemen's Land for stealing pigs.[77] Her *ADB* article continues:

> The extensive Quinn and Kelly clans tended to skirt the fringes of the law, and for Ellen and Red financial difficulties, several moves, further births and mounting police attention set a definitive pattern. Red began drinking heavily. In 1865 he stole a calf and served four months in gaol. The following year he died, an alcoholic, of oedema, leaving Ellen with seven children aged from 18 months to 13 years.

> As she struggled to raise her children on inferior farmland, she became notorious for her sometimes-violent temper, resulting in several court appearances. After moving her family into the far north-east of Victoria to stay near relations, she leased a selection of 88 acres (35.6 ha) there and sold 'sly grog' to make ends meet. The bushranger Harry Power became a family friend, introducing 14-year-old [son] Ned to the life of a bandit. In 1869 Ellen took a lover, Bill Frost, and became pregnant, he promising marriage. The baby—her ninth—was born in March 1870, but Frost did not keep his word. Trouble with the law increased, with several of Ellen's siblings and offspring suffering periods of imprisonment.

> Late in 1872, with Ned in prison, she met George King, a 23-year-old Californian horse-thief, and once more fell pregnant ...[78]

And so on ...

Things went from bad to worse when young Ned turned out to be a psychopathic killer well outside the range of the usual rural petty crims.[79] Ellen was conveniently in prison to see Ned before his execution. Big crime then went back to Melbourne where it belonged. Ellen Kelly became respectable in old age though never well-off, and died in 1923.

Ned Kelly's few writings show a more than Irish-sized chip on the

article/114837871

77 Grantlee Kieza, *Mrs Kelly* (Sydney: HarperCollins 2017), chs 1–2.

78 Jacqueline Zara Wilson, 'Kelly, Ellen (1832-1923)', *Australian Dictionary of Biography,* Supplementary Volume (2005): http://adb.anu.edu.au/biography/kelly-ellen-13021

79 Russ Scott and Ian MacFarlane, 'Ned Kelly—stock thief, bank robber, murderer—psychopath', *Psychiatry, Psychology and Law* 21 (2014): 716–746.

shoulder. Like some later mass murderers, he was given to writing spiels of garbled history in manifestos full of imported resentments to 'justify' his murders:

> I have been wronged and my mother and four or five men lagged innocent and is my brothers and sisters and my mother not to be pitied also who has no alternative only to put up with the brutal and cowardly conduct of a parcel of big ugly fat-necked wombat headed big bellied magpie legged narrow hipped splaw-footed sons of Irish Bailiffs or english landlords which is better known as Officers of Justice or Victorian Police who some call honest gentlemen.[80]

That is from Kelly's 'Jeriliderie letter', written at the time he held up Jerilderie from Saturday to Monday (allowing mass to be said on the Sunday).[81] In another letter he wrote, 'thank God my conscience is as clear as the snow in Peru.'[82]

While the Kelly gang were certainly not church-going folk, the clergy did manage to insert themselves into the story at the last moment. On 28 June 1880, the Irish-born priest Fr Matthew Gibney was travelling by train through Glenrowan. He learned that Ned and his gang had been surrounded in Mrs Jones' Hotel and were shooting it out with police. He left the train and tended the apparently seriously wounded Kelly, heard his confession and gave him the last rites. Although Kelly advised against it, Gibney entered the burning hotel to minister to the remainder of the gang. He found three of them dead and anointed the remaining one shortly before he died.[83]

The Kelly clan were by no means typical of the community among which they lived, the poor selectors of north-east Victoria. Methodist and Catholic farmers who mostly got on well, they were mostly law-abiding and patriotic folk, contributing to one another's churches and charities. They saved money by not throwing it away on alcohol, and when they did have a quiet drink it was mostly in licensed premises, not in illegal shanties like Mrs Kelly's. Two respectable Protestant selectors went bail surety for Mrs Kelly when

80 Ned Kelly, Jerilderie letter (1879), 30: https://www.nma.gov.au/explore/features/ned-kelly-jerilderie-letter/transcription
81 https://trove.nla.gov.au/newspaper/article/5932022; Mecham, *"John O'Brien"*, 116–7.
82 Ned Kelly, Cameron letter (1878): http://kellygang.asn.au/wiki/Cameron_Letter
83 VE Callaghan, 'Gibney, Matthew (1835–1925)', *Australian Dictionary of Biography:* http://adb.anu.edu.au/biography/gibney-matthew-6305/text10873; a fictional story of priest and horse-thief in Banjo Paterson, 'Father Riley's horse': http://www.wallisandmatilda.com.au/father-rileys-horse.shtml

she was in Beechworth jail with a newborn baby.[84] Even in Kelly country, respectability was the norm.

Child slavery?

Other than horse thieving, one sin for which rural Australia provided particular opportunities was child slavery. In Australia's best-known rural memoir, *A Fortunate Life,* Bert Facey is sold into slavery aged eight by his grandmother, though he doesn't use that word.[85]

Child slavery could occur in closed institutions, such as the agricultural schools for migrant orphans, Tardun and Bindoon.[86] But equally hidden from prying eyes were remote farms, where there was little to prevent poor farmers working young relatives non-stop.

Mary Ann Corrigan, born in Enniskillen, arrived in Australia aged 21 on an assisted passage in 1878 and gained employment on a pastoral property in south-eastern New South Wales. Because of some unspecified problem, she went to the newly-established convent of St Benedict in Queanbeyan and was taken in and did housework. On a visit to relatives in Bathurst she met her future husband, a blacksmith, and they married in the Catholic cathedral there in 1884. She named her firstborn Joseph Benedict, the rather unusual second name believed to indicate gratitude for her time at the convent; the nuns embroidered his christening robe. When young Ben was five and with two younger brothers, his paternal grandfather called and suggested Ben come to stay with him for a while on his small farm at Limekilns, a tiny village well out of Bathurst on the Sofala Road. He was to stay there for nine years, and it was not a pleasant time. Old Patrick Chifley had come from the bottom of the heap in County Tipperary and as a boy barely survived the potato famine. He had not long before buried the last of three wives. A daughter kept house but labour was needed to work the considerable number of acres (by Irish standards) that Patrick had accumulated. 'The old Tartar',

---

84　Doug Morrissey, *Ned Kelly: Selectors, squatters and stock thieves* (Redland Bay: Connor Court, 2018), especially chs 2–3.

85　AB Facey, *A Fortunate Life* (Fremantle: Fremantle Press, 2018), ch. 5.

86　Barry M Coldrey, *The Scheme: The Christian Brothers and childcare in Western Australia* (O'Connor WA: Argyle-Pacific Publishing, 1993), ch. 12; Royal Commission into Institutional Responses to Child Sexual Abuse, Case Study 11: Christian Brothers, 2014, https://www.childabuseroyalcommission.gov.au/case-studies/case-study-11-christian-brothers;　general discussion of institutions in Richard Hil, Joanna Penglase and Gregory Smith, 'Closed worlds: Reflections on institutional care and child slavery in Australia', *Children Australia* 33 (2008): 12–17.

as Ben later called Patrick, was demanding and Ben's life for nine years was a tough round of milking cows, cutting firewood, bagging potatoes and general dogsbody. He slept on a chaff-bag bed in a four-roomed wattle and daub shack with earth floors. He did attend the local state school (as was compulsory) but its quality was poor and available better schools in Bathurst were not considered. At home he learned he was 'the descendant of a race that fought a long and bitter fight against perjurers and pimps and liars'.[87]

Ben survived to become an educated man, economic theorist and prime minister. But with some residual resentment against banks.

Conclusion

Catholic rural Australia did maintain a distinctive culture—distinct both from rural Protestant culture and city Catholicism. Forged in poverty and Irish heritage, it also took advantage of economic opportunities and freedoms not available in Ireland. Those who wished to maintained a strong Catholic devotion in circumstances where churches were distant and priests present only intermittently.

---

87 David Day, *Chifley: A life* (Pymble: HarperCollins, 2002), 3–37; D B Waterson, 'Chifley, Joseph Benedict (Ben) (1885–1951)', *Australian Dictionary of Biography*: http://adb. anu.edu.au/biography/chifley-joseph-benedict-ben-9738

SAINT MICHAEL THE ARCHANGEL, WOLLOMBI:
THE CHURCH THAT MOVED—AND WAS PAID FOR—THREE TIMES
Gael Winnick*

St Michael the Archangel in Wollombi is a very early church from colonial times in New South Wales and as such is important in the history of Catholicism in this country. The Australian Catholic University commissioned a book about the church which was written by Alison Plummer with myself and launched in 2019. This paper is my telling of the story.

St Michael's is a Catholic church which is owned by a trust on behalf of the community of the Wollombi Valley. It was moved once and paid for three times and has three foundation stones incorporated into the church.

The connection between the Australian Catholic Historical Society and St Michael's was highlighted in 1992 when the Society gifted a portrait of John Bede Polding to the Friends of St Michael's. A further connection is found in the St Michael's trust deed which states that should the trust be dissolved the ACHS has responsibility to apply the assets to an appropriate tax-exempt organisation.[1]

My involvement with St Michael's goes back to my first time in the church which was at the re-opening Mass in October 1999 with Bishop Michael Malone. However, I did know the story of the sale of the church in the early 1990s as it was much discussed at that time at the Catholic Theological Union where I was studying for my degree in Theology. Some years after the re-opening, seeing an ageing congregation and conscious of the strenuous efforts of many people to save St Michael's, I asked if I might conduct research with a view to investigating the possibility of applying for state heritage listing to preserve the church. The Friends of St Michael's had no wish to pursue state heritage listing but they were agreeable to me researching the story of the church on my own, which is what I have been doing for about ten years.

Having set myself a task I promptly ran into brick walls. I could find

---

1   Trust Deed for Friends of Saint Michael's: (3) In the event of the Association being dissolved the amount which remains ... shall be applied by the Australian Catholic Historical Society in accordance with their powers to (an organisation) which is exempt from income tax under section 23 of the *Income tax Assessment Act*.

*   Gael Winnick is co-author with Alison Plummer of *The Church that would not Die, St Michael the Archangel, Wollombi*, published by the Australian Catholic University, Strathfield, New South Wales.

Interior, Saint Michael the Archangel, Wollombi, photograph John Harrison

no records, nothing, despite attempts by archivists, historical societies, historians, parish secretaries and many others. What happened to the records? Their fate is unknown. Were they washed away by floods or consumed by fire? There were several floods in the first St Michael's, St Mary's Cathedral burned in 1865 as did Branxton presbytery later on. Many records in the early days must have got wet and damaged in saddle bags

As no progress was being made I asked around for someone who might know about early rural Catholic churches. The name of a man with a weekender in the Wollombi Valley was suggested but I was unable to obtain contact details so I emailed John Carmody, President of the Australian Catholic Historical Society. "Who is Greg Craven?" The response: "The Vice Chancellor of the Australian Catholic University." So began the collaboration between the Vice Chancellor and myself with a book on the history of the church of St Michael as the outcome. As well as being the instigator of the whole project I have been involved right up to and including significant input into the development and writing of the book.

At the same time as trying to find records of the early church, I was gathering the stories of people who were involved with St Michael's in the 1990s. This led to numerous interviews that were to form the basis of a film begun by Ken Martin, film maker, photographer and Wollombi Valley resident, and myself. Ken's gorgeous photos enhance the book. The film is not proceeding, but the interviews were made available for the book and have been invaluable.

When it became evident that the Vice Chancellor and the Australian Catholic University, with great generosity, would be commissioning a book, I asked Alison, who is an author, journalist, editor, and also a Wollombi resident and married to Ken Martin, if she would write it. We are fortunate that Alison not only crafted the wonderful writing but also had oversight of the design and production of the book.

The Wollombi Valley is in the lower Hunter Valley about 30km west of Cessnock. The first peoples, whom we honour and recognise as traditional custodians of the land, have been here for tens of thousands of years and regard nearby Mount Yengo as a special place.

In the early years of the Sydney colony a land route north presented difficulties because of the Hawkesbury River, so a route was found further inland and the Great North Road was built between 1826 and 1836 by convicts.[2] The road split at Wollombi which became the administrative centre of the district.

In the 1830s and 1840s the European population comprised free settlers, convicts, ex-convicts and ex-soldiers who had been granted land. These ex-soldiers included Napoleonic war veterans. The Catholics were mainly Irish.

In January 1840 Father John Lynch, parish priest of West Maitland, rode into Wollombi where he celebrated Mass for the people, *'many of whom had to come a distance of fourteen or fifteen miles'*[3] over rugged terrain. That same day *'A subscription was entered into and men set to work, to erect a church (probably a timber building) on a piece of land, the gift of an inhabitant.'*[4]

Bishop Polding, having ridden from Sydney in late September 1840, arrived in the Wollombi Valley, processed into the village accompanied by prominent Anglicans including the Wiseman brothers, and proceeded to lay the foundation stone for a permanent sandstone church.[5] The writing on the

---

2   https://convicttrail.com.au/
3   *Australasian Chronicle*, 21 January 1840, 2.
4   *Australasian Chronicle,* 21 January 1840, 2.
5   *Australasian Chronicle,* 8 October 1840, 2.

stone is carved in such a way that the stone needs to stand on its narrow end to be read. Did it stand upright on the land while waiting for the building to begin? It is over 1500 mm tall and 265 mm wide and is now incorporated into the existing church on its side. 1840 was only about twenty years since the first priests had worked officially in the colony. In 1842, about 18 months after the laying of the foundation stone, tenders were called for the erection of the church[6] and the first Mass was celebrated in 1843.[7] If there was an architect for the first church he has not been found.

The Anglican church of St John the Evangelist, designed by the architect Edmund Blackett, was opened in 1849, six years after St Michael's, so for around 170 years we have had St John the Evangelist and St Michael the Archangel benignly watching over Wollombi.

Where were people buried? In the early years burials occurred next to the original church where floods still uncover headstones. The Wollombi burial ground, divided equally between Protestants and Catholics, was gazetted in 1846.[8] The Catholic section was consecrated by Archbishop Polding in 1864.[9] It has not been possible to establish if burials were still taking place in the churchyard between 1846 and 1864. By the 1980s the Anglican section had been so well patronised that the Cessnock City Council, which has charge of the cemetery, made a strip in the Catholic section for Anglicans. What do the Anglicans buried in Catholic consecrated ground make of this?

Between 1843 and 1893, except at the end of that period when there were letters from the parish priest at Branxton to the Bishop, most of the records we have are newspaper reports. The Great North Road was superseded by steam transport to the Hunter River and the world bypassed Wollombi but bushrangers roamed, wheat was grown until the rust arrived and pubs came and went bust. And the faithful went to Mass, with the *Maitland Mercury* commenting that the number and faithfulness of Catholics is astonishing. *"Catholics are noted in all parts of the country for their punctuality at divine service."*[10]

Floods are a feature of life in the Wollombi Valley with its steep sides and

---

6 *The Hunter River Gazette; and Journal of Agriculture, Commerce, Politics, and News* (West Maitland, 19 March 1842), 2.

7 *The Maitland Mercury and Hunter River General Advertiser,* 6 May 1843, 2.

8 *Maitland Mercury,* 20 June 1846, 4.

9 *Maitland Mercury,* 21 June 1864, 3.

10 *Maitland Mercury,* 21 June 1864, 3.

narrow valleys. However, the flood of March 1893[11] was massive with water said to be over the top of the church.[12] As a result, the church was deemed unstable and the decision was taken to move it to higher ground next to the post office in the village.[13]

On 22nd October 1893 a new foundation stone was laid by Bishop Murray who thanked everyone for the *'£415 (which) was promised and placed upon the stone.'*[14] This was a considerable sum as there was a depression at the time. As well as the new foundation stone two others were also incorporated into the new church: the 1840 original and its Latin translation.

Following the laying of the foundation stone in October 1893 *'Father Rogers specially thanked the non-Catholic subscribers for their thoughtfulness and liberality,'*[15] thus highlighting the ecumenism which has been prominent throughout the history of settlement of the Wollombi Valley. The earliest record we have is a report that when the Catholics resolved to erect a church in January 1840 *'several of the Protestant inhabitants have kindly promised to contribute towards (it) with a liberality of spirit highly honourable to them.'*[16] In September 1840 at the laying of the foundation stone Bishop Polding *'congratulated (the people) on the peace and harmony which reigned throughout the district and prayed that no evil spirit would come, and by his foul breath excite the storm of religious strife.'*[17]

Polding's prayers were answered. I have been unable to find any record whatsoever to suggest anything other than amicable relationships with all denominations, particularly in the 19th century where the newspaper reports are more numerous. There was always reciprocity with fundraising, socialising, entertainment, always doing together what they could. This was highlighted in 2006 with Anglicans and Catholics in the Wollombi Valley signing a covenant to work together, eighteen months before the Anglican diocese of Newcastle and Catholic dioceses of Maitland-Newcastle and Broken Bay signed their covenant. To this day good relations continue with

11 *Maitland Mercury,* 14 March 1893, 2.
12 Letter Father Rogers to Bishop Murray 13th March 1893 with permission Diocese of Maitland-Newcastle.
13 Letter Father Rogers to Bishop Murray 16th March 1893 with permission Diocese of Maitland-Newcastle.
14 *Maitland Mercury,* 24 October 1893, 5.
15 *Maitland Mercury,* 24 October 1893, 5.
16 *Australasian Chronicle,* 9 June 1840, 3.
17 *Australasian Chronicle,* 17 October 1840, 2.

Anglicans always outnumbering Catholics in St Michael's on Good Friday for the Stations of the Cross.

Is the existing church a rebuild of the original or a new design altogether? The local stories tell of a rebuild, stone by stone, using original material. It appears to have about the same footprint as the first church which was reported to be about forty feet long[18] although it is not known how this was measured. We do not know if the first church had a sanctuary. The external measurement of the existing nave is thirty six feet eleven inches.

A reason why the footprint may be considered to be about the same as the original is that the building was erected very quickly. The tenders were called in August 1893 by architect Frederick Menkens,[19] the tender was awarded in early September 1893[20] and the foundation stone was laid by Bishop Murray on 22nd October 1893.[21] The church was finished in February of the following year and opened in March by the Bishop.[22] It is difficult to see how a significant amount of new dressed stone could have been available in such a short time for a new design.

In the absence of records we looked at nearby St Patrick's church at Nulkaba in the hope that it could provide some clues. The first St Patrick's was dedicated by Bishop Polding in 1840[23] and replaced by a stone one in the early 1890s. Both the 1890's churches, St Patrick's and St Michael's, were in the same parish with Father Rogers as the parish priest. There are significant similarities between them; windows, skirtings, altars, the round arch. This is not surprising as architect Frederick Menkens was involved with them both. He called for tenders for St Michael's[24] and supervised the building of St Patrick's.[25]

The sacristy of St Michael's is intriguing. The original church did not have one; however money to construct one had been raised before the flood.[26] The external rear wall of the existing church is not in alignment

18 *Maitland Mercury,* 6 May 1843, 2.
19 *Newcastle Morning Herald and Miners' Advocate,* 18 August 1893, 8. No reference to St Michael's has been found in the Menken's papers.
20 *Newcastle Morning Herald and Miners' Advocate,* 7 September 1893, 8.
21 *Maitland Mercury,* 24 October 1893, 5.
22 *The Maitland Daily Mercury,* 22 March 1894, 2.
23 *Australasian Chronicle,* 17 October 1840, 2.
24 *Newcastle Morning Herald,* 18 August 1893, 8.
25 *Maitland Mercury,* 20 September 1892, 5.
26 John W Delaney City of Cessnock, 1788–1988 Roman Catholic Church History, 45,

across the sanctuary and sacristy. Where those walls abut, there is a recess is 230mm. The corbels on the sacristy side of the sanctuary are 230mm while they are 460mm on the other side. The manner in which the sacristy is attached differs in both churches. It seems the sacristy of St Patrick's was a planned addition[27] but it appears to have better proportions in relation to the rest of the church than does St Michael's, the sacristy of which appears disproportionately large giving it almost a "stuck on" appearance. Could that sacristy have been added later, as was St Patrick's?

When Trevor Howells, renowned in the heritage world, came to Wollombi I said I had come to the point where, in the absence of paper records, the stones would have to talk but that I could not understand what they had to say. He said not to worry and pointed to a rough stone just above ground level on the north west corner indicating that this would have been a footing stone located underground on a flat site, which happens to be the terrain of the first site.

Stained glass quatrefoil window of St Michael the Archangel, photograph, Mitchell Winton, courtesy of the Wollombi Valley Chamber of Commerce.

The rooflines of the old and new St Michael's are different and the embellishments which were current in the 1890s are evident in St Michael's so in a sense it is a church of the 1890s. It is fair to say that Menkens left his stamp on St Michael's.

In the wall above the altar there is a stained glass quatrefoil window of St Michael the Archangel. Its provenance is a mystery. Was it originally intended for that round space in St Michael's? Was it in the original church? Who designed it? The best guess at the moment is Franz Xaver Zettler from Munich who designed windows for the Branxton church in 1880s/1890s.

St Michael's has been in two dioceses, Sydney and Maitland, which

'Wollombi Catholic Church had never had a sacristy. Father T Rogers in 1892 decided to add a sacristy at a cost of £150-0-0'.

27 *Maitland Mercury,* 20 September 1892, 5, 'Provision has also been made for a sacristy'.

became Maitland-Newcastle, and six parishes; presumably it was first in Sydney, then East Maitland, West Maitland, Wollombi-MacDonald River (1856 and 1871), Branxton from 1871 and Cessnock from 1905 where it remains.[28] St Patrick's church at Nulkaba, which dates from about the same time as St Michael's in 1840,[29] became the parish church of Cessnock on the establishment of the parish in 1905. The new church in Cessnock, St Joseph's, was opened in 1954. In the years following the Second Vatican Council the parish priest of Cessnock initiated changes to the churches in the parish including St Michael's which had altar rails removed and pews replaced. The painted timber altars were replaced by a marble one made from the altar rails from St Joseph's.

In May 1990 the people who assembled for Mass at St Michael's were appalled to read in the bulletin that this was to be the last Mass at the church which would close immediately. There had been no warning, not a hint that this might happen. Despite being questioned the priest would give no explanation as he scurried to his car. Subsequently the reasons given for the closure were that Masses at Wollombi were no longer pastorally desirable, a shortage of priests, and falling attendances.[30] The falling attendances was a reference to the previous Easter when there had been a flood which meant bridges were under water, roads were cut and people were unable to get to church. For about the next twelve months the church remained closed and locked.

This was a very difficult period for the Cessnock parish and it is in this context that St Michael's was sold.[31] In April 1991 changes were made in St Joseph's church at Cessnock with regard to the placement of the altar, pews and the Blessed Sacrament. These changes had been flagged and many people were supportive but many people in Cessnock were distressed.

In late April 1991, a few days after the re-arrangement at St Joseph's, St Michael's was stripped of everything that could be moved; the tabernacle, stations of the cross, altar, statues, everything but the pews.[32] The statues, facing backwards with fabric streaming behind, were seen attached to the

---

28 John W Delaney, *City of Cessnock, 1788–1988: Roman Catholic Church History*, (Manuscript, Cessnock: c. 1988).
29 *Australasian Chronicle*, 17 October 1840, 2.
30 Letter to Cessnock parishioners from the parish priest, Vince Ryan, 11 May 1991.
31 Cessnock parish at that time is story waiting to be told.
32 *The Cessnock Herald*, 8 May 1991, front page.

back of a cabin of a utility as it raced around the cemetery. It was surreal, like a Fellini movie, witnesses reported. There was no warning, no recognition of the fact that many items had been donated by families still in the valley. Much of what was taken was sold. The sacristy cabinet was recovered many years later and donated to the church.

One item not taken was the bell. It appears a local man backed his truck up to the bell and with a friend got it down and took it to his property where he hid it. It was so well hidden it took him about two years to remember where it was but he eventually retrieved, restored and hung it next to the church. The official story is that nobody knows what happened to the bell. I am assured that it was not stolen, but taken for restoration and safe keeping.[33]

To the outcry in Cessnock regarding the changes to St Joseph's were added rumours about the possible sale of St Patrick's at Nulkaba and St Michael's at Wollombi. The story of the uproar in Cessnock and the proposed sale of the two churches became widespread.[34] Cessnock parishioners were concerned about the changes to St Joseph's and the possible sale of the churches, while Wollombi folk focused on the fate of St Michael's. Bishop Clarke was inundated with letters, and also petitions, including two from Cessnock in May 1991 totalling more than 300 signatures.[35] A petition from Wollombi with around 200 signatures apparently received no response from the Bishop. Many people in the Wollombi Valley and beyond became involved, including the ACHS whose president, Brian McAteer, wrote to the Bishop in 1991 saying in part:

> *I regard St Michael's, Wollombi, as a shrine to John Bede Polding, James Murray, the pioneer priests who worked in the district under difficult conditions and the Catholic settlers who travelled long distances to publicly demonstrate their faith by attending at Mass.*[36]

One of the difficulties with the whole process with regard to decisions regarding St Michael's was the lack of consultation. There is no record of any consultation at all with the people of the Wollombi Valley regarding the sale. On the contrary a delegation from St Michael's which went to see the Bishop was assured that nothing would happen without consultation. But it

---

33 Author's conversation with Michael Reilly.
34 Multiple newspapers.
35 As quoted in *Concerned Parishioners Newsletter*, 8/9 June 1991.
36 Letter from Brian McAteer, President of the Australian Catholic Historical Society, to Bishop Clarke 24 May 1991.

did. July 10th 1991 brought confirmation of the sale, the reasons for which were given later by the parish priest who was reported as saying:

> *money from the sale of the churches, plus insurance money was used to pay the parish debt, not to finance changes to St Joseph's*[37]

However in May 1991 it had been stated the money would be used in Cessnock for the church and school among other needs.[38]

The sale of both churches took place on September 7th 1991 attended by a huge crowd, many of whom were from Cessnock, with some holding placards. St Patrick's was sold in the morning after which the crowd proceeded to Wollombi for the afternoon sale of St Michael's.

The auction, which was held in the church, began with someone rolling thirty 20 cent pieces up the aisle and saying, 'Here's your thirty pieces of silver and that's all you're going to get.'[39] During the auction the bell of St John's was tolling in solidarity with its sister church. St Michael's was bought for $120,000 which was the reserve. The winning bid was made by an individual on behalf of the community. The sale, with a large picture and article, made the front page of the *Sydney Morning Herald*.[40] The months between the sale and settlement were busy ones, with fundraising and the formation of the Trust, which by settlement became the owner of St Michael's.

The church, however, was in need of restoration. Apart from general dilapidation there was earthquake damage from the 1989 earthquake and problems with drainage causing rising damp. A decision was made to dynamite some rock which was close to the church and obstructing the drainage. This did not go smoothly as it appears the powder factor was not calculated very well with the resulting explosion being a lot bigger than intended and one wall of the sanctuary was bowed right in and needed straightening.[41]

The internal wall was damaged by the explosion, which turned out to be a blessing in disguise, as wonderful decorative wall painting was discovered underneath the paint. When could this decoration have been painted? Just four

---

37 *Newcastle Herald,* 2 October 1991, front page.
38 Letter to Cessnock parishioners from parish priest 11 May 1991.
39 Author's conversation with Daryl Heslop.
40 *Sydney Morning Herald,* 10 September 1991, front page.
41 Author's conversation with Michael Reilly.

years after the church was completed the *Freemans's Journal* commented on St Michael's *'pretty sanctuary'*[42] so perhaps it had been painted by then. It is difficult to imagine a report of a 'pretty sanctuary' if the walls were whitewashed. When could this decoration have been covered over? It must have been many years ago as there seems to be no living memory of a 'pretty sanctuary'.

The second St Michael's at the time of building in the 1890s was in the Branxton parish with Father Rogers being the parish priest, and at least two other churches in that parish, built around that time, also had wonderful wall decorations. These churches were St Paul's at Glendon Brook and St Brigid's at Branxton, unfortunately the wall decorations of the latter were subsequently painted over. One story involving the restoration of St Michael's concerned the young woman who made the stencils to replicate the original pattern and painted the damaged walls. At eight months into her pregnancy she was still getting up on the high scaffolding, to the alarm of many.

After a great deal of effort by many people, Bishop Michael Malone reopened St Michael's in October 1999. My recollection is that before the Mass began he apologised to the people of the Wollombi Valley for the great wrong done to them in selling the church. Word got about that the church was reconsecrated at this re-opening Mass but this was not the case. When it was closed it was not deconsecrated and it is very doubtful if it was ever consecrated in the first place.

St Michael's is recognised as a Catholic church by the Diocese of Maitland-Newcastle, it is financially independent with fundraising continuing and is managed by the Friends of St Michael's. St Michael's is owned by a trust for the people of the Wollombi Valley. Its life is always in the context of the Wollombi Valley. The church is in really good shape with a new roof, guttering and downpipes, the drainage has been fixed and the stonework has been repointed. We are grateful to the parish priest of Cessnock, Father James Lunn, who comes to celebrate Mass monthly and also on the fifth Sundays. Around about the feast of St Michael each year the Bishop comes for Mass.

The first church was paid for by July 1847, due we are told, to the enthusiastic promotion of temperance by Father Lynch.[43] Four years after

---

42 *Freeman's Journal*, 1 January 1898, page 20.

43 *Sydney Chronicle*, 14 July 1847, 3, 'Among the persons present were not a few who had

the opening of the second church £100 was still owing from the £600 it had cost.[44] Following the 1991 sale there was still money outstanding to two generous families so in 2006 wonderful leadlight windows depicting the story of creation were designed and sold as memorial windows enabling St Michael's to be debt free.

To our knowledge, St Michael's is the only Catholic church in Australia that was sold, bought by a community and re-instated as a Catholic place of worship. Of course, this is not only the story of a church but of an amazing community.

I wish to express my thanks for the friendship and the generosity of many people who shared memories and mementos so the story of St Michael's could be told. My thanks also to the Australian Catholic Historical Society for inviting me to tell the story.

Particularly I wish to acknowledge and honour all the people who have been involved with St Michael's from the 1830s until today. The people who worshipped there, who built, moved, rebuilt, maintained, loved, bought, and worked to have it reopened as a Catholic place of worship.

Now you know something of St Michael's the invitation is extended to all to come to Wollombi and see our little church for yourselves.

---

profited considerably by following the temperance maxims which are so ably advocated and so unceasingly put forth by the rev. chairman. These persons, in a generous and grateful spirit, contributed liberally from the means which improved conduct had placed at their disposal.'

44 *Freeman's Journal*, 1 January 1898, 20.

'HUMBLY RELYING ON THE BLESSING OF ALMIGHTY GOD': PATRICK MCMAHON GLYNN—FROM IRISH LAWYER TO AUSTRALIAN STATESMAN

Dr John Kennedy McLaughlin*

This is an edited version of an Address delivered to a meeting of the Australian Catholic Historical Society on Sunday, 21 July 2019, in Sydney.

Patrick McMahon Glynn was an instance, by no means unusual—let alone unique—of an Irishman in the nineteenth century achieving a successful career in his chosen profession and in politics in Australia.

Glynn was born on 25 August 1855 at Gort in County Galway. He was the third of the eleven children of John McMahon Glynn and Ellen née Wallsh. John was a merchant, who conducted a large general store in the town square of Gort. The Glynns were Catholics.[1]

When Glynn was born Ireland was still experiencing the aftermath of the Great Famine of the late 1840s, and was only a generation removed from the final repeal in 1829 of the Penal Laws against Catholics. For more than a century after the defeat of the Catholic King James II by his nephew and son-in-law, the Protestant William of Orange, at the Battle of the Boyne in 1690 the practice by Catholics of

Patrick Glynn, Australian politician, in 1898.

their religion resulted in the religion of the vast majority of the population being (at least in theory) largely proscribed.

In Ireland, as throughout the British Isles, it was necessary for the younger sons of the gentry or the landowning classes to seek their way in life through their own efforts. But for almost a century after 1690 Catholics officially were precluded from practising the professions of law and medicine and from holding commissions in the armed Services.

* John Kennedy McLaughlin, AM, BA, LL M (Sydney), Ph D (Monash), was formerly an Associate Judge of the Supreme Court of New South Wales, and has held academic appointments at the University of Sydney (Faculty of Law) and at the University of Technology, Sydney (Faculty of Law).

1 Gerald O'Collins, *Patrick McMahon Glynn, a Founder of Australian Federation* (Melbourne, 1976), Chapter 1, 'The Glynns of Gort', 1–10.

As the eighteenth century advanced, and especially after Irish Catholics had declined to support the restoration of the House of Stuart at the time of the Jacobite rising in Scotland in 1745, the Penal Laws in Ireland, and their enforcement, were gradually relaxed. The extent to which the statutory prohibition from their practising the profession of the law could be evaded by Catholics is uncertain. The prohibition which had obtained, in the case of solicitors, since 1698; and, in the case of barristers, by regulation since 1704 and by statute since 1727, was repealed in 1792. At the same time as those restraints were being removed by statute, the arrangements for legal education at the King's Inns in Dublin were also undergoing change and improvement. But even after 1792 Catholic barristers had to wait until the final repeal of the Penal Laws in 1829 before the prohibition against their appointment as King's (or Queen's) Counsel was removed.

Throughout the late eighteenth century and for most of the nineteenth century the majority of Irish lawyers came from the upper-middle class. They were not the landowning gentry. Neither were they from the working class, let alone from the impoverished peasantry. As the nineteenth century advanced some, as in the case of Glynn himself, came from the prosperous merchant class. There was one characteristic that most of the lawyers had in common—certainly, almost all the barristers. They were graduates of Trinity College, Dublin (the University of Dublin). The prohibition against Catholics taking degrees at Trinity was removed by an Irish statute of 1793. Nevertheless, they could not hold professorships, fellowships or scholarships until all religious tests were abolished in 1873. But for the ensuing century the Catholic Church in Ireland attempted (not always with any significant success) to deter its adherents from attending that great seat of learning. It was not until 1970 that the Church ceased threatening its members with excommunication if they attended Trinity, unless with special permission from their Bishop.

The usual path to a career at the Irish Bar was first, to graduate from Trinity, then, having enrolled and kept terms at the King's Inns in Dublin and at an English Inn of Court in London, to be called to the Bar by each institution. When the King's Inns was founded in 1542, under the auspices of King Henry VIII, the English barristers succeeded in imposing upon Henry, and he upon the Irish profession, a condition to the effect that no barrister should practise before the superior courts in Ireland who had not been called to the Bar by one of the English Inns of Court. In consequence of that restriction, which continued until 1886, it was necessary for the Irishman to keep terms (fewer than in the case of an English barrister) in London; and, having been called to the Bar by an English Inn, on condition that he would practise only in Ireland, then to be called by the King's Inns, and thus become a member of the Irish Bar.

Patrick Glynn received his primary education from the Sisters of Mercy in Gort. Then for three and a half years he was a boarder at the French College (later known as Blackrock College), conducted by the French Order of the Holy Ghost Fathers at Blackrock on the outskirts of Dublin. There he did well academically. Then he proceeded along the foregoing path for a career at the Bar, although, interestingly, upon leaving school he became an articled clerk to a Dublin solicitor for three years, before entering Trinity. Perhaps he was then undecided upon which branch of the profession he would enter. Although a committed Catholic for all his life, Glynn perceived no problem in pursuing his tertiary studies at Trinity, where he graduated BA in 1878. There is no evidence that Glynn either sought or received any episcopal permission to attend Trinity.[2] The following year he was called to the English Bar (Middle Temple), then to the Irish Bar, and immediately commenced practice as a barrister in Dublin.

In Ireland there was an over-supply of young men qualifying for and embarking on a career in the legal profession. Glynn soon discovered that not only was he competing with many other young men commencing in legal practice, but that the Irish Bar had become a 'closed shop' (that is, where new members of a profession were accepted by their already established colleagues on the basis of family, social or political connections, rather than for actual or potential professional merit). Glynn realised that, having no such connections, professional success in his homeland would be extremely difficult. On 4 September 1880, the day he sailed from London for Melbourne, he recorded in his diary that 'the good opinion [of many friends], the flattering hopes of others, and a not altogether empty brief bag ... during sixteen months' membership of the Irish Bar' did not prove 'a sufficient inducement to remain at home ... In Ireland energy or ability are only one of the requisites for professional success; there must be many accidental

---

2 O'Collins, *op. cit.*, n 1, 12–13.

advantages.'[3] With probably greater accuracy, he had told his mother several months earlier, 'Here [in Ireland] Prejudice, interest and cliqueism is nearly everything.'[4]

Australia was the obvious destination, as Glynn had kinsfolk, both paternal and maternal, living in Melbourne, Sydney and Adelaide (in which last city his maternal grandmother Agnes Wallsh had died only two years previously). Other kinsfolk also subsequently came to Australia, two of this brothers (both doctors) settling in South Australia. In his diary he recorded that he 'would be most happy to go to Australia. There seems a field there for a good speaker, here it is narrow and chances of opening few.'[5]

At the Melbourne Bar (where he was admitted soon after his arrival —as an Irish barrister he was entitled to automatic admission in Victoria) Glynn's short career was even less successful than in Dublin. He found that professional work was no more available to a new barrister than in Ireland. To his brother James in Dublin he wrote, 'Trying to get business here as a stranger is like attacking the devil with an icicle.'[6] He received no encouragement from Sir Redmond Barry, a Judge of the Supreme Court of Victoria, and probably the foremost Irishman in Melbourne at that time. Barry (whom Glynn described as 'a swindle', saying, 'He is a spruce old fellow, and no use to any man.'[7]) advised Glynn 'to go back at once'.[8] For a time Glynn managed to subsist in Victoria by selling life insurance and copies of a legal publication.

But even while despondent in Melbourne Glynn had thoughts of a career in politics. Whilst a generation earlier Sir Charles Gavan Duffy (a future Premier of Victoria) had regarded the law as a means to a career in politics,[9]

3 Diary of P M Glynn, 4 September 1880, *Glynn Papers*, National Library MS 4653, quoted in O'Collins, *op. cit.*, n 1, 18.
4 P M Glynn, Dublin, to his mother Ellen Glynn (née Wallsh), 21 June 1880, in Gerald Glynn O'Collins (ed.), *Patrick McMahon Glynn: Letters to his Family (1874–1927)* (Melbourne, 1974), 6.
5 Loc. cit., n 3.
6 P M Glynn, Melbourne, to his brother James Glynn, 25 April 1881, in O'Collins, *op. cit.*, n 4, 24.
7 P M Glynn, Melbourne, to his mother Ellen Glynn, 28 October 1880, in O'Collins, *op. cit.*, n 4, 21.
8 P M Glynn Melbourne, to his sister Elizabeth (Mrs O'Donnell), 2 January 1881, in O'Collins, *op. cit.*, n 4, 23–24.
9 Sir Charles Gavan Duffy, *My Life in Two Hemispheres*, 2 volumes (London, 1898; facsimile edition, Dublin, 1969), Volume I, 59.

Glynn regarded politics as a possible means to a successful career in the law. In January 1881 he wrote to his sister Elizabeth in Dublin, 'If I get on—the devil thank the colony. I can't see how I am to do so without becoming a politician; and as such ought to succeed if I get a chance.'[10] However, it was in South Australia, not in Victoria, that Glynn's aspirations were fulfilled. In South Australia, to which Colony he removed two years later and where the legal profession was not divided between barristers and solicitors, Glynn ultimately achieved success both in the law and in politics.

It was largely through the encouragement and influence of his mother's sister Grace Wallsh, who had migrated to Australia in the 1860s, that Glynn obtained a professional opening in South Australia, and was soon established as a partner and then as principal of the firm of lawyers which he had joined. Grace was a nun, Sister Bernard in the Order of St Joseph, in which she was an early and influential companion of the foundress, Saint Mary McKillop, in establishing the Order and of which she herself later became the Superior-General. At the time of Glynn's arrival in Australia Sister Bernard was stationed in Adelaide. When the ship in which he was travelling called at that city on its way to Melbourne, Glynn had the opportunity of spending 'a jolly few hours' with her and with his uncle Johnny Wallsh (Grace's brother).[11] Subsequently Sister Bernard was transferred to Sydney, and it was there that she met Malcolm Henry Davis, of the Adelaide firm of solicitors, Hardy and Davis, who wanted 'a Roman Catholic Irishman' to open a branch office for them at Kapunda.[12] That was a town located some 47 miles north of Adelaide, at a time when there were few Catholic lawyers practising in South Australia, let alone Irish Catholic lawyers. Through his aunt's good offices Glynn met Davis in Melbourne, and was ultimately engaged by the latter's firm, practising first at Kapunda, from August 1882, and later, after

---

10 P M Glynn, Melbourne, to his sister Elizabeth, 2 January 1881, in O'Collins, *op. cit.*, n 4, 23.

11 P M Glynn, Melbourne, to his mother Ellen Glynn, 28 October 1880, in O'Collins, op. cit., n 4, 18. The spelling Wallsh (with the double LL) of the surname of the maternal aunt and uncle of Patrick McMahon Glynn is that used by Glynn's grandson, Gerald Glynn O'Collins, SJ, in his biography of his celebrated ancestor (op. cit., n 1), although on at least one occasion Glynn himself used the spelling Walsh (with one L) to refer to his paternal uncle (P M Glynn, Melbourne, to his mother Ellen Glynn, 28 October 1880, *loc. cit., supra*).

12 P M Glynn, Adelaide, to his mother Ellen Glynn, 5 July 1882, in O'Collins, *op. cit.*, n 4, 52; O'Collins, *op. cit.*, n 1, 33. The discovery of copper at Kapunda in 1843 had precipitated a mining boom in that town.

his entry into Parliament, in Adelaide, from September 1888.

Davis (who was Catholic, but English, not Irish) and his partner, Arthur Marmaduke Hardy, must have thought that Kapunda was a good opening for a branch office of their firm. Since 1860 the town had been accessible by rail from Adelaide, and until the copper mines had ceased operation in the 1880s Kapunda was the chief country town in South Australia. An early settler and administrative official of the Colony, Boyle Travers Finniss, who became the first Premier of South Australia under Responsible Government, recorded the copper mines at Kapunda and at Burra Burra (the latter located about 100 miles to the north of Adelaide) as 'the wonders of the world'.[13] Kapunda was of sufficient importance to be one of the destinations for Australia's first Royal visitor, Prince Alfred, Duke of Edinburgh, in November 1867. The great and unqualified enthusiasm of the welcome which His Royal Highness received in Kapunda suggests a total absence of any Fenian sympathy among the Irish population of the town—a contrast to the situation in New South Wales, where four months later a self-proclaimed Fenian attempted to assassinate him.[14] Probably the Prince's only disappointment in his visit to Kapunda was that his expressed interest in viewing the mines was thwarted by the fact that all the miners and other workers had been given a holiday in order to welcome the Royal visitor.[15]

The desire of Davis and Hardy to employ a 'Roman Catholic Irishman' suggests that by the early 1880s a significant proportion of the town's population of about 3000 came within either or both of the categories Catholic and Irish, and could be expected to bring their legal work to a fellow countryman and co-religionist. As early as 1850–1851 the Catholic church was one of only two places of worship in Kapunda (the other being the chapel of the sect called 'The Howling Methodists', whose tenets, according to the local chronicler of the period 'are not patronized in the township'[16]).

13 Boyle Travers Finniss, *The Constitutional History of South Australia ... 1836–1857* (Adelaide, 1886), 80.

14 *Adelaide Observer*, Saturday 9 November 1867, 5; Patrick O'Farrell, *The Irish in Australia*, revised edition (Kensington, NSW, 1993), 209–210; Keith Amos, *The Fenians in Australia, 1865–1880* (Kensington, NSW, 1988), chapter 3, 'The O'Farrell Incident'. Almost fifteen years later Henry O'Farrell's brother, Peter Andrew Charles O'Farrell, who had previously been a leading solicitor and land speculator in Melbourne, attempted to shoot Archbishop James Alipius Goold, of Melbourne, at Brighton, Victoria, on 21 August 1882 (O'Farrell, *op. cit., supra*, 100).

15 *Kapunda Herald*, Friday, 10 August 1900, 4.

16 E M Yelland (ed.), *Colonists, Copper and Corn in the Colony of South Australia 1850–*

Cornish settlers, especially the skilled miners, also constituted a significant part of the population of Kapunda, where the continuing rivalry between the Cornish (often Methodist and sometimes Orangemen) and the Irish (usually Catholic) on occasion descended into violence. For example, the unexpected defeat of Glynn in the 1893 election gave rise to local rioting in the town. As Glynn informed his mother very shortly after his arrival, many of the farmers in the vicinity of Kapunda were Irishmen from County Clare, and some even from the area of Gort in County Galway, where Glynn had been born and his family resided. However, he continued to his mother, '[t]he Catholics as usual are the poorer class—the protestants the wealthy and fashionable.'[17] Michael Davitt, the Irish Land League agitator, who visited Kapunda in the 1890s, wrote that it felt as though 'Kapunda was somewhere in Connaught'.[18]

At the time of Glynn's arrival there was only one other solicitor practising in the town, and several years after the establishment of that branch office, there were only three lawyers recorded as practising in Kapunda, Glynn and Hardy being two of them (although Hardy was essentially located in the firm's Adelaide office).[19] In Kapunda Glynn soon achieved the professional success which had eluded him in Dublin and in Melbourne. As his biographer, his grandson, the Reverend Gerald Glynn O'Collins, has observed, Glynn would not have been a total stranger with the people of Kapunda, as Sister Bernard had previously been stationed there as Superior of the local convent and school and his uncle Johnny Wallsh had been a regular visitor to the town.[20] Less than a year after his arrival Glynn in April 1883 became the editor of the local newspaper, the *Kapunda Herald*, regularly writing editorials and leading articles for that and for other publications. Soon he was speaking and writing in support of the Land Nationalisation Society, of which he was one of the founders,[21] and was flirting with the opinions of the American economist Henry George, based on the idea of a single tax. Combining his

1851 by Old Colonist (Melbourne, 1970), 138–139.

17 P M Glynn, Kapunda, to his mother Ellen Glynn, 26 September 1882, in O'Collins, *op. cit.*, n 4, 56.

18 Quoted in Philip J. Payton, *The Cornish Miner in Australia* (*Cousin Jack Down Under*) (Trewolsta, Kernow, Cornwall, 1984), 71.

19 Robert Haden Smith, *Law List of Australasia* (Melbourne), 1882, 179; 1886–1887, 192.

20 P M Glynn, Kapunda, to his mother Ellen Glynn, 26 September 1882, in O'Collins, *op. cit.*, n 4, 55 at 56.

21 George E. Loyau, *Notable South Australians* (Adelaide, 1885), 246.

legal practice with journalism and involvement in local affairs, it is hardly surprising that in 1887 the voters of Kapunda elected Glynn to the House of Assembly of South Australia as one of the two members for the electorate of Light. Interestingly, both were Catholics.[22] Despite his earlier stated ambition of using politics as a means for professional success in the law, it is as one of the Fathers of Federation and as a successful politician in the early years of the Commonwealth of Australia that Glynn is now remembered.

Political parties of the kind with which we are now familiar did not exist in South Australia at that time. A candidate would offer his own individual policies, often, in a general way, aligning himself with policies of other candidates. Glynn was a supporter of Free Trade, a stand, however, which was not very popular with South Australian voters in the late 19th century. He supported payment of salaries for members of Parliament. Otherwise, the self employed or members of the working classes could not afford to enter Parliament. He also argued for female suffrage and for reform of the Colony's Upper House. In these areas he could be regarded as being a liberal. One matter of particular interest to Glynn, both in the South Australian Parliament and later in the Commonwealth Parliament, was the control and use of Australia's inland rivers. He was a leading member of the South Australian Royal Commission on the waters of the River Murray from 1887 to 1891, and in the Commonwealth Parliament he strongly supported the *River Murray Waters Act* of 1915.

Glynn's parliamentary career was not without its set-backs. First elected in September 1887, he lost his seat in 1890. This was a bitter defeat, which in a letter to his mother on 29 April of that year he ascribed to '1st bribery, 2nd religious Bigotry because I supported the Catholic claims to school grants, 3rd misrepresentation among the ignorant German louts, of whom about 600 are on the Roll [for the electorate of Light], 4th the treachery of my opponents'.[23] Early in 1892 Glynn came close to giving up his parliamentary ambitions when he was offered the post of Resident (the equivalent of Administrator) of the Northern Territory, which was then attached to South Australia. Negotiations broke down on the matter of salary, probably with

---

22 Glynn described his colleague, Jenkin Coles (later, as Sir Jenkin, a long-serving Speaker of the House of Assembly), as 'an able administrator, wealthy, formal Catholic, a friend, but a thoroughly unscrupulous candidate' (P M Glynn, Kapunda, to his mother Ellen Glynn, 2 April 1887, in O'Collins, *op. cit.*, n 4, 108).

23 P M Glynn, Adelaide, to his mother Ellen Glynn, 29 April 1890, in O'Collins, *op. cit.*, n 4, 131.

little regret on Glynn's part.[24] In 1893 he stood again for Light, without success, but in 1895 he was returned in a by-election for the seat of North Adelaide (by then he was no longer residing in Kapunda). That was the first election in Australian history to be held under universal adult suffrage, with women entitled equally with men. Glynn lost his seat at the general election in the following year, but won it back in a byelection in 1897, and held it until he entered the first Commonwealth Parliament in 1901.

Glynn was very briefly South Australia's Attorney-General in the short-lived Government of Vaiben Louis Solomon, which subsisted for only seven days in 1899. More importantly, however, Glynn, an enthusiastic supporter of Federation, was elected one of the ten Representatives from South Australia to the Federal Convention of 1897–1898, where he was an influential and respected participant. At that Convention Glynn was described by Alfred Deakin (in whose ministry he was later to serve as Attorney-General of the Commonwealth) as 'a little Irish barrister, large-nosed and florid, with a brogue as broad as he was long and the figure of a jockey and the reputation of a hard and reckless rider'.[25] Deakin omitted to mention Glynn's very large and distinguishing moustache. Glynn was an extremely able lawyer, with a sound knowledge of constitutional law. His speeches in Parliament and at the Federal Convention were models of careful preparation. His arguments were always presented with eloquence and supported by impeccably researched facts. He was regarded as one of the most widely read parliamentarians of his day, whose knowledge of the works of Shakespeare (quotations wherefrom were often included in his speeches) was both wide and deep.

The inclusion in the proposed Constitution of a reference to the Deity had engaged the interest not only of the Federal Convention of 1897–1898, but also of many members of the public and especially leaders of religious denominations. The first session of that Convention was held in Adelaide in March and April of 1897. On the last day of business, 8 April, Dr John Quick, one of the Victorian Representatives, a learned and rather solemn barrister, suggested that in the proposed Preamble to the Constitution there should be inserted the words 'invoking Divine Providence'. That suggestion was rejected without a division.[26]

---

24 P M Glynn, Adelaide, to his mother Ellen Glynn, 26 January 1892, in O'Collins, *op. cit.*, n 4, 142 .

25 Alfred Deakin, *The Federal Story* (Melbourne, 1944), 59.

26 J A La Nauze, *The Making of the Australian Constitution* (Melbourne, 1974), 128.

But that was not the end to the matter. There was organised petitioning to the Convention, on topics as diverse as appeals to the Privy Council, the control and sale of alcoholic liquors and Almighty God. It was the view of many that the presence of Almighty God in the Preamble to the Constitution Act would assist the peace, order and good government of the new Commonwealth, and nearly identical amendments to the draft Constitution had been suggested by the Legislatures of the five Colonies represented at the Convention (Queensland sent no Representatives). New South Wales, South Australia and Tasmania had suggested that the Preamble should include the phrase 'acknowledging Almighty God as the Supreme Ruler of the Universe'; Western Australia preferred 'grateful to Almighty God for their freedom, and in order to secure and perpetuate its blessings'; whilst the Victorians merely expressed 'reliance' on God's blessing. Over fifty petitions received in Adelaide, Sydney and Melbourne prayed for a recognition of God, most commonly in the Preamble. Many went further to request the prescription of a prayer before the daily sessions of Parliament and the insertion of a power to appoint days of national thanksgiving and humiliation. Those petitions came from ordinary citizens, from general assemblies, from councils of churches, from Methodist conferences; but most of all they came from 'Members' or 'congregations' of evangelical and Protestant churches; Primitive Methodists, Baptists, Congregationalists, the Salvation Army, Presbyterians and Anglicans. The Colonial Legislatures themselves had been petitioned, in the words of Professor J. A. La Nauze, 'in most Colonies moderately, in Victoria immoderately, for there the rain of Presbyterian petitioners seemed to testify to the presence of an able campaign-director'.[27] The Catholic Bishops in Victoria and South Australia aligned themselves with the Protestants. As Professor La Nauze has observed, 'There had never before been such a demonstration of common purpose among the Churches of Australia.'[28]

Nevertheless, it was the South Australian Representative Glynn, a devout Catholic—not a Representative from New South Wales or Victoria, Colonies with large Catholic populations—who was responsible on 2 March 1898 for inserting into the Preamble to the Constitution the words 'humbly relying on the blessing of Almighty God'. When he moved with studied eloquence the

27 La Nauze, *op. cit.*, n 26, 224.
28 La Nauze, *op. cit.*, n 26, 225.

insertion of that phrase, there was no overt opposition and the motion was carried without a division. In this Glynn was motivated by sincere religious belief as well as by political pragmatism, recording in his diary for that date,

> Today I succeeded in getting the words 'humbly relying on the Blessing [*sic*] of Almighty God' inserted in the Preamble. It was chiefly intended to secure greater support from a large number of voters who believe in the efficacy for good of this formal Act of reverence and faith.[29]

Nevertheless, some of the Representatives, including even Edmund Barton, had certain reservations. One Representative who expressed his concern was another Irish lawyer, Henry Bournes Higgins, one of the Representatives from Victoria. Higgins was born in Ireland, at Newtownards in County Down, where his father, the Reverend John Higgins, although brought up in the Church of Ireland, was a Wesleyan minister. The Higgins family emigrated to Australia in early 1870, when Henry was aged 18. He graduated from the University of Melbourne (where he was influenced by the teachings of the great Professor W. E. Hearn), and practised at the Victorian Bar from 1876. Higgins shed the Wesleyanism of his father, and spiritually moved towards agnosticism. That opposition to organised religion and the intrusion of religion into government, which Higgins regarded as being exclusively a secular domain, was manifest in the Federal Convention of 1897–1898. There he often found himself at odds not only with the other Victorian delegates, including Alfred Deakin, but with almost the entirety of the Convention.

During the debate on Glynn's proposal Higgins achieved a victory for principle in the matter of religion. He considered that the recognition of the Almighty in the Preamble might alarm many people, since it now gave some positive warrant to Australian Courts (as had been the case in America) to justify intolerant or restrictive legislation. Despite Barton's scepticism, the majority of the Convention were convinced that what Higgins called a 'safeguard against religious intolerance' would do no harm and might win some votes in favour of Federation, thus Glynn's amendment being passed without a division. It was the concern of Higgins that this reference to the Almighty in the Preamble might suggest an implied power in the Commonwealth Parliament to legislate regarding religion. Higgins therefore

---

29 Glynn Diary, 2 March 1898, National Library, MS 558, quoted in La Nauze, *op. cit.*, n 26, 226.

proposed what was to become section 116 of the Constitution, leaving the States free, if they wished, to legislate for religious intolerance.[30] That section provides,

> The Commonwealth shall not make any law for establishing any religion, or for imposing any religious observance, or for prohibiting the free exercise of any religion, and no religious test shall be required as a qualification for any office or public trust under the Commonwealth.

There were certain parallels between the later careers of Glynn and Higgins. Each entered the first Commonwealth Parliament as a member of the House of Representatives. Each held office as Attorney-General of the Commonwealth. Higgins had won his parliamentary seat as an independent, but with Labour support. He was appointed Attorney-General in the first Labour government of Australia, that of Christopher Watson in 1904. As such, Higgins found himself in the anomalous position of being a member of a Labour cabinet but not of the Labour Party caucus. However, the political career of Higgins lasted for only five years and was overshadowed by his great achievements as a Justice of the High Court of Australia, to which he was appointed in October 1906, being also from 1907 the President of the Commonwealth Court of Conciliation and Arbitration. But probably the achievement for which Higgins, as one of the Founding Fathers, should be most truly honoured was the insertion into the Constitution of section 116, that great safeguard against religious intolerance and the intrusion of religion into the powers of the Commonwealth, thereby ensuring, so far as the Constitution and the laws of the Commonwealth can do so, that there should in Australia be a total division between Church and State.

Thus it came about that one Irish lawyer, a Catholic, was responsible for the Almighty being recognised in the Constitution of the Commonwealth, whilst another Irish lawyer, brought up as a Wesleyan, but by then committed to no religious belief, was responsible for ensuring that such recognition should not impinge upon the nation or its people.

Thus far Glynn's professional and political career has been recounted. It is appropriate to refer also to his personal life. In appearance Paddy Glynn, as he was universally known, was a dapper little man, about 5 feet 4 inches (163 centimetres) tall. Many years after Glynn's death Sir Robert Menzies, who was professionally acquainted with him in the 1920s, described Glynn

---

30 La Nauze, *op. cit.*, n 26, 228–229.

as 'looking like a black beetle and talking like a silver-tongued angel'.[31] He was a non-smoker, at a time when most men smoked pipes or cigarettes. In 1883 he gave up alcohol for a limited period as a result of a bet with a friend, but at the end of that period he remained a lifelong teetotaller.

During his early years in Australia especially while he was in Melbourne and subsequently living in Kapunda, Glynn followed a rather lonely bachelor existence, residing in boarding houses. His time being occupied with establishing himself professionally, there was little opportunity for social relaxation, although he did attend the regular dances at Kapunda, and he was a keen and fearless horse rider. Matrimony could not be contemplated until he had established himself professionally and had become financially independent, and also there were few Catholic young ladies in Kapunda.

But in September 1898 during the Sydney session of the Federal Convention Glynn, somewhat to the surprise of his fellow Representatives, embarked upon what the *Bulletin* described as his meteor-like rush into matrimony.[32] Within the space of a single week he wrote a letter of proposal to Abigail Dynon of Melbourne, was accepted by telegram, hurried down to Melbourne, was married there on Saturday, 11 September at St Francis's Church, before returning to the Convention in Sydney on the following Monday. His best man was King O'Malley, a colleague in the South Australian House of Assembly (who was later to be Glynn's colleague in the Commonwealth Parliament from 1901 until 1917, where they were of different, and often opposing, political persuasions). Abigail was the beautiful daughter of Irish born parents, who had prospered in commerce in Melbourne. Glynn had met her only once, a year or so before, in Melbourne, when he asked her to 'wait for him'.[33] She did so. The marriage was happy and successful, producing three sons and five daughters, although two of those children died in infancy.

In 1901 Glynn was elected to the first House of Representatives as a Free Trader. In that election South Australia was not divided into electorates. All its MPs were elected for the State as whole, just as in the case of present day election of Senators. In 1903 he was returned unopposed for the division of Angas, won easily against a Labor candidate in 1906, was unopposed again

---

31 *Bulletin* (Sydney, 22 March 1961; H Whitington, 'Patrick McMahon Glynn, KC, 1855/1931: a further character from Kerwin Maegraith's court sketchbook', *Law Society Bulletin*, 8/11 December 1986, 339. See also Collins, *op. cit.*, n 1, 274.

32 *Bulletin* (Sydney), 25 September 1897.

33 O'Collins, *op. cit.*, n 1, 125–129.

in 1910, 1913 and 1914, won against a Labor candidate in 1917, and lost his seat to Labor in December 1919. During his time in the Commonwealth Parliament Glynn held a number of ministerial portfolios. He was Attorney-General under Alfred Deakin in 1909–1910, Minister for External Affairs (as the Foreign Minister was then called) under Sir Joseph Cook in 1913–1914, and Minister for Home and Territories (where he was the only Catholic) in the Nationalist Government under William Morris Hughes from 1917 until his defeat at the end of 1919. Glynn was a loyal and enthusiastic supporter of the Crown and the British Empire, and vigorously encouraged Australia's role in the First World War. He supported Home Rule for his native Ireland, to the extent however that Ireland should remain loyal to the British Crown. In the 51 years since Glynn had departed Ireland, when aged 25, he chose to return to his homeland on just one occasion, very briefly in 1916 (to see his octogenerian mother) while he and his wife, at the invitation of the Empire Parliamentary Association, were visiting France and the United Kingdom, as part of a delegation to inspect the War administration.

After the death of Mr Justice O'Connor in November 1912 there were rumours that Glynn might be appointed to fill that vacancy on the High Court of Australia. Glynn did not appear particularly enthusiastic at the prospect, noting in his diary that there was greater attraction in making the law, rather than in interpreting it, so he was not pursuing the position.[34] When in the following month the High Court bench was expanded to allow for the appointment of two additional Justices, thus creating three vacancies, it was reported that Glynn 'was regarded as a certainty for elevation to the Bench'.[35] It should be recalled that Glynn was a conservative Free Trader, albeit with a liberal outlook on many matters, and that it was the Fisher Labour government that was making the appointments. As Professor Anne Twomey has observed, 'It is hard to imagine a government today appointing an opposition member to the High Court.'[36] The probable reason why he was not appointed was that political difference, there being powerful Ministers opposed to him within the Labour Government. Another critic of the

---

34 Diary of P M Glynn, 12 October 1912, loc.cit., n 3, quoted in O'Collins, *op. cit.*, n 1, 234.

35 *Sydney Morning Herald*, 25 November 1912, 8.

36 Anne Twomey, 'Lawyer, Catholic and liberal conservative', in Anne Henderson, *Federation's Man of Letters: Patrick McMahon Glynn* (Redland Bay, Queensland, 2019), 111–112.

rumoured appointment was the Chief Justice of South Australia, Sir John Gordon, who rejected the offer of the appointment himself. Gordon wrote to the Commonwealth Attorney-General that Glynn was 'a good fellow', but that his 'mental outlook always seems to ... resemble scrambled eggs— wholesome enough, but messy'.[37] That was a most unfair and inaccurate statement regarding Glynn's abilities as an astute lawyer and a skilled politician. Glynn however was not disappointed, and was content to remain in Parliament. In the event there has never been a Justice of the High Court from South Australia.

After his electoral defeat at the end of 1919 Glynn (who had been appointed King's Counsel in July 1913) resumed full-time legal practice in Adelaide. He was the last of the Founding Fathers to sit in the Commonwealth Parliament. In 1927 he attended the opening of the new (now the Old) Parliament House, as one of the three survivors of the 1901 session. The other two were Hughes, still an MP (and to remain one until his death in 1952) and O'Malley.

Glynn died of pneumonia on 28 October 1931, at the age of 76, survived by two sons and four daughters (his wife having predeceased him in the previous year). In the words of his grandson and biographer, the Reverend Gerald O'Collins, Glynn was 'A person of extraordinary integrity and industry, his oratorical powers, humour and learning made him a consistently popular speaker for literary and national societies. The more eloquent his speech, the thicker became his brogue. He could quote Shakespeare to illuminate any political, legal, business or social occasion.'[38]

Since his death, now the better part of a century ago, Glynn has rather faded from public memory. Interestingly, however, in very recent times he and his achievements have been commemorated by the inauguration at the Australian Catholic University of the P M Glynn Institute on 13 October 2016. The object of that entity is to examine challenges facing government, society as a whole and Christianity in Australia. It aims to develop research in such areas as education, healthcare, human rights and immigration, and so to be in a position to formulate workable and worthwhile proposals for

---

37 Troy Simpson, 'Appointments that might have been', in Tony Blackshield, Michael Coper and George Williams (eds.), *The Oxford Companion to the High Court of Australia* (Oxford, 2001), 24.

38 Gerald O'Collins, 'Glynn, Patrick McMahon (1855–1931)', *Australian Dictionary of Biography*: http://adb.anu.edu.au/biography/glynn-patrick-mcmahon-paddy-6405/text10949

a healthier and more humane Australian life. The Institute has established the Gerald Glynn O'Collins Oration, named in honour of Glynn's grandson. The Reverend Gerald Glynn O'Collins, AC, born in Melbourne in 1931, is a Jesuit priest, and a most highly distinguished scholar, educator, writer and theologian. The first Oration, entitled 'Federation's Man of Letters: Patrick McMahon Glynn', was delivered by Anne Henderson in 2019. That Oration, together with responses thereto by scholars and commentators has been published in book-form.[39] Glynn and his achievements are thus now being rightly recalled to public memory.

Paddy Glynn was one of those young Irish lawyers of the nineteenth century who, perforce, had to make their livelihood beyond the over-crowded profession in their native land. In Australia, which he embraced unreservedly as his home, Glynn was outstandingly successful as a lawyer, as a parliamentarian—indeed, a statesman—and as one of the Fathers of Federation.

---

39 Henderson, *op. cit.*, n 36.

THE IRISH WOMEN'S CLUB: CUMANN NA MBAN IN SYDNEY
1919–1935

Anne-Maree Whitaker*

In this decade of centenaries for Ireland, 2018 marked a century since the event which historians have described as 'a turning point' – the general election of December 1918.[1] If the Easter Rising was planned and executed by a tiny minority, as some claimed, the crushing victory of Sinn Féin in the election two years later provided hard evidence that the Irish people overwhelmingly supported their ideals. The old Irish Parliamentary Party, which had supported Home Rule as a constitutional means to attain self-government, was reduced from 73 seats in 1910 to just six in 1918. In East Mayo Sinn Féin's youthful Easter Rising veteran Eamon de Valera annihilated the IPP's 67-year-old leader John Dillon, winning 66 per cent of the vote.[2]

The 1918 election was also the first which extended the franchise to women over the age of 30. While attention has naturally focused on Constance Markievicz as the first woman elected to the UK Parliament, less well known is the mobilisation of thousands of Irish women as canvassers, lobbyists and election agents. This was in addition to the impact of their votes, as about 36 per cent of the new electorate was female, and in some constituencies women voters were in the majority.[3] The London *Times* commented: 'These great majorities are not due to any complete turnover of the old electorate, but to the votes of the women and of the large number of young men who now have the vote for the first time ... The women voted for Sinn Fein in whole regiments and their enthusiasm was extraordinary. Everywhere the Sinn Fein organisation was almost perfect'.[4]

The organisation which mobilised Irish women was Cumann na mBan, usually translated as Irish Women's Council. It was founded in 1914 and was 'a unique and peculiar nationalist group in that its membership consisted

---

1 Kieran Waldron, 'The General Election of 1918 – a Turning Point in our History', *Cathair na Mart (Journal of Westport Historical Society)* 35 (2018): 8–15.
2 Waldron, 'General Election of 1918', 13–14.
3 Senia Pašeta, 'Feminist Political Thought and Activism in Revolutionary Ireland, c 1880–1918', *Transactions of the Royal Historical Society*, 27 (2017): 208.
4 'Sinn Féin triumph in Ireland', *The Times*, 30 December 1918, 10.

* Anne-Maree Whitaker is a professional historian with a special interest in Australia's Irish and Catholic history. She was a Councillor of the ACHS from 1995 to 2005.

entirely of women and girls'. While nationalism was widespread throughout Europe, no comparable women's nationalist group was founded elsewhere. Following the Easter Rising the organisation was out of the public eye until the threat of conscription of Irishmen into the British Army in mid-1918. Cumann na mBan played a major public role in organising opposition to conscription through parades and church-door petitions, and this experience naturally lent itself to election campaigning. Cumann na mBan went on to become the most influential women's organisation in twentieth-century Ireland.[5]

Following the Sinn Féin success at the election, its new members of parliament declined to take their seats in Westminster. Many of the newly-elected were in British prisons, but those who were free to do so met on 21 January 1919 at Dublin's Mansion House to form a separate Irish Parliament known as Dáil Éireann (meaning 'assembly of Ireland'). During the two-hour sitting, Dáil members adopted a Constitution and read out a Declaration of Independence, first in Irish, then in French and, finally, in English. This declaration ratified the Irish Republic that had been proclaimed on Easter Monday 1916 and ordained 'that the elected Representatives of the Irish people alone have power to make laws binding on the people of Ireland, and that the Irish Parliament is the only Parliament to which that people will give its allegiance'.[6]

Meanwhile in Australia in the dying days of World War I seven men were imprisoned without trial for alleged membership of the Irish Republican Brotherhood, the secret organisation which had been behind the Easter Rising. On 17 June 1918 the men were arrested in Sydney, Brisbane and Melbourne, and held in Darlinghurst Gaol in Sydney. They were all office bearers of the Irish National Association, formed in 1915 to promote Irish independence from British rule, or, as their constitution expressed it, 'to assist Ireland to achieve her national destiny'.[7] A public enquiry was held, which turned into slapstick when a police officer asserted that 1798 leader Wolfe Tone led a rebellion in England in 1916 and Robert Emmet (who was

---

5   Cal McCarthy, *Cumann na mBan and the Irish Revolution*, (Cork: Collins Press 2014), 1, 5, 92–96.

6   Parliament of Ireland: https://www.oireachtas.ie/en/visit-and-learn/history-and-buildings/history-of-parliament-in-ireland

7   Garrath O'Keeffe, 'Australia's Irish Republican Brotherhood', *Journal of the Royal Australian Historical Society*, 83/2 (1997): 136–152.

executed in 1803) was killed in a car accident in 1917.[8] All but one of the seven internees were released on 19 December 1918 while Albert Dryer was held until 11 February 1919.

In February 1919, under the headline 'A Patriotic Society', the *Catholic Press* newspaper reported:

Last month was witnessed in Sydney the inauguration of a branch of the Cumann na mBan. The meeting held for the purpose in the rooms of the I.N.A., Station House, was a very enthusiastic and successful one. After the aims and objects of the association were explained, it was decided by the ladies to place themselves under the patronage of Ethna Carbery, and that the branch be known as An Craob Ethna Carbery (the Ethna Carberry branch). The following ladies were elected office-bearers: President, Miss B. O'Grady; vice-presidents, Miss M. Ryan and Miss Sheehan; secretary, Miss Amy Ryan; treasurer, Miss May Maloney; committee, Mrs Cheetham, Miss Madeline Sheehy, Miss Mary Organ, and Miss Kathleen Weber. The names of Mrs J. Murphy and Miss Darcy have since been added to the committee. When the ban has been lifted from the holding of meetings, the Cumann na mBan will meet in the I.N.A. rooms (sixth floor), Station House, at 8 p.m. sharp on Wednesdays, and special attention will be given the Irish language, industry, literature, &c. Information as to membership, &c., can be had from the secretary, Miss A. Ryan, I.N.A., sixth floor, Station House.[9]

Beatrice O'Grady, Madeleine Sheehy and Amy Ryan will be discussed later in this paper. Cork-born Mary Organ was the sister of IRB couriers Andrew and Matthew Organ, while Kathleen Weber was the half-sister of INA secretary Albert Dryer.

Ethna Carbery, after whom the branch was named, was an Irish nationalist poet and journalist who was credited with a major contribution to the Irish cultural revival before her death in 1902 at the age of 35. Her link to Sydney was through one of the Darlinghurst internees, Liam McGuinness, who knew her and her father in Belfast as well as her husband Seumas MacManus.[10]

The organisation's first event was held at the Surryville Hall in June 1919

---

8 'Mr Justice Harvey's Inquiry', *Freeman's Journal* [Sydney], 22 August 1918, 23.
9 'Cumann na mBan in Sydney: A Patriotic Society', *Catholic Press*, 27 February 1919, 17.
10 'Death of Mrs Seumas MacManus', *Freeman's Journal* [Dublin], 3 April 1902. 'Mr William F McGuinness', *Catholic Press*, 1 August 1935, 17.

and combined an evening playing the card game euchre with dancing and a fancy dress competition depicting characters from Irish history and legend. The admission fee was two shillings and the evening included euchre from 8 pm to 10 pm, dancing from 8 pm to midnight to the music of the Surryville Orchestra, and supper at 10.30pm. The event was promoted by the *Catholic Press* newspaper's social column, which reported: 'The gathering, to an onlooker, must have been most interesting, to hear the dancers greet each other in the soft, rich tones of the Gaelic language, and to watch them as they moved gracefully in their picturesque attire through the dances.'[11]

The activities described were identical to many other fundraising events held for Catholic church causes and organisations such as the Irish National Foresters and the Hibernian Australian Catholic Benefit Society. Groups which held events at the Surryville Hall in the late 1910s and early 1920s included the St Vincent de Paul Society, Labor party branches, trade unions, football clubs and the Catholic parishes of St Kieran's Golden Grove and St Benedict's Broadway. The hall later became the University of Sydney Union and was replaced by the Wentworth Building in 1972.

The fancy dress competition was not a feature of the regular monthly fundraisers but was repeated on special occasions. Among these were nights devoted to the poetry of Thomas Moore and Ethna Carbery in 1928, when the evening's entertainment of recitations, music and song featured works by the chosen writer.[12] It is difficult to gauge numbers at these events, but one newspaper report listed names of 70 persons in attendance, noting 'and many others'. Attendees were predominantly but not exclusively female.[13] Funds raised by the Sydney branch of Cumann na mBan were sent to head office in Dublin to assist Republican prisoners and their families; fundraising for special tributes was conducted separately.[14]

Contributing to the ongoing success of Cumann na mBan was the support of the *Catholic Press* newspaper. Its social editor, who used the nom-de-plume 'Eblana', was Miss Margaret O'Brien who fulfilled the role from the

11 'Social News and Gossip by Eblana', *Catholic Press*, 5 June 1919, 13 and 26 June 1919, 12.

12 'Cumann na mBan: Ethna Carbery night', *Catholic Press*, 26 July 1928, 21; 'Cumann na mBan: Tom Moore Night', *Catholic Press*, 23 August 1928, 35.

13 For example 'In the Winter Garden: Social Chat and Catholic Doings', *Freeman's Journal* [Sydney], 6 October 1921, 16.

14 'Rev Father E Teehan farewelled by Cumann na mBan', *Catholic Press*, 3 February 1927, 16.

paper's founding in 1895 until her death in 1937. Margaret was the niece of Monsignor James O'Brien who was the rector of St John's College at Sydney University from 1888 to 1915, and the founder of the *Catholic Press* newspaper. Her column consistently reported on Cumann na mBan events and more importantly, promoted coming activities including their monthly ceilidh.[15]

The Cumann was also active at other Irish community occasions. For a number of years they had a float in the St Patrick's Day Parade which went from St Mary's Cathedral to the Sydney Showground at Moore Park. The office bearers also represented the group at events such as requiem masses for Cathal Brugha in July 1922, Irish President Arthur Griffith in August 1922, and the former Cumann na mBan President Constance Markievicz in July 1927, at the welcome to coadjutor Archbishop Michael Sheehan in November 1922 and the funeral of Monsignor Joseph Collins in June 1926.[16]

Aside from cultural promotion and fundraising, the Sydney Cumann na mBan occasionally donned uniforms like their Irish sisters. One such occasion was the welcome to Melbourne's Archbishop Daniel Mannix in August 1921. During a visit to Europe the previous year the British Navy intercepted Mannix's ship off the coast of Cornwall to prevent him landing in Ireland; the archbishop famously quipped: 'The greatest victory the Royal Navy has had since Jutland'. The event made world headlines and cemented the archbishop's status as a hero to Australia's Irish community. When he arrived in Sydney by train, it was reported: 'The Cumann na mBan took a very prominent part in the welcome to Archbishop Mannix. The members, in uniform, met at the Railway Station, headed by two of the members representing 'Hope' and 'Liberty', and carrying flags of Ireland. They were loudly applauded by onlookers as they marched to the cathedral, where they formed a guard of honour to his Grace as he proceeded to the steps of the High Altar.'[17]

The first speaking tour of Australia by Irish political activists following

---

15 'All About People', *Catholic Press*, 17 June 1937, 20.

16 'Irish National Association', *Freeman's Journal* [Sydney], 13 July 1922, 23; 'Arthur Griffith', *Catholic Press*, 24 August 1922, 21; 'Cumann na mBan', *Catholic Press*, 28 July 1927, 25; 'Archbishop Sheehan welcomed by Irish National Association', *Catholic Press*, 23 November 1922, 18; 'Death of Right Rev. Monsignor Collins', *Catholic Press*, 1 July 1926, 14.

17 'Social News and Gossip', *Catholic Press*, 25 August 1921, 10.

the Easter Rising and resulting War of Independence and Civil War occurred in 1923. The Irish Envoys, as they became known, were Father Michael O'Flanagan and John Joseph O'Kelly (also known by his pen-name 'Sceilg'). O'Flanagan was a former Vice-President of Sinn Féin, while O'Kelly had been a prominent member of the First Dáil elected in 1918. After a fairly tumultuous tour, characterised by conflict with Australia's Catholic bishops, the Envoys were arrested at Waverley in Sydney's eastern suburbs and deported in July 1923.[18] Arrested with them was 23-year-old Australian-born vice-president of the Irish National Association, Seán or Jack Clancy. At the time of the arrests on 30 April three Sydney residents posted bail sureties. O'Flanagan's surety was Bondi wine merchant Christopher Boland. O'Kelly's surety was John Sheehy, long-time Sydney Irish community activist and father of Cumann na mBan president Madeleine Sheehy. Seán Clancy's surety was Cumann na mBan committee member and future president Amy Ryan.[19]

The following year a far more successful tour occurred when Linda Kearns and Kathleen Barry arrived in November 1924 and spoke extensively in the mainland eastern states before their departure in March 1925. Both women had impeccable Republican credentials as activists, organisers and speakers. Linda Kearns was a trained nurse who set up a casualty station during the Easter Rising to care for injured Volunteers. She later endured imprisonment and hunger strike before escaping in 1921. Kathleen Barry was the sister of Kevin Barry, who in November 1920 became the first IRA member executed by the British since 1916. Kathleen had a strong Republican record in her own right, fighting on the anti-Treaty side in the Civil War. The women travelled through Victoria, New South Wales and Queensland during their four-month visit, speaking at meetings and appealing for funds to assist prisoners and their dependants.[20] Kathleen Barry attended the Sydney Cumann's Christmas fundraiser in December 1924, before both women

---

18 Mark Finnane, 'Deporting the Irish Envoys: domestic and national security in 1920s Australia', *Journal of Imperial and Commonwealth History*, 41/3 (2013): 403–25.

19 'Envoys Arrested', *Daily Telegraph*, 1 May 1923, 5. This is not the same edition as the one on Trove; clippings of both editions are in the Irish Envoys file at NSW State Archives, Police Special Bundle 7/6723. The press report names O'Kelly's surety as John Sheedy, but the 1923 *Sands Directory*, 385, confirms the occupant of the address given was John Sheehy.

20 Anne-Maree Whitaker, 'Linda Kearns and Kathleen Barry Irish Republican Fundraising Tour, 1924–25', *Journal of the Australian Catholic Historical Society*, 37/2 (2016): 208–211.

attended a farewell fundraising harbour cruise organised by Cumann na mBan in March 1925, shortly before their departure from Australia.[21]

Now to turn from the events in which Cumann na mBan featured to the people who made up its ranks. The women who became active in the Sydney Cumann came from a variety of backgrounds. Some were Irish-born while the Australian-born mostly had at least one parent born in Ireland. A majority of the committee members were unmarried, which is perhaps not surprising in an era when married women had large families which took up a good deal of their time. Mrs Sara Murphy who served on the committee and as an event organiser had a family of six (three of whom became religious brothers), while Mrs Annie Hess who was Treasurer for a number of years had seven children born between 1925 and 1939 (one of whom became a nun).[22] The committee members were mainly aged in their forties, although some were much younger. The first committee included 23-year-old Kathleen Weber, sister of INA secretary Albert Dryer, while Madeleine Sheehy was elected President in 1922 at the age of 22.

The person described as the founder of Cumann na mBan in Sydney was Liam McGuinness, at 29 the youngest of the Darlinghurst internees. McGuinness was born in Belfast and lost his father at an early age. At the age of 13 in 1902 he joined the newly formed Na Fianna Éireann and came under the influence of its founder, poet and author Bulmer Hobson. He also became involved with Hobson's Ulster Literary Theatre, acting in plays and mingling with the cultural nationalists who were associated with it such as Robert Johnson and Seumas MacManus, the father and husband of the writer Ethna Carbery. McGuinness also went on rambles in the glens of Antrim with Roger Casement, met the legendary Fenian Jeremiah O'Donovan Rossa, and gave Seán McDermott the first republican book he read.

Liam emigrated to Sydney in 1912 and joined a number of Irish bodies including the Irish National Association and the Gaelic League, and became known as an Irish dancing teacher. A concert was organised in his honour in 1935, prior to him leaving Sydney to live in Lithgow. Former Cumann na mBan President Amy Ryan was one of the organisers, and the event raised £39 which was formally presented to McGuinness. Albert Dryer later wrote

---

21 'A Notable Visitor', *Catholic Press*, 25 December 1924, 23; 'Cumann na mBan', *Catholic Press*, 12 March 1925, 12–13.

22 'Unusual Tribute at Requiem', *Catholic Weekly*, 12 June 1947, 6; death notice, *Sydney Morning Herald*, 26 October 1960, 56.

of him: 'In all departments of Irish activities his wise and sustained enthusiasm proved a very significant factor in promoting the cause of Ireland's independence, as well as of her culture. His associates regarded as inspiring his personality and labours for the cause.'[23]

Many Catholic priests in the 1920s were not afraid to declare their opinions on Irish politics and Anglo-Irish relations. One of the best-known was Dr Patrick Tuomey,[24] not least because he was charged in 1918 with 'having delivered a speech on September 4 last calculated to cause disaffection and encourage disloyalty' and fined £30. Tuomey was undeterred by

Rev Dr Patrick Tuomey with group of women, Sydney, c 1925. [Dryer papers, National Library of Australia]

this punishment and continued to express his views on political topics. His popularity with the Irish National Association saw them make a presentation on his departure for the Southern Highlands in 1917, and on his return to Sydney in 1922 he slipped easily back into Irish social and political circles.[25] He was particularly associated with Cumann na mBan, and it is possible a photograph from Albert Dryer's papers in the National Library includes women who were active in the organisation.[26]

---

23 'Mr William F McGuinness', *Catholic Press*, 1 August 1935, 17; 'Irish Testimonial Concert', *Catholic Press*, 26 September 1935, p 8; Witness Statement of Albert Thomas Dryer, Bureau of Military History, Ireland, WS 1526, 17.

24 Tuomey has been described as part of the 'apostolic succession' of Irish priests which began with O'Flynn, Therry and McEncroe: Father Edmund Campion, eulogy at the funeral of Father Michael O'Sullivan, Mary Mother of Mercy Chapel, Rookwood Cemetery, Sydney, 1 August 2019.

25 'Remarkable Irish Priest Mourned', *Catholic Press*, 24 February 1955; Witness Statement of Albert Thomas Dryer, Bureau of Military History, Ireland, WS 1526, 10–12.

26 Picture, 'Reverend Dr Patrick Tuomey surrounded by a group of people in a garden,

Beatrice O'Grady was elected first president of the Sydney Cumann in 1919 and remained in the position for three years. She was single and 40 years of age. Beatrice's father John was born in Newmarket on Fergus, County Clare, and emigrated with his parents and siblings to Sydney in 1855 at the age of 14.[27] Her father's occupation was listed in electoral rolls as 'independent means' and he had made his fortune as a wine and spirit merchant. Obviously his wealth was sufficient to allow Beatrice and his three other daughters to remain unmarried and out of the workforce. They shared the family home with their brothers who were also unmarried, but employed as clerks and salesmen. Beatrice joined the third order of St Francis in 1898 at the age of 20. This was a lay organisation for Catholics of both sexes, who lived 'in the world' and could marry and take employment. Beatrice soon became the order's novice mistress, a role which involved instructing new members in their duties and obligations. She continued in this position for several decades, and was still actively involved in the order at the time of her sudden death in 1952.[28]

Margaret Madeleine Sheehy (1899-1999), President 1922–23, later known as Dr Margaret Jones [NSW State Archives]

Following Beatrice O'Grady the presidency was held for a few months in 1922 by 39-year-old Mrs Sara Murphy, who had served on the committee since 1919. She was born Sara Kehoe in Wexford, and married Joe Murphy in Gorey in 1913 before emigrating to Sydney with their first child the following year. Sara and Joe were enthusiastic participants in Cumann na mBan social events, but probably the demands of their family of six made it

---

Sydney? approximately 1925', Albert Dryer papers, National Library of Australia.

27 NSW death certificate 1918-13349.

28 'Well-Known Tertiary Dies', *Catholic Weekly*, 9 October 1952, 9.

difficult for Sara to commit too much time to a senior leadership role.[29]

Later in 1922 the Presidency passed to 22-year-old Australian-born Madeleine Sheehy. Her father John Sheehy had arrived in Sydney in around 1890, and had a long history of activism in Irish community affairs. He was born in Ballingarry, County Limerick, and had qualified as a lawyer in Dublin but did not practise in Sydney, instead taking the role of General Secretary to

Amy Ryan (1878–1957), President 1924–1926, bail surety for the Irish Envoys 1923 [private collection]

the Irish National Foresters benevolent society.[30] Madeleine, also known as Margaret, was educated at St Scholastica's College, Glebe and went on to study medicine at the University of Sydney. At the event to welcome noted Gaelic scholar and Coadjutor Archbishop Michael Sheehan to Sydney in November 1922 Madeleine gave an address of welcome in Gaelic on behalf of Cumann na mBan.[31] After graduating in April 1923 she had to move to Toowoomba to gain a residency, and later worked at Kenmore Hospital in Goulburn before her marriage to Cecil Jones in 1928. She retired from the workforce after her marriage, apart from a stint of war service, and died in 1999 just short of her 100th birthday.[32]

The fourth President of Cumann na mBan was 48-year-old Miss Amy Ryan, who held the office from November 1923 until January 1927. Amy's father James Ryan was from Kilmanagh, County Kilkenny, and had arrived in the 1850s as a teenager with his mother and siblings to join his father in

---

29 'Mr. Joseph A. Murphy', *Catholic Press*, 10 July 1930, 36; 'Unusual Tribute at Requiem', *Catholic Weekly*, 12 June 1947, 6.

30 'Presentation to Mr John Sheehy', *Freeman's Journal* [Sydney], 10 November 1921, 22; 'All About People', *Catholic Press*, 30 October 1941, 2.

31 'Archbishop Sheehan welcomed by Irish National Association', *Catholic Press*, 23 November 1922, p 18; Gregory Byrnes, 'Archbishop Sheehan – a biographical sketch', *Journal of the Australian Catholic Historical Society*, 14 (1992): 32.

32 'Dr Margaret Jones', *Sydney Morning Herald*, 27 July 1999, 20.

Numbaa in the Shoalhaven district of southern New South Wales. James was a farmer and also served as mayor of the town for many years.[33] Amy and her sisters Alice and Ellen moved to Sydney where they shared houses. Amy was employed as a stenographer, Alice was a teacher and Ellen was a dressmaker.[34] At the time of the arrest of the Irish Envoys and a supporter in 1923, Amy Ryan was one of three bail sureties. She suffered a period of ill-health in 1927 and 1928, relinquishing the presidency of Cumann na mBan, but recovered and in 1935 was one of the organisers for the Liam McGuinness concert.[35] She died in 1957 and was buried in the Nowra General Cemetery.[36]

As with many community organisations Cumann na mBan declined and eventually ceased. Part of the reason for this was the progression of events in Ireland, and part also related to the health and availability of activists in Australia. The Cumann began to use the name 'Irish Women's Club' in 1926, although the monthly ceilidhs seem to have continued until around mid-1930.[37] A notice in September 1935 announced a 'reunion dance' at a favourite venue, St Benedict's church hall in Broadway. The event was probably inspired by the benefit organised for their founder Liam McGuinness the previous month, but does not seem to have been repeated.[38] The last mention of the organisation in the press was a farewell for Annie and George Hess and their seven children when they left for Melbourne in 1939. Annie Kehoe's involvement in Cumann na mBan dated from before her marriage to George Hess in 1924, and she had been the group's treasurer for many years.[39]

Cumann na mBan in Ireland was set up with four objects:
1. To advance the cause of Irish Liberty;
2. To organise Irishwomen in the furtherance of this object;
3. To assist in arming and equipping a body of Irishmen for the defence of Ireland;

33 'Numba', *Freeman's Journal* [Sydney], 1 September 1921, 35.
34 Electoral roll 1913, district Enmore, sub-district Enmore, 137 Alice Street, enrolment numbers 2729; 2730; and 2733.
35 'Cumann na mBan', *Catholic Press*, 23 February 1928, 13; 'Complimentary Concert', *Catholic Press*, 11 July 1935, 8.
36 NSW death registration 2937/1957, Brigid Amy Ryan.
37 'Cumann na mBan Christmas Party', *Catholic Press*, 9 December 1926, 36; 'Cumann na mBan', *Catholic Press*, 12 June 1930, 20;
38 'Cumann na mBan Reunion Dance', *Catholic Press*, 5 September 1935, 25.
39 'Saying Farewell', *Catholic Press*, 5 January 1939, 25; 'Wedding Bells', *Catholic Press*, 8 January 1925, 13.

St Patrick's Day Parade float 1926: Erin Giver of Faith to Nations
[private collection].

4. To form a fund for these purposes to be called the 'Defence of Ireland Fund'.[40]

The organisation in Sydney obviously did not undertake the same range of activities as in Ireland. First aid classes and the purchase of weapons were left to those at home. The Sydney Cumann undertook a mixture of cultural promotion, political action and fundraising while also providing a social milieu for women of Irish birth or descent. It might be asked what women activists in Ireland thought of this antipodean offshoot? The answer comes indirectly during the visit of Kathleen Barry in 1924 and 1925. Kathleen attended the Sydney Cumann's Christmas party in 1924 before her visit to Melbourne in late February-early March 1925 when the Kevin Barry craobh of Cumann na mBan was established.[41] Sadly the Melbourne branch had a 'very unprofitable, undignified existence of a few months', according to Máire McKee.[42] Nevertheless, Kathleen obviously believed that the Sydney

40 McCarthy, *Cumann na mBan and the Irish Revolution*, 18.
41 'A Notable Visitor', *Catholic Press*, 25 December 1924, 23; 'Irish Relief and Reconstruction Fund', *Advocate*, 19 February 1925, 25.
42 Máire McKee to Kathleen Barry, 2 February 1926, P94/68, University College Dublin Archives: http://www.ucd.ie/t4cms/p0094-moloney-kathleen-barry-descriptive-catalogue.pdf, 23.

model was successful and worth replicating in other parts of Australia.

Patrick O'Farrell famously declared that the Irish Civil War was 'a profound disillusionment and embarrassment' to Irish-Australians, and created in them a feeling of 'hostility or at least unwillingness to be identified with or involved in things Irish.'[43] Clearly this brief history of Cumann na mBan in Sydney in the 1920s shows that the opposite was true, and that a vibrant Irish cultural and political scene continued.

---

43 Patrick O'Farrell, 'Irish Australia at an End: the Australian League for an Undivided Ireland 1948–54', *Tasmanian Historical Research Association Papers and Proceedings*, 21/4 (1974): 144.

Daughters of Our Lady, Queen of the Apostles—The First and Only Order of Aboriginal Sisters in Australia, 1938—1951: History, Context and Outcomes

Christine Choo*

Abstract

The story of the Daughters of Our Lady, Queen of the Apostles, the first and only order of Aboriginal[1] sisters in Australia, is deeply enmeshed with the story of the evangelisation of the Aborigines in the West Kimberley by Roman Catholics. Beagle Bay Mission was established by the Trappists in 1890, then in 1901 it was taken over by the Pallottine order whose mission was to evangelise the Aboriginal people of the area. In response to Papal directives, one of the Pallottines' most important aspirations was to establish an Aboriginal ministry to their own people. The Daughters of Our Lady, Queen of the Apostles was created in 1938 by Bishop Otto Raible SAC, Catholic Bishop of the Kimberley (1927–1959), with an enthusiastic group of young Aboriginal women in Beagle Bay Mission. It lasted for eleven years.

Acknowledgement of Country

This paper was first presented on country of the *Whadjuk* people of the *Noongar* nation and I wish to pay my respects to their past, present and emerging Elders.

I also wish to pay my respects to the *NjulNjul*, the *Nigena* (*Nyinina*) and other Aboriginal peoples of the Kimberley as the topic of this paper refers to them and their ancestors.

I sincerely appreciate living on *Whadjuk boodja*, having come here from Malaysia in 1967 and been welcomed by the Aboriginal people of this land.

Introduction

It was the *NjulNjul* people of Beagle Bay who encountered the Catholic missionaries to the West Kimberley region in the last decade of the 19th century, and it was at Beagle Bay that the first permanent Christian mission was established in the Kimberley. For the missionaries, the 'frontier' was

---

1 I use 'Aboriginal' to refer to Indigenous people of Australia, and the Kimberley. The term 'Indigenous' is used only when it is specifically mentioned in the references or discussions to which I refer in the paper.

* Christine Choo BA, MSocWk, MPhil (Australian Studies), PhD (UWA). Historian, Social Researcher and Independent Scholar, Perth, Western Australia. An earlier version of this article was presented as a paper at the World Heritage Day Lecture Series – 'Catholicism on the Margins' in Perth on 18 April 2019. This article is refereed.

more than the physical environment, it included the 'frontier' of spiritual endeavour, where they set out to evangelise the Aboriginal peoples. The early history of the Catholic Church in Western Australia is deeply enmeshed with the Church's mission to the Aboriginal peoples, and the story of the order of Aboriginal (native) sisters, Daughters of Our Lady, Queen of the Apostles, established in Beagle Bay by Bishop Otto Raible in the 1930s, lies at the heart of the evangelisation method.

In this paper I document a brief history of the Daughters of Our Lady, Queen of the Apostles, which survived for eleven years between 1939 and 1951, and place the order in the ecclesial and social contexts in which it emerged. The Catholic Church and the wider community of Australia are largely unaware of the existence this order of Aboriginal women and its contribution to the Church. Not only was it established in the north-west of Australia, far from the focus of the Church in the south and east, but it was an order exclusively for Aboriginal women established at a time when Aboriginal people had no legal rights on their own land colonised by Europeans.

There is no mention of the Daughters of Our Lady, Queen of the Apostles in *The History of the Catholic Church in Western* Australia by D. F. Bourke, published by the Archdiocese of Perth in 1979.[2] Maria Rosa MacGinley, whose history of women religious in Australia was published in 1996, devoted five paragraphs to the 'Daughters of Mary Queen of Apostles'. MacGinley drew on the work of Mary Durack, J C Dunphy, Margaret Zucker and research notes provided by Sister Brigida Nailon CSB who wrote the history of the Pallottines in Western Australia.[3] In Nailon's history, *Nothing is wasted in the household of God*, the opening of 'a convent for native sisters' was limited to four short paragraphs; the native sisters were referred to again

---

2   D F Bourke, *The History of the Catholic Church in Western Australia* (Perth: Archdiocese of Perth, 1979).

3   Maria Rosa MacGinley, *A Dynamic of Hope: Institutes of Women Religious in Australia*, (Sydney: Crossing Press/Institute of Religious Studies: 1996), 311–313; Mary Durack, *The Rock and the Sand*, (London: Constable: [1969] 1985); J C Dunphy [nd] 'The Pomegranate: A History of the Sisters of St John of God', unpublished manuscript (in possession of author M R MacGinley); Margaret Zucker, *From Patrons to Partners: A History of the Catholic Church in the Kimberley, 1884–1984*, (Fremantle: University of Notre Dame Press: 1994), 114–115; Brigida Nailon CSB, *Nothing is wasted in the Household of God: Vincent Pallotti's Vision in Australia 1901–2001*, (Richmond: Spectrum Publications: 2001).

briefly in the context of their presence in Balgo Mission, and their eventual formal closure in 1953.[4]

In Chapter 6 of *Mission Girls*, based on my own research in the 1990s on Aboriginal women on Catholic missions in the Kimberley, I drew on a range of sources to tell the story of Bishop Otto Raible's dream of establishing an order of Aboriginal sisters to minister to their own people.[5] I interviewed a number of women who had joined but were then reluctant to speak of their experiences in the order. However, in more recent times former members have shared some of their experiences for the St John of God Heritage Centre in Broome.[6] The biography of Katie Fraser, one of the first young women to join the order, offers further insight into the life of one member of the order, though Katie herself was reluctant to speak of her time as a nun. Katie's story is told as a joint biography and family history in her daughter Cindy Solonec's PhD thesis.[7]

On 20 April 1939, *The Advocate* newspaper in Melbourne published an article about the forthcoming establishment of the order in Beagle Bay with the acceptance of the first postulants[8].

First Australian Native Nuns. Foundation at Beagle Bay

WHAT promises to be the first congregation of Australian aboriginal nuns is soon to be established at the Beagle Bay Mission of the Pallottine Fathers in the Kimberleys, Western Australia. In June, six or seven native young women, educated by the Sisters of St. John of God, will become postulants in a new religious congregation, to be known as the Sisters of Our Lady, Queen of the Apostles. His Lordship Bishop Raible, P.S.M., Vicar-Apostolic of the Kimberleys, has taken the step after careful consideration, following constant requests over a long period by the native girls themselves to enter the religious life. At present they are undergoing special study and training, before

---

4 Nailon: (2001), 139 and 199.

5 Christine Choo, *Mission Girls: Aboriginal Women on Catholic Missions in the Kimberley, Western Australia, 1900–1950*, (Crawley: UWA Press: [2001] 2004).

6 St John of God Heritage Centre. 2015. Sisters of Mary Queen of the Apostles. *Kimberley Community Profile*, Sep 2015, 14–15; St John of God Heritage Centre, Broome. 2016. *Native Sisters. The Blue Sisters 1939–1951: Sisters of Mary Queen of the Apostles*. Video Recording. Produced by Julie Bailey for SSJG Heritage Centre, Broome: https://heritage.ssjg.org.au; Also exhibits at the SSJG Heritage Centre.

7 Jacinta Solonec, *Shared lives on Nigena country: A joint Biography of Katie and Frank Rodriguez, 1944–1994*. PhD Thesis, University of Western Australia (2015).

8 A 'postulant' is a candidate for entry into a religious order.

beginning their postulancy. Their habit will be blue and white, with the initials of the congregation, and they will wear sandals. But they will not take vows and will be free to leave whenever they desire. The Beagle Bay Mission is one of the oldest established in Australia, being founded by the Holy See in 1887.[9]

Although other newspapers throughout Australia ran similar articles in the following weeks and on a few other occasions, the Daughters of Our Lady, Queen of the Apostles, the first and only order of Aboriginal women in Australia, seems to have slipped into oblivion, out of the consciousness of Australia's Catholic community and wider public.

Church in the Kimberley – Beagle Bay Mission

Beagle Bay Mission was established in 1890 by Trappist monks (an order of Cistercian cloistered monks who follow the Rule of St Benedict) from Sept Fons in France, with the encouragement of Bishop Matthew Gibney of Perth who had a particular interest in Aboriginal people and their welfare. As early as 1892 the Trappists recognised the need for the presence of nuns to assist in the education of 'the young female savages and even the incorrigible boys' and were hoping that the a few sisters of the newly established French order, Religieuses de Notre Dame des Missions (Sisters of Our Lady of the Missions, established in Lyon in 1861), would join them in Beagle Bay. However, this was not to be. After nearly a decade of hard work in Beagle Bay where the environment was not conducive to the life of the contemplative order, the Trappists left suddenly on orders from France. After a long search for suitable missionaries to replace them, Bishop Gibney arranged for the Pallottines to take responsibility for the mission in April 1901.

The Pallottines belonged to the order of male missionaries, the Pious Society of Missions, PSM (Pious Society of Missions, later named Society of the Catholic Apostolate, SAC), which was founded in Italy by Vincent Pallotti in 1835.[10] One of their aims was 'to carry the faith where it was unknown'. They were an apostolic order whose priests and brothers sent to

---

9   *The Advocate* (Melbourne), Thursday 20 April 1939, 4.

10 The Society of the Catholic Apostolate, Regina Mundi (Queen of the World) Region, also known as Pallottine Fathers and Brothers, is an integral part of the Union of Catholic Apostolate, a people inspired by St. Vincent Pallotti's (1795–1850) vision of everyone being called by God to be disciples of Jesus, continuing the work of Jesus here on earth 'urged on by the love of Christ' (2Cor 5:14). Website: https://www.pallottine.org.au/ See also: https://en.wikipedia.org/wiki/Vincent_Pallotti

the Kimberley were practical men who could turn their hand to any form of labour. Their plan was to evangelise the Aborigines through work and prayer. The Pallottine approach to evangelisation, similar to that of the Benedictines in New Norcia, was to settle families close to the mission and to remove the children from their families into dormitories located in the mission compound in order to give them a basic education. Men and boys were trained in trades and young women mainly in domestic work.[11] The Pallottines soon recognised that they needed female missionaries to help to run the girls' dormitory and the school.

On 6 June 1906, nine sisters of St John of God, under the leadership of Mother Antonio O'Brien, arrived at Beagle Bay Mission from Ireland via Kalgoorlie and Subiaco. The sisters were responsible for the care of the children in the dormitories; they taught them in school, and worked with the women and older girls on household chores for the priests, brothers, sisters and children in their care. With the arrival of the St John of God sisters the number of children who were brought under the care of the mission increased dramatically as this period coincided with the introduction of state-sanctioned removal of Aboriginal children, particularly 'half-caste' children, under the *Aborigines Act* of 1905 (WA). The number of children cared for at Beagle Bay Mission increased steadily. At the end of 1913 there were 147 children being cared for at the Mission.[12] In 1936 there were at least 124 children in the mission dormitory, most of whom were half-castes removed from their families and placed there under legislation.[13]

In addition to the maintenance of their own religious life, the St John of God sisters were also responsible for the care of the church and preparation for religious services. In 1908 the sisters moved away from the strict control of the male hierarchy in Beagle Bay to Broome where they established a

---

11 This approach to evangelization was practiced in the Benedictine missions at New Norcia and in Drysdale River Mission in the Kimberley, and later at the Pallottine mission in Balgo. Christine Choo and Brian F McCoy, 'Mission Dormitories: Intergenerational Implications for Kalumburu and Balgo, Kimberley, Western Australia', In Patricia Grimshaw & Andrew May eds., *Missionaries, Indigenous Peoples and Cultural Exchanges*, (Brighton, U.K. & Portland, Oregon: Sussex Academic Press: 2010). See also: Christine Choo, 'Mixed Blessings: Establishment of Christian Missions in the Kimberley', in Cathie Clement, Jeffrey Gresham and Hamish McGlashan eds. *Kimberley History: People, Exploration and Development*, (Perth: Kimberley Society: 2012).

12 Nailon, (2001), 40.

13 Choo, *Let the Children Come to Me* ([2001] 2004), chapter 5.

Members of the Sodality of the Children of Mary – Mia Charles, Margo Joseph, Emelda Taylor, Carmen Haslem, Philomena Wudi, Agnes Wright, Cecilia Rose Jnr, Susan Dolby, Monica Stracke, Teresa Dann, Martha Hughes, Laura Booty, Magdalene Kelly–with Father John Herold. Beagle Bay Mission, circa 1934–1936. Photograph (SSJG-0002521) courtesy of Sisters of St John of God Heritage Centre, Broome

convent and a school. From the 1930s they worked in the Kimberley with people with Hansen's Disease (leprosy) and other illnesses. The sisters have maintained a deep and ongoing relationship with many Aboriginal women in the Kimberley.[14]

Because of their close contact with the children in the dormitories the St John of God nuns became the surrogate mothers and sisters of the young Aboriginal girls in their care, all of whom lived away from their own families. They were closely involved in nurturing the young women's faith development and became significant role models for them. Girls and young women on the mission were baptised and brought up as good Catholics – they attended mass and the sacraments and assisted with the preparation of the altar for daily mass; at mass they sang hymns and responded in Latin; they collaborated closely with the priests, brothers and deacons as supporters

---

14 *Sisters, Pearls and Mission Girls* (Rebel Films, 2002). Viewed 13 Mar 2019: https://slwa.kanopy.com/video/sisters-pearls-and-mission-girls

in the evangelisation of their own people. Older girls cared for the younger girls, including their own siblings.

From as early as 1911, the missionaries encouraged the young women to join the Sodality of the Children of Mary, an association within the Church founded in the 1830s in France, that encouraged prayer and devotion to Mary, the mother of Jesus. Sodality members met regularly for prayer and on these occasions they wore a distinctive uniform of a white dress with a belt and a blue cape. Mission girls' membership of the Sodality of Mary shaped their spirituality and religious practice.[15]

Wider Ecclesial Context

In this discussion of the only religious order of Aboriginal women in Australia, it is important to examine the wider ecclesial context including the place of women's religious orders, and expectations of these orders in the Catholic Church in the 19th and early 20th centuries.

From the mid-1800s a number of directives from the Popes instructed the Church on the necessity to reach out as missionaries beyond the borders of their diocese. On 18 September 1840, Pope Gregory XVI published his Encyclical Letter, *Probe Nostis – On the Propagation of the Faith*, in which he encouraged the rebirth of missionary endeavour in the Church. He encouraged the development of male and female missionary orders, in both the lay and clerical spheres, and urged the bishops to extend their missionary endeavour to the whole world.[16] Nearly eighty years later, on 30 November 1919, Pope Benedict XV issued an Apostolic Letter, *Maximum Illud – On the Propagation of the Faith Throughout the World*, which identified the need for Catholic missions to train local clergy and to reach out to the indigenous populations.[17] Pope Pius XI, on 28 February 1926, published an Encyclical Letter, *Rerum Ecclesiae – On Promoting the Sacred Missions*, which focussed on the foundation, consolidation and independence of the new churches with native clergy and lay leadership, and respect for native values.[18] It envisaged the development of native Catholics who would provide

---

15 St John of God Heritage Centre, Broome (2016).

16 Gregory XVI. 1840. *Probe Nostis—On the Propagation of the Faith* (18 September 1840).

17 Benedict XV. 1919. *Maximum Illud: Apostolic Letter on the Propagation of the Faith Throughout the World*, Translated by Thomas J M Burke, S J (Washington, DC: National Catholic Welfare Office: 30 November 1919).

18 Pius XI, *Rerum Ecclesiae—On Promoting the Sacred Missions*. © Copyright–Libreria

leadership in the Church and their country. The Encyclical made special mention of the work of women (the Pope was referring to missionary sisters who ventured to lands far beyond their convents in Europe):

30. We must not go further without saying something about the work that is being done by women, for since the very earliest days of the Church they have always been remarkable for their diligence and zeal in assisting the preachers of the gospel. We want to single out here, and single out for Our highest praise, those many women who have vowed their virginity to God and have gone to pursue their vocation on the missions. There they have devoted themselves to the education of children and to a great many other works of charity and devotion. This recognition of their achievements will, We hope, encourage the sisters and inspire them to further efforts on behalf of the Church. We hope too that they will hold fast to the conviction that the usefulness of their work will increase in proportion to the care they give to their own spiritual perfection.[19]

These Papal directives created the broad ecclesial context for the extension of missionary work to indigenous peoples, and for the role of women missionaries.

In Australia, one of the significant outcomes of the Third Plenary Council of the ecclesiastical hierarchy who gathered in Sydney between 2 and 10 September 1905 was the call for the evangelisation of the Aboriginal people of Australia, particularly the north west. The 'Acts' of the Third Plenary Council record that on Saturday 9 September 1905 'a brief report by the Right Reverend Bishop of Perth dealing with the missions to the Aborigines in Western Australia, was read by the Secretary of the Council'. The report, which indicated that the Western Australian government was prepared to support the work of the missions, was unanimously endorsed by all present at the Council who recommended to the Holy Father that a new mission to the north of Western Australia be approved. The Pope's formal approval was given on 17 June 1907.[20] The Benedictine monks of New Norcia established a mission at Pago in the far north of Western Australia in 1908.[21]

Editrice Vaticana (28 February 1926).

19 Pius XI, *Rerum Ecclesiae* (1926).

20 E Perez, OSB. [nd] *Fifty Years of the Drysdale River–Kalumburu–Benedictine Mission.* Handwritten draft. Benedictine Archives, New Norcia, Western Australia, BA 01039.

21 Perez, E OSB, *Kalumburu, 'Formerly Drysdale River' Benedictine Mission North-Western Australia: A Golden Jubilee Publication (1908–1958)* (New Norcia: New

The popes' encyclicals of 1840, 1919 and 1926 provided a new challenge to women in religious life in the Americas, Africa, Asia and the Pacific, where missionary activity coincided with the westernising influence. Wherever the sisters went they welcomed women from local communities who wanted to join their orders. They also helped to establish orders of indigenous sisters, with the hope that they would contribute to the development of leadership of the young, non-Western churches.[22]

Globally, in most locations where they were established, native sisters reached out to those in greatest need in their communities. Some Western missionaries believed that the conversion of the women would lead to the conversion of the nation and they worked hard to bring young women into their schools; women and girls were taught European domestic skills and needlework. Some missions established orphanages where they educated young girls and prepared them for marriage to male converts. By joining a religious order, the native sisters challenged the marriage systems and customs of their communities.[23]

The feminine culture of the nuns conflicted with a masculine culture of clericalism, authority and obedience in the Church. The western nuns and native sisters remained under the control of the male hierarchy in almost all aspects of their religious practice and work. While missionary clergy welcomed the practical assistance the sisters gave them in mission work, and valued sisters as co-workers, there was a tradition of clergy using sisters as sacristans and housekeepers who washed, ironed, mended and sewed for priests and brothers, often in addition to their work as teachers and nurses. As McNamara states:

> By implication, nuns were being realigned as subalterns at the lower ranks of the clergy rather than being placed at the elite peak of the laity. By the twentieth century, Rome was taking women religious

---

Norcia Abbey Press, 1958); 1.

22 Jo Ann Kay McNamara, 'Sisters in Arms: Catholic Nuns through Two Millennia', (Cambridge, Massachusetts: Harvard University Press, 1996), 586.

23 McNamara (1996), 594.

more seriously and spending more effort to define their position. ... In 1906, Pius X established the Sacred Congregation for Religious with supervisory powers over congregations that had escaped diocesan control by direct ties to Rome. All religious communities were commanded to revise their constitutions to conform to the details of convent life prescribed in the new canon law code of 1917.[24]

Paradoxically these requirements imposed further burdens on religious congregations of women, even as the congregations were working to champion the rights and change conditions under which local women were living.[25]

In the early 20th century, congregations of native sisters were formed in Papua and New Guinea. On 27 October 1912, at the Cathedral of Vunapope in New Guinea, His Lordship Dr Couppe, MSC, inducted five young native girls as postulants in the newly created Society of the Daughters of Mary Immaculate or 'Little Sisters', which came under the guidance of the Sisters of Our Lady of the Sacred Heart (OLSH). The Sisters went regularly to bush stations close to Vunapope; they taught in village schools, visited and attended to the sick. They made altar-breads and assisted the 'Blue Sisters' (OLSH) in washing, ironing, and repairing altar and house linen, and they cared for the Mission cemetery. In 1920 a branch of this order was established in Tapo or Tanui, another mission station not far from Vunapope where the native sisters taught in the school.[26]

On 1 December 1918, the Congregation of the Handmaids of Our Lord (Ancilla Domini – A.D. Sisters) was founded in Papua by the Vicar Apostolic of Papua, Archbishop Alain Marie Guynot de Boismenu, MSC. Six young women (five from Papua and one from Thursday Island) formed the original group who came under the Daughters of Our Lady of the Sacred Heart (OLSH) for their formation who made their first profession on 30 November 1920. Their role was to support the priests, especially those working in remote and isolated areas. They opened schools, provided some medical services, took care of the church, gave religious instruction, visited villagers, created vegetable gardens, cooked and did house-keeping for the priests. They also cared for orphaned babies.

---

24 McNamara. 1996, 613–614.
25 McNamara. 1996, 615.
26 Joseph Madigan MSC. Why Not Become Nuns? The Native Sisters in Our Island Missions. *Freeman's Journal* (Sydney, NSW: 1850–1932): Thursday 22 July 1926, 11.

Although women's religious orders have worked in Aboriginal communities throughout Australia, including in some of the most remote areas, very few Aboriginal women have joined the religious orders as nuns. In Western Australia, only four Aboriginal young women are known to have joined an existing religious order, the Benedictine Missionary Sisters based in the Benedictine monastery town of New Norcia. Their situation was different from that of the young women of Beagle Bay as the girls from New Norcia joined an established order of nuns who had come from Europe to work with the Benedictine monks in New Norcia and Kalumburu (formerly Drysdale River Mission) in the Kimberley. Sister Veronica Willaway OSB, daughter of Harold and Philomena Willaway who had both been brought up in New Norcia, was the only one of the four who remained in the order. She joined the Benedictine Sisters in 1958 and made her final vows in 1966 at the age of 21. When the Benedictine Sisters withdrew from Australia, she was transferred to Spain and eventually to the USA in 1991.[27]

It is within this broad ecclesial context that the Daughters of Our Lady, Queen of the Apostles, was established in Beagle Bay by Bishop Otto Raible in 1939.

Establishment of Daughters of Our Lady, Queen of the Apostles

Father Otto Raible arrived in Beagle Bay in 1928 and was ordained Bishop in May 1935. One of Bishop Raible's priorities, in line with the directives from the Vatican, was to establish a ministry with Aboriginal priests and nuns who could serve their own people.[28] By then there were three generations of Catholics at Beagle Bay who were well schooled in religious practices including attendance at daily mass and benediction, the daily recitation of the rosary and participation in spiritual retreats. They held a special devotion to the Sacred Heart, and young women and teenage girls were encouraged in Marian devotion through the Sodality of the Children of Mary.

In 1938 Bishop Raible led an enclosed retreat for 27 members of the

---

27 Willaway, Sr Veronica OSB, 'My memories as a Benedictine Sister at New Norcia', *New Norcia Studies*, 6 (September 1998): 42–44; Katharine Massam, 'To name and remember: The Benedictine Sisters of New Norcia Reunion with past pupils, October 2001', *New Norcia Studies* 10 (September 2002): 26–32.

28 Bill Worth, 'Bishop Otto Raible SAC, part 1, 'Church of the Kimberley–Heroes in Faith', *Kimberley Community Profile* (St John of God Heritage Centre Broome: May 2015): 11: https://heritage.ssjg.org.au/Assets/historical-articles/KCP-May-2015-Raible-part-1.pdf

Children of Mary at which he had encouraged the participants to consider becoming nuns. Four of the girls responded by requesting to become nuns to work with their own people. This was the Bishop's dream. He immediately sought permission from the Holy See at the Vatican to establish a new congregation of sisters at Beagle Bay, and wrote to the mother general of the St John of God sisters in Wexford in Ireland to inform her of these plans. Bishop Raible was inspired by the establishment of the Native Sisters in the Vicariate of Rabaul in 1912 and sought the advice of the Bishop of Rabaul on the establishment of the order in Beagle Bay.[29]

Under the Rules of the Society of Native Sisters, Daughters of Our Lady, Queen of the Apostles, the first aim of the Daughters was to try to make themselves more holy every day 'by imitating what Our Lord Jesus Christ had done, especially by being poor, chaste and obedient'.[30] As their special work, the Daughters would 'help our poor pagan brothers and sisters, the natives of Australia, so that they also may know God, love Him and so save their souls'. They would do this 'by assisting the priests in their work, wherever it [would] be required, in schools and orphanages, homes for the aged and poor, and by nursing the sick'. They would 'take special care of the native women and girls, so that they become good Christian women and mothers.' And their work would be confined to 'the Australian full blood and half caste natives' and any Catholic girl of 'at least one half of aboriginal blood' could be admitted if she had 'the right intention, [was] bodily and mentally fitted for missionary work and [was] of a sociable disposition'. Girls of twelve years and over could be admitted as aspirants[31], and the age of admission to the novitiate was eighteen years. The candidate entered her postulancy, a time of special probation, six months before admission to the novitiate. The right of admission and dismissal rested with the Bishop, and prior to her admission, inquiries would be made about 'her character and piety, and also about her people'. During the years prior to their reception, candidates received thorough instruction in their Faith and were also taught general knowledge and given training in 'certain useful trades'. The girls wore a

29 St John of God Heritage Centre, Broome. 2016; St John of God Heritage Centre, 2015. Sisters of Mary Queen of the Apostles, 14–15; Nailon (2001), 433.

30 Brigida Nailon CSB. [?1987] 'Land of Wait and Wonder. Resource Notes on the Establishment of Roman Catholic Missions in the Kimberley'. Archives of the Diocese of Broome. [unpublished]. Included as Appendix F in Choo, *Mission Girls*.

31 An 'aspirants' was a girl who showed interest in and hoped to join the Sisters.

habit comprising a long garment of unbleached calico with blue trimming and other features that distinguished them from other girls at the mission. (Refer to Appendix 1 for the text of the Rules).

The postulants' religious instruction commenced in January 1939 with Bishop Riable urging them to follow a strict routine to enhance their spiritual life:

> Then His Lordship gave us some advice what we should do in order to prepare ourselves for our new Vocation. He told us to go to Holy Mass every day and receive Holy Communion if possible, make a visit to the Blessed Sacrament each day and to make some little sacrifices every day. Then he gave us a little book in which we should mark every day, if we had done these things faithfully during the day. He also gave us a Catechism and New Testament each

Daughters of Our Lady, Queen of the Apostles in their blue-trimmed habit - Vera Dann, Katie Rodriguez, Biddy Kelly and Mary Albert Snr.

The first four to join (included Lucy Dolby/ Sr Ursula who left just prior to May 1942) completed six months of Postulancy and on 22 June 1942 received from His Grace Archbishop Prendiville the holy habit and received their religious name. Mary Magdalene Albert was accepted as a postulant the same day Beagle Bay Mission, 24 May 1942. Photograph (SSJG-0002085) courtesy of Sisters of St John of God Heritage Centre, Broome

and told us that Father Francis would give us some lessons regularly.[32]

In 1939 the aspirants to the sisterhood were placed under the care of Sister Mary Augustine McCarthy SSJG. She was assisted Sister Gerard SSJG who was appointed mistress of novices[33] in October 1940, and Sister Catherine

---

32 'Chronicle of the Regina Apostolorum Convent (Native Sisters) Beagle Bay Mission, November 1938–23 December 1951, referred to in Nailon CSB. [?1987], 'Land of Wait and Wonder'.

33 A 'novice' is a person who has been received into a religious order for a period of

Daughters of Our Lady, Queen of the Apostles, Veronica aka Vera Dann (Sr Elizabeth Dann), Brigid aka Biddy Kelly (Sr Frances Kelly), Catherine aka Katie Fraser (Sr Agnes Fraser/Rodriguez) and Lucy Dolby (Sr Ursula Dolby), with Bishop Otto Raible. Beagle Bay Mission, circa 1942–1946. Photograph (SSJG-0003108) courtesy of Sisters of St John of God Heritage Centre, Broome

Hayes. Their newly renovated convent ('Blue Convent', and former hospital) was blessed and opened by Bishop Raible on 6 January 1940, the Feast of the Epiphany. The first four postulants in 1940 were Katie Fraser, Lucy Dolby, Veronica (Vera) Dann and Brigid (Biddy) Kelly.[34] On 22 June 1940, as part of the Jubilee celebrations marking the 50th anniversary of the Catholic mission at Beagle Bay, four of the original six girls who had expressed interest in joining became novices and received the holy habit of the Daughters of Our Lady, Queen of the Apostles. The same day four other girls entered the

probation prior to taking vows.

34 St John of God Heritage Centre. 2015. Sisters of Mary Queen of the Apostles, identifies the first four postulants as Lucy Dolby (Sr. Ursula), Brigid Kelly (Sr. Francis), Veronica Dann (Sr. Elizabeth) and Magdalen Albert (Sr. Anne).

Aspirants, Postulants and Novices of Daughters of Our Lady, Queen of the Apostles, Biddy James, Margaret Albert Snr, Olive Dann, Alice Henry, Flora Baird, Anastasia Peters, Biddy Kelly, Mary Leonie Sibosado, Mildred Baird. Four who wear capes and medals have taken formal promises. The other seven girls are aspirants who have not progressed to making promises. Beagle Bay Mission, circa 1947/1948. Photograph (SSJG-0071666) courtesy of Sisters of St John of God Heritage Centre, Broome

society—postulant Magdalene Albert, and three aspirants—Mary Leonie Sibosado, Martha John Baptist and Benedicta Dann.

The presence of high-ranking members of the Church hierarchy at the ceremony, including the Apostolic Delegate from Rome and Archbishop Prendiville of Perth, gave the Daughters the official sanction of the Church and recognition as an important achievement in the life of the Church in the Kimberley.[35] Therefore, the girls who joined the Daughters bore the heavy burden of the expectations of so many people who had a vested interest in the success of the order.

---

35 *The Record*, 27 June 1940.

The aspirants, postulants and novices were separated from the other young mission girls. They lived like the Sisters of St John of God who worked on the mission, with the same food, routine of work and prayer, and the same work caring for the Beagle Bay Church and the male missionaries, cooking, cleaning and preparing the church for services and working with the St John of God Sisters caring for children in the dormitories and teaching them in school. The girls were taught religious studies, music and singing in Latin. Katie Fraser (Sister Agnes) taught at the school. Biddy Kelly (Sister Frances) played the organ and the violin and could speak German, the mother tongue of the Pallottine missionaries. Other girls on the mission looked up to the Daughters and wanted to be like their friends who had joined.[36] Two of Katie Fraser's sisters, Edna and Gertie, also stayed at the Convent with their older sister while they attended school because their parents had left Beagle Bay.[37]

While the structures and routines of religious life gave the girls status within the mission, they were still lower in the hierarchy in relation to the European priests, brothers and nuns who worked there.[38] The postulants and novices continued to live sheltered lives at Beagle Bay with little or no contact beyond the confines of the mission. As children they had left their families in 'the Colony' around the mission compound to live in the mission dormitory from where they moved straight to the convent when they joined the Daughters. Their lives were dominated by religious concerns. Under the Rules of the order the first allegiance of an aspirant, postulant or novice was to God and that allegiance would inform her relationship with her parents and family: 'She must behave in a way that is pleasing to God because God said in the fourth commandment to honour Father and Mother. She can show her love to her parents and relations by praying for them.'[39] The change in the way the young women had to relate to parents, family and friends placed an enormous emotional burden on them.

The reflections of Sister Veronica Willaway OSB, who at the age of

---

36 St John of God Heritage Centre, Broome, 2016.

37 Solonec (2015), 93.

38 This was noted in a letter from the Commissioner of Native Affairs to the Honourable Minister for the North West, in relation to Katie Fraser when, in 1943 at the age of 23, she applied for an exemption from the *Native Administration Act* of 1936 (WA). The Commissioner stated that '… [her vows were] in no way comparable to those taken by the members of the Order of St. John of God', thus suggesting that Katie's status was inferior to that of the European sisters. Solonec (20150: 94.

39 See Appendix 1, Section B: Training.

fourteen joined the Benedictine Missionary Sisters at New Norcia Mission where she grew up, articulate some of the challenges faced by a young Aboriginal woman who entered a religious order. The young women who joined the Daughters in Beagle Bay would also have encountered these challenges.

> After I entered, the thing that was the hardest was having to see the Benedictine Sisters and the Monks on a different level of life. All my young life I was taught to respect them as my elders, teachers, care givers, religion teachers, nurses and providers; now I was being called to be their sister through St. Benedict. In my new life I was also being asked to be changed – I was no longer one of the crowd, but starting to be a religious and because of this I needed to be respected by friends and peers in this new status. This overnight change was difficult for most of us, as I was so young and I was among them in school and during recreation periods. Years later, all my friends and peers were very proud of me because I was the second Aboriginal Sister in the Congregation ...[40]

During World War II when the German missionaries were interned as enemy aliens, and when the Aboriginal community from Broome was evacuated to Beagle Bay, the novices and postulants worked even harder on the mission as numbers of residents grew.[41] Soon after the war ended, in 1946, Katie Fraser left the Daughters.

Although no equivalent order or group of Aboriginal men was created at Beagle Bay, baptised Aboriginal men and women were encouraged to participate fully as active laity, engaged in the life of the mission community as workers and family members. Bishop Raible was committed to extending the missionary work of the Pallottines beyond Beagle Bay to the nomadic Aboriginal people of the semi-desert region south of Halls Creek and along the Canning Stock Route. After a failed attempt to set up a centre at Rockhole in the late 1930s, a small group of mission men and women working with one of the Pallottine brothers was sent by Bishop Raible to find a suitable location for the new mission. They established Balgo Mission on the edge of the Great Sandy Desert in 1942.[42] After the war, on 22 September 1947,

---

40 Willaway (1998), 42
41 Choo, ([2001] 2004), chapter 6.
42 Choo and McCoy (2010), 171–72.

Daughters of Our Lady, Queen of the Apostles, Mary Leonie Sibosado and Emily Charles, with Sister Gerard Gath and Indigenous families. Beagle Bay Mission, 1946. Photograph (SSJG-0071665) courtesy of Sisters of St John of God Heritage Centre, Broome

three of the Daughters set off for Balgo Mission.[43] They were Barbara Cox, Vera Dann and Josephine Sibosado, who joined the team of mission workers from Beagle Bay who were already there. Their departure for Balgo was reported on the radio by the Australian Broadcasting Commission and in the Perth secular press.[44] The Daughters were sent to Balgo in place of the St John of God sisters because it was considered too isolated and the conditions too harsh for the non-Aboriginal sisters. The Daughters worked alongside members of the Pallottine community and with other Aboriginal lay people from Beagle Bay who were sent to work there.

---

43 D Breslin, 'Aboriginal Nuns'. *West Australian*, 11 Oct 1947, 4. Versions of this article from Beagle Bay were published in other Catholic newspapers in Australia in October 1947; Brian McCoy, *Holding Men: Kanyirninpa and the health of Aboriginal men* (Canberra: Aboriginal Studies Press, 2008), 53.
44 'Aboriginal Nuns to Evangelise Fellow Natives', *Southern Cross*, 10 October 1947, 5.

This new venture was to be the test of the evangelisation method of sending Aboriginal missionaries to reach out to other Aboriginal people. However, Bishop Raible failed to take into account the cultural, language and social differences between the coastal people of Beagle Bay and desert people of Balgo, and the inexperience of the young Daughters due to their isolation in Beagle Bay. Although the Daughters' work at Balgo was similar to that at Beagle Bay, they experienced severe culture shock as they were not prepared for the harsh conditions and isolation among the nomadic desert people, so different from their own. They were also not prepared for their relative independence in Balgo. In this alien environment they were faced with enormous challenges without the support of the St John of God sisters and their own community and families.

One of the challenges that the young women faced was the possibility of sexual encounters, even exploitation by other workers, lay and religious, in the isolation of Balgo and other distant communities. This situation was referred to by Mary Durack in her book about the Church in the Kimberley, *The Rock and the Sand*, published in 1969, when she suggested that the young women who were sent to Balgo were driven 'to seek reassurance in the company of the few lay helpers, white or coloured, who came their way'.

> In any event within fourteen months not even the folds of the religious habit could conceal the fact that earthly romance had, where most were concerned, proved stronger than the spiritual romanticism of the religious life. One or two said they were prepared to persevere but the truth could no longer be denied. The time and conditions had not been ripe or the young people yet strong and secure enough for the grand experiment by which the bishop had set such store.[45]

The pregnancy of an Aboriginal nun is also referred to in the musical, *Bran Nue Dae* by Jimmy Chi and Kuckles of Broome, in which one of the characters, Aunty Theresa, a deeply pious Aboriginal woman, admits that she had a child to a German missionary who took the child away.[46] However, this issue, that is the pregnancy of members of the Daughters, remains a topic that is too sensitive to be discussed or acknowledged openly by the women themselves or by the Church hierarchy. Other challenges may have included the strict regime of religious practice imposed on the young women

---

45 Durack ([1969] 1985), 272.
46 Chi, Jimmy and Kuckles, *Bran Nue Dae: A Musical Journey* (Paddington & Broome: Currency Press & Magabala Books, 1991).

within the hierarchy of nuns, brothers and priests at the mission, and the emotional distance that was required of them as religious women.

Finally, as one by one the young women left the order, each for her own reason, the Bishop withdrew the Daughters from Balgo. The convent of the Daughters of Our Lady, Queen of the Apostles closed in December 1951 when Sister Mary Clare, the only remaining postulant, was granted a dispensation from her promises. None of the young women was professed as a sister, and the women remained circumspect about the reasons for their decision to leave the Daughters. The closure of the order marked another milestone in the life of the Catholic mission in the Kimberley and a great disappointment to Bishop Raible, as he recorded:

> [Sister Mary Clare] took off her habit with a sad heart, for she had a real vocation. The Bishop declared the Society dissolved, burying his most cherished hopes with it.[47]

Outcomes—'Nothing is wasted in the household of God'[48]

The women who formed the first and only religious order of Aboriginal women in Australia, the Daughters of Our Lady, Queen of the Apostles, were a product of their time and their environment. They had been brought up at Beagle Bay Mission as Catholic girls, deeply involved in religious practices including attending mass and other religious services, reciting the rosary and praying daily. They were actively involved in music and singing in Latin at liturgical services; their training had given them the opportunity to deepen their faith and share their ministry in the wider community. Their training had also given them some prestige and privilege in their community.[49]

After the former Daughters re-entered the wider Catholic community in the Kimberley, most maintained their commitment to the Catholic faith and continued to identify with the Catholic Church. Those who kept their faith married and raised their children as Catholics and were the strength of the Catholic community and their families. They and their families actively participated in the life of the Church in the Kimberley, contributing as catechists and support workers, readers, singers and musicians in liturgical

---

47 Bishop O Raible in *Chronicle of the Regina Apostolorum Convent.*
48 'Nothing is wasted in the Kingdom of God' is remembered as one of Bishop Raible's sayings. Nailon (2001), 276.
49 St John of God Heritage Centre, Broome. 2016.

celebrations.[50] Nonetheless, the faith and commitment of others were shaken by their experiences as Daughters.

Katie Fraser (formerly Sister Agnes) is a good illustration. After Katie left the Daughters in 1946, after seven years with them and before they were sent to Balgo, she worked at Liveringa Station where she met Frank Rodriguez, a former Spanish Benedictine novice who had been granted dispensation from the New Norcia monastery some years earlier. Katie and Frank married not long after they met. Katie's daughter, Cindy Solonec notes:

> The Rodriguez marriage remained strong throughout their lives and with their Catholic convictions unfaltering they continued to be involved in the Church. They had lived by the mantra 'the family that prays together, stays together'. Their faith contributed not only to the stability of their family but also to the close-knit congregation. They attended services and special events and Frank sometimes stood as a sponsor for an adolescent at Confirmation time (for instance). He also attended parish meetings while they both had a reasonably active social life within the parish. ... it was their interaction with their children regardless of where we lived that was most prominent for the remainder of their lives. ... Our Catholic upbringing ensured that Christian values and morals remained a significant influence in our behaviours for many years.[51]

The family remained connected to the Catholic community, in spite of the fact that the importance of the Catholic tradition waned for some Frank and Katie's descendants and family members. As Cindy Solonec states, although Frank was disappointed in this situation, '... he understood the change in attitudes among his descendants as secular influences and further education challenged our worldviews'.[52]

The women who had been Daughters of Our Lady, Queen of the Apostles, each in her unique way, contributed to the evangelisation of Kimberley Aborigines through the establishment of a network of Catholic families within the community. They were women raised on sound Christian principles who expressed these principles practically in the way they lived.

---

50 'Sisters of Mary Queen of the Apostles', *Kimberley Community Profile* (St John of God Heritage Centre: September 2015): 14–15; 'Native Sisters: The Blue Sisters 1939–1951: Sisters of Mary Queen of the Apostles' (St John of God Heritage Centre, Broome: 2016). Video Recording. Also exhibits at the SSJG Heritage Centre.

51 Solonec (2015), 190.

52 Solonec (2015), 195.

Although not exactly according to the Bishop's dream, the women's lives did fulfil the Church's approach – to encourage Indigenous people to minister to their own.

Appendix 1

Daughters of Our Lady, Queen of the Apostles – Rules, Outline of their Training, and Form of the Ceremony of Dedication

A.   RULES OF THE SOCIETY OF NATIVE SISTERS (DAUGHTERS OF OUR LADY, QUEEN OF THE APOSTLES)

Chapter 1: On the Aim of Our Society

1. Our Patroness is Our Lady, Queen of the Apostles. We call ourselves 'Daughters of Our Lady, Queen of the Apostles'.

2. She was so holy, because she followed the example of her Divine Son so perfectly. We, her children, will therefore try first and with all our hearts, to make ourselves more holy every day, by imitating what Our Lord Jesus Christ had done, especially by being poor, chaste and obedient.

3. Secondly, as our special work, we will help our poor pagan brothers and sisters, the natives of Australia, so that they also may know God, love Him and so save their souls.

4. We will do this by assisting the priests in their work, wherever it will be required, in schools and orphanages, homes for the aged and poor, and by nursing the sick. We will take special care of the native women and girls, so that they become good Christian women and mothers.

5. Our work is confined to the Australian full blood and half caste natives.

Chapter 2: Who Can Be Admitted to the Society?

1. Any Catholic girl of at least one half of aboriginal blood can be admitted if she has the right intention, is bodily and mentally fitted for missionary work and is of a sociable disposition.

2. The right of admission and dismissal rests with the Bishop.

3. Before admitting any postulant inquiries must be made about the character and piety, and also about her people.

4. Girls that have completed their twelfth year can be admitted as aspirants.

5. The age for admission to the novitiate is 18 years. For grave reasons the Bishop can dispense from this rule. Six months before the reception into the novitiate the candidate enters her postulancy, a time for special probation.

6. During the years preceding the reception the candidates receive a thorough instruction in their holy Faith. They also will have lessons in general knowledge and will be trained in certain useful trades.

Chapter 3: Our Habit

1. Our habit separates us from the world and reminds us that we are consecrating our lives to God. We will therefore have a great reverence for our holy habit.
2. Our habit consists of a long garment of unbleached calico. The sleeves are short, reaching near the elbow. We wear a cape of the same material with a collar, open in front and with blue bindings. The cincture is of blue webbing with two ends hanging down at left side about fifteen inches. The veil is of light blue material with a white forehead band.
3. Long church sleeves are worn at Holy Mass and whenever the Blessed Sacrament is exposed.
4. The professed Sisters wear a scapular of unbleached calico with blue lining on the same occasions.
5. While at work outside the convent, we wear a plain cape and veil. A medal of our Lady on blue cord reminds us of Our Patroness.

Chapter 4: On What We Do While We Are Novices

1. We are made novices on the day when we receive the holy habit. We make retreat for three days beforehand.
2. The time of the Novitiate lasts two years. For just reasons the Bishop can make it longer but not for more than six months.
3. During the time of the Novitiate we learn all about our holy vocation. The rules are explained to us, and we try to keep them faithfully.
4. The Novices will take special care to find out their faults and to correct them.
5. They will particularly try by every possible means to make their love of the Lord grown in their hearts.
6. By acts of humility and self denial, and especially by perfect obedience the Novices will prepare themselves for their life's work.
7. The Novices will not speak to anyone outside the Convent except what their various duties require. They can receive visitors once a month.

Chapter 5: On the Promises

1. We do not make public vows. We feel ourselves bound to our holy vocation by the love of Christ, which we renew every day, when we offer Holy Mass with the priest.
2. Moved by this love of Our Lord, we promise to be poor, chaste and obedient.

3. We make another promise, namely to persevere in the Society for a certain time.

4. We also promise to work in the Missions for the natives of our own country wherever our Superiors may send us.

5. After the Novitiate we make the promises for one year over a period of five years. After this we dedicate ourselves for periods of three years, until we make our dedication for life. This cannot be made before we reach the age of thirty-five.

6. The Promises bind under pain of venial sin only.

7. Form of Dedication:

O most holy Virgin, my mother and queen,

Comforted by thy motherly love, and guided by thy gentle hand,

I, Sister . . . .

approach the altar of God to give my own self, body and soul, to Jesus.

To Him I give over my body and promise to be chaste.

To Him I give over my soul and promise to be obedient.

For the love of Our Lord I promise to do missionary work amongst my native brothers and sisters, and to stay in the society of the Daughters of Our Lady, Queen of the Apostles for one year (for three years / for life) and live according to the rules of this Society.

Unholy though I am of this holy vocation, I throw myself at Thy feet, O Jesus. With thy holy grace I am ready to do what Thou wilt.

Amen

B. TRAINING

1. What is the most important thing in the life of a young sister?

That she tries very hard to be obedient to her Superior because by doing so she would be obedient to God himself.

And another thing she tries to be cheerful and happy because she is serving God himself.

2. Who must take first place in her heart?

Well, our Lord must take the first place in her heart, and his heavenly Mother, because we are Our Lord's brides and we've given our lives for him.

3. How must she behave towards her parents and relations?

She must behave in a way that is pleasing to God because God said in the fourth commandment to honour Father and Mother. She can show her love to her parents and relations by praying for them.

4. What should be the first thing a Sister does when her Superior gives her a correction?

When her Superior gives her a correction she must take it in the spirit of love because the Superior is taking the place of God himself.

5. Why should every Sister have a Spiritual Director?

Every Sister should have a Spiritual Director because he can help her in all her difficulties and can always give her advice to overcome them all.

C. CEREMONY FOR DEDICATION (PRAYERS FROM THE RITUAL TRANSLATED FROM LATIN)

Opening Prayers

1. *Prayer to the Holy Ghost*
2. *O God! You have given the Holy Spirit to your Apostles whilst they prayed with Mary, the Mother of Jesus with one mind. Give us, that under the protection of this our Mother and Queen, we may serve your Majesty faithfully and spread, by word and example, the glory of Your Name.*
3. *Lord Jesus Christ! You have set on fire the hearts of your handmaids with such a fervour of love [by] that they are willing to follow your footsteps by saving the souls of the Natives, give to them, we pray, to persevere un such a wholesome resolution and may they deserve a Heavenly Blessing for their labour.*

Blessing of the Scapular

Lord Jesus Christ! You said: My yoke is sweet and my burden is light – bless and make holy this Scapular in honour of the Blessed Virgin, Queen of Apostles, and grant that she who is going to wear it may persevere under your cross joyfully and faithfully and may be ever conscious of her holy vocation.

Prayers after the Litanies

For the spreading of the greater glory of your most Holy Name, and for the eternal salvation of souls may the dedication of your handmaid be acceptable to You. Filled abundantly with your love may they persevere faithfully in your Holy service.

Lord Jesus Christ! You have deigned to make your most holy Mother the Queen of the Apostles, pour out over these Your Handmaids, whom you have enrolled under your Missionaries, your abundant bounty; so that protected and guided by the same Queen they may live up to their vocation with all their heats and finally may receive the crown of an Apostle.

127

Source:

[Brigida Nailon, CSB. [?1987] 'Land of Wait and Wonder: Resource Notes on the Establishment of Roman Catholic Missions in the Kimberley', Archives of the Diocese of Broome.]

References

Aboriginal Nuns to Evangelise Fellow Natives, *Southern Cross* (Adelaide, SA: 1889–1954), 10 Oct 1947, 5.

Benedict XV. 1919. *Maximum Illud: Apostolic Letter on the Propagation of the Faith Throughout the World.* 30 November 1919. Translated by Thomas J. M. Burke, S.J. Washington, DC: National Catholic Welfare Office: http://www.svdcuria.org/public/mission/docs/encycl/mi-en.htm

Bourke, D F, *The History of the Catholic Church in Western Australia (* Archdiocese of Perth, 1979)

Breslin, D 1947, 'Aboriginal Nuns', *West Australian*, 11 Oct 1947, 4.

Chi, Jimmy and Kuckles, *Bran Nue Dae: A Musical Journey* (Paddington & Broome: Currency Press & Magabala Books, 1991).

Choo, Christine. [2001] 2004. *Mission Girls: Aboriginal Women on Catholic Missions in the Kimberley, Western Australia, 1900–1950.* Crawley. University of Western Australia Press.

Choo, Christine. 2012. Mixed Blessings: Establishment of Christian Missions in the Kimberley. In Cathie Clement, Jeffrey Gresham and Hamish McGlashan eds. *Kimberley History: People, Exploration and Development. Proceedings of the Kimberley Society Kimberley History Seminar, University of Western Australia, 27 March 2010.* Perth: Kimberley Society.

Christine Choo and Brian F. McCoy SJ. 2010. Mission Dormitories: Intergenerational Implications for Kalumburu and Balgo, Kimberley, Western Australia. In Patricia Grimshaw & Andrew May eds., *Missionaries, Indigenous Peoples and Cultural Exchanges*, Brighton, U.K. & Portland, Oregon: Sussex Academic Press.

Clement, Cathie, Jeffrey Gresham and Hamish McGlashan eds. 2012. *Kimberley History: People, Exploration and Development. Proceedings of the Kimberley Society Kimberley History Seminar, University of Western Australia, 27 March 2010.* Perth: Kimberley Society.

Dunphy, J. C. [nd] 'The Pomegranate: A History of the Sisters of St John of God', unpublished manuscript (in possession of author M. R. MacGinley).

Durack, Mary. [1969] 1985. *The Rock and the Sand.* London. Constable.

Gregory XVI. 1840. *Prope Nosti—On the Propagation of the Faith*: http://www.

papalencyclicals.net/greg16/g16probe.htm

Grimshaw, Patricia and Andrew May eds. 2010. *Missionaries, Indigenous Peoples and Cultural Exchanges*, Brighton, U.K. & Portland, Oregon: Sussex Academic Press.

MacGinley, Maria Rosa. 1996. *A Dynamic of Hope: Institutes of Women Religious in Australia*. Sydney. Crossing Press/Institute of Religious Studies.

Madigan, Joseph MSC. Why Not Become Nuns? The Native Sisters in Our Island Missions. *Freeman's Journal* (Sydney, NSW: 1850–1932), Thursday 22 July 1926, 11.

Massam, Katharine. 2002. To name and remember: The Benedictine Sisters of New Norcia Reunion with past pupils, October 2001. *New Norcia Studies* No. 10, September 2002, 26–32.

McCoy, Brian. 2008. *Holding Men: Kanyirninpa and the health of Aboriginal men*. Canberra. Aboriginal Studies Press.

McNamara, Jo Ann Kay. 1996. *Sisters in Arms: Catholic Nuns through Two Millennia*. Cambridge, Massachusetts. Harvard University Press.

Nailon, Brigida. CSB. [?1987]. *Land of Wait and Wonder. Resource Notes on the Establishment of Roman Catholic Missions in the Kimberley*. [Draws on 'Chronicle of the Regina Apostolorium Convent (Native Sisters) Beagle Bay Mission, November 1938–23 December 1951'] Archives of the Diocese of Broome. [unpublished]

Nailon, Brigida. CSB. 2001. *Nothing is Wasted in the Household of God: Vincent Pallotti's Vision in Australia, 1901–2001*. Richmond, Victoria. Spectrum Publications.

Perez, E. OSB. [nd]. *Fifty Years of the Drysdale River – Kalumburu – Benedictine Mission*. Handwritten draft. Benedictine Archives, New Norcia, Western Australia, BA 01039.

Perez, E. OSB. 1958. *Kalumburu, 'Formerly Drysdale River' Benedictine Mission North-Western Australia: A Golden Jubilee Publication (1908 – 1958)*. New Norcia. New Norcia Abbey Press.

Pius XI. 1926. *Rerum Ecclesiae – On Promoting the Sacred Missions*. © Copyright–Libreria Editrice Vaticana: http://w2.vatican.va/content/pius-xi/en/ encyclicals/documents/hf_p-xi_enc_28021926_rerum-ecclesiae.html

Sisters, Pearls & Mission Girls. 2002. Video Recording. Director, David Batty; producer Jeni McMahon; writers, Jeni McMahon, David Batty. Rebel Films Pty. Ltd. & Film Finance Corporation Australia. Viewed 13 Mar 2019. Source: https:// slwa.kanopy.com/video/sisters-pearls-and-mission-girls

Solonec, Jacinta (aka Cindy). 2015. *Shared lives on* Nigena *country: A joint*

Biography of Katie and Frank Rodriguez, 1944–1994. PhD Thesis, University of Western Australia.

St John of God Heritage Centre Broome. 2015. Bishop Otto Raible SAC. Part 1. Church of the Kimberley – Heroes in Faith. By Bill Worth. *Kimberley Community Profile*, May 2015, 11: https://heritage.ssjg.org.au/Assets/historical-articles/KCP-May-2015-Raible-part-1.pdf

St John of God Heritage Centre, Broome. 2015. Bishop Otto Raible SAC. Part 3. Church of the Kimberley – Heroes in Faith. By Bill Worth. *Kimberley Community Profile*, Aug 2015, 11: https://heritage.ssjg.org.au/Assets/historical-articles/KCP-2015-Aug-Raible-Part-3.pdf

St John of God Heritage Centre, Broome. 2015. Sisters of Mary Queen of the Apostles. *Kimberley Community Profile*. September 2015, 14–15: https://heritage.ssjg.org.au/Assets/historical-articles/KCP-2015-Sept-Native-sisters.pdf

St John of God Heritage Centre, Broome. 2016. *Native Sisters. The Blue Sisters 1939 – 1951: Sisters of Mary Queen of the Apostles*. Video Recording. Produced by Julie Bailey for SSJG Heritage Centre, Broome: https://heritage.ssjg.org.au

The Advocate (Melbourne, Vic.: 1868–1954) Thursday 20 April 1939, 4.

The Record (Perth, WA: 1874) 27 June 1940.

The Society of the Catholic Apostolate. Website: https://www.pallottine.org.au/

Willaway, Sr. Veronica OSB. 1998. My memories as a Benedictine Sister at New Norcia. *New Norcia Studies*, No. 6, September 1998, 42–44.

Zucker, Margaret. 1994. *From Patrons to Partners: A History of the Catholic Church in the Kimberley, 1884–1984*. Fremantle. University of Notre Dame Australia.

Acknowledgement

I wish to thank the following for their assistance and support:

Odhran O'Brien, Archivist and Director, Archives of the Catholic Archdiocese of Perth, and Dr Marco Ceccarelli, Director, Centre for Faith Enrichment, Western Australia, for the invitation to participate in the World Heritage Day 2019 Seminar: 'Catholicism on the Margins' on 18 April 2019, where I presented this paper;

Dr Cindy Solonec, for reading a draft of this paper and sharing her insightful comments;

Sr. Pat Rhatigan SSJG and the Sisters of St John of God Heritage Centre in Broome, Western Australia, for their permission to use photographs in their collection; and the referees who provided feedback prior to publication.

ABSENCE OR AMNESIA: WAS THE GOLDEN WEST REALLY FREE OF 'THE NOXIOUS WEED OF SECTARIANISM' THAT BLIGHTED EARLY TWENTIETH-CENTURY AUSTRALIA?

Jeff Kildea*

Introduction

In October 1918, prominent Perth printer and soon-to-be editor of Perth's Catholic newspaper the *WA Record*, Pat Bryan, told a meeting of the Catholic Young Men's Society:

> Western Australia, in comparison with the East, is reasonably peaceful at all times. We have not suffered from sectarian strife as have Melbourne and Sydney.[1]

The year before, the writer of the *Record*'s 'While the Billy Boils' column put it more colourfully:

> It is good to live in W.A. All the Catholic papers from 'the other side' tell of parsons with straws in their hair blasting and fuming at the unmindful Church and doing dervish dances around the reeking cauldrons of sectarianism.[2]

Although much has been written on sectarianism in Australia, most of the literature relates to the eastern states, with scant reference to Western Australia, thus lending credence to these contemporary claims.[3]

But were they true? Had Western Australia somehow avoided 'the noxious weed of sectarianism' that plagued the eastern states in the early 1900s.[4] Or are these assertions evidence of self-delusion or wishful thinking? For sectarian conflicts did occur in the west, such as the disruption of the Twelfth of July celebrations at Coolgardie in 1897 and at Boulder in 1901 by rioters brandishing hurleys, and sectarian influence did exist in politics,

---

1 *W. A. Record*, 26 October 1918, 3.
2 *W.A. Record*, 4 August 1917, 10.
3 The classic study of sectarianism in Australia, Michael Hogan, *The Sectarian Strand: Religion in Australian History*, (Melbourne, Penguin, 1987), hardly mentions Western Australia, while D F Bourke, *The History of the Catholic Church in Western Australia*, (Perth: Archdiocese of Perth, 1979), hardly mentions sectarianism (cf. 123–4).
4 *W.A. Record*, 7 February 1914, 13.

* A paper given by Dr Jeff Kildea, Adjunct Professor in Irish Studies, University of New South Wales, at the 2019 World Heritage Day Conference: 'Catholicism on the Margins' held at St Mary's Cathedral, Perth, 18 April 2019.

affecting Irish-Catholic politicians such as Patrick Lynch and Hugh Mahon.[5]

In this paper I will describe sectarianism as it existed in early twentieth-century Australia and examine whether Western Australia really did avoid it or whether the state's sectarian past has been ignored, downplayed or simply forgotten.

What is sectarianism?

In his PhD thesis entitled 'Proddy-Dogs, Cattleticks and Ecumaniacs', Ben Edwards wrote, 'The most common and simplest usage of the term sectarianism refers to prejudice, discrimination, bias or hatred of another individual or group based on their religious beliefs or affiliation'.[6] Edwards then made three important points about sectarianism in Australia:

- firstly, it was much more than a religious conflict—it was 'a complex interaction of religious identity and rivalry, class, ideology and ethnicity';

- secondly, it was not synonymous with anti-Catholicism— 'Sectarianism, in the Australian context, has not been a one-sided prejudice and the rivalry has not always been simply between Catholics and Protestants'; and

- thirdly, as its European antecedents demonstrate, 'sectarianism has been a regular fixture within the armoury of social and political conflict throughout the centuries, serving as a conduit for the expression of not only religious rivalry but of other social cleavages and grievances'.

Sectarianism in the Australian context

In early twentieth-century Australia religious affiliation was generally identified with the three main national or ethnic groups that constituted the nation's European society: the English, the Irish and the Scots. Competition between religions in nineteenth and twentieth- century Australia reflected

---

5   *Kalgoorlie Miner*, 12 July 1897, 3; and 15 July 1901, 5; Danny Cusack, 'With an Olive Branch and a Shillelagh: the Political Career of Senator Paddy Lynch, 1867–1944', (PhD Thesis, Murdoch University, 2002), 81–82, 90–92; Jeff Kildea, *Hugh Mahon: Patriot, Pressman, Politician*, 1: (Melbourne, Australia: Anchor Books, 2017), 212; *Menzies Miner*, 6 April 1901, 3.

6   Benjamin Edwards, 'Proddy-Dogs, Cattleticks and Ecumaniacs: Aspects of Sectarianism in New South Wales, 1945–1981' (PhD thesis, University of New South Wales: 2007), 2. It was published in 2008 by Acorn Press in Melbourne under the less colourful title, *Wasps, Tykes and Ecumaniacs*.

complex ethnic rivalries, particularly those between Irish Catholics, on the one hand, and English Anglicans and Scots-Irish Presbyterians on the other. The society comprised two distinct communities: one was British in origin and Protestant in faith, the other Irish and Catholic. Through most of the nineteenth century the Irish made up about one quarter of the immigrants to Australia while the British made up three quarters. Furthermore, the Irish were mostly Catholics and Catholics were mostly Irish by birth or descent so that in the period under review Catholics were about 23 per cent of the population Australia-wide, though they differed from state to state with New South Wales having the highest proportion at more than 25 per cent and South Australia the lowest with just over 14 per cent. Western Australia was about the average.

But a word of caution. While it is broadly true that in early twentieth-century Australia to be Catholic was to be Irish and to be Irish was to be Catholic, it is nevertheless a generalisation. One needs to bear in mind that a significant minority of the Irish in Australia were Protestants and a significant minority of Catholics were not of Irish birth or descent.[7]

While Edwards rightly reminds us that sectarianism was not a one-way street, it is equally important to understand that the reciprocity was not symmetrical. Sectarianism as practised by Catholics tended to be existential: the Catholic Church insisted that it alone was the repository of religious truth, thus precluding ecumenical engagement; its marriage laws discouraged marriage across religious lines; and its maintenance of a separate education system committed the Church to an attitude of estrangement from aspects of Australian society.[8]

On the other side, sectarianism as practised by Protestants tended to be reactive, condemning Catholic exclusiveness, particularly in education, questioning Catholic loyalty to the Crown and warning against Catholic domination of the instruments of state power. Let me give some examples:

On exclusiveness, the *Methodist* newspaper declared in 1911 that the Catholic Church through its school system 'seeks to segregate its young people, and to bring them up under influences which imbue their minds with

---

7   In round figures Catholics accounted for some 85 per cent of Irish emigration to Australia, see Oliver MacDonagh, 'Emigration from Ireland to Australia: an Overview' in Colm Kiernan (ed.), *Australia and Ireland 1788–1988: Bicentenary Essays* (Dublin: Gill and MacMillan, 1986), 121–137, 132.

8   Patrick O'Farrell, 'Protest without Anarchy. The Church in Australian History', *Bulletin of Christian Affairs*, 1/5 (1970): 3–16, 11.

the narrowest and most bigoted notions, separating them in the most sacred relations of life from the rest of the citizenship of the State'.[9]

On loyalty, the *Australian Christian World* in 1910 told its readers, 'there is very widespread conviction that the loyalty of Roman Catholics to the British Crown is of the thinnest quality and may in time prove the undoing of Australia'.[10]

On Catholic domination, the *Methodist* newspaper, in an article in 1916 headed 'The Roman Catholic Menace' warned its readers: 'Roman Catholicism is subtly working ... to secure ascendancy and control. That church is working in the interests of disloyalty and of sectarian advantage, and is throwing dust in the eyes of Protestant electors all the time, especially of the working classes'.[11]

The net result was to make Catholics both exclusive and excluded – exclusive because of the characteristics of Irish Catholicism as practised in Australia and excluded because of feelings of hostility toward them by reason of their racial origin and their despised Papist religion. Although the Irish in Australia wished to be accepted as part of the broader Australian community, they were not prepared to do so on any terms and certainly not terms that denigrated their Irishness or their Catholicity.[12]

But, once again, a word of caution. For the most part Catholics and Protestants coexisted peacefully. It was mostly charismatic individuals, on both sides, who stirred up trouble. As against the headline-grabbing rantings of these sectarian warriors, there are many stories of interdenominational cooperation, particularly in rural areas.

Divisive Issues

The issues that most clearly divided the two communities in the first quarter of the twentieth century concerned Catholic demands for state aid, support for Irish self-government and opposition to conscription for overseas service during the First World War, with each issue feeding into Protestant concerns about Catholic exclusiveness, disloyalty and plans for domination.

9 *Methodist*, 21 January 1911, 1.

10 *Australian Christian World*, 23 December 1910, 2.

11 *Methodist*, 25 November 1916, 25.

12 Jeff Kildea, '"A veritable hurricane of sectarianism": The Year 1920 and Ethno-Religious Conflict in Australia', in Colin Barr and Hilary M Carey, *Religion and Greater Ireland: Christianity and Irish Global Networks, 1750–1950* (Montreal: McGill-Queen's University Press, 2015), 363–382.

State aid

State funding of denominational education had existed from the mid-1830s. In most of the Australian colonies it was reformed in the 1850s and abolished in the 1870s upon the establishment of free, secular and compulsory education systems administered by the colonial governments. While Protestant denominations accepted the education settlement, Catholics defied it, retaining and expanding their own network of schools funded by the Catholic people and made viable by the dedication of unsalaried teaching brothers and nuns.

Even after the reforms took hold, the Catholic church continued to agitate for a return to the old system, much to the annoyance of Protestants and secularists who, objecting to the exclusivist tendency of Catholic education and social life, were not about to give succour to what they regarded as breeding grounds of disloyalty. This agitation increased in the 1910s as Catholics in the east began to challenge the education settlement with aggressive political campaigns for state aid led by Catholic Federations, recently established in four of the six states, with tens of thousands of members across a vast parish network. As a result, sectarian tensions ratcheted up.

Irish self-government

At about the same time events in Ireland also strained interdenominational relations. From the 1870s the Australian Irish had supported the campaign for Irish home rule, receiving envoys from the Irish Parliamentary Party who regularly visited the country on fund-raising tours, often provoking protests from Protestant empire loyalists. When in 1912 the British government announced its intention to legislate for Irish home rule, a major controversy erupted in Australia between supporters and opponents of the proposal, who divided generally along ethno-religious lines.

And it was not long before debate about home rule became entwined with local issues, particularly the demand by Catholics for state aid for their schools. At a meeting held at the Sydney Town Hall on 14 March 1912 to protest against the British government's proposal, a banner on the platform proclaimed, 'Mark the men who support bursaries to Roman Catholic schools.' And even though it was supposed to be a meeting about home rule, William Robson MLC complained in his speech that the state government was giving in to the unreasonable demands of the Catholic Church which was 'trying to get hold of educational powers'.[13]

In August 1914 the outbreak of war acted as a circuit breaker for Australia's escalating sectarian tensions. Catholics joined with Protestants to support the war effort. For the next twenty months talk of Irish Catholic disloyalty subsided, at least in public, as Catholics and Protestants lined up together at the recruiting offices to enlist in the Australian Imperial Force and to help the British Empire defeat Germany.[14] But the fragile truce in the sectarian conflict was broken following the Easter rising in Dublin in April 1916.

When news of the outbreak of violence began to reach Australia, Irish-Australian Catholics at first deplored the rising as misguided and a threat to the promised implementation of home rule. However, following the execution of the leaders and the imposition of martial law, Irish Catholics began to criticise British rule in Ireland, provoking a Protestant backlash. Sectarianism, which had lain dormant since the outbreak of war, flared up and intensified as criticism of Britain was regarded by many Protestants as disloyal to the British Crown, already under threat from without but now also from within.[15]

Conscription

It was in this highly-charged atmosphere that the first conscription referendum was held. In October 1916 the voters rejected conscription by a narrow margin;[16] they would do so again in December 1917 by an increased

---

13 *Freeman's Journal*, 21 March 1912, 31, 36; *Sydney Morning Herald*, 15 March 1912, 9.

14 The absence of public attacks on the Irish Catholic community in the first 20 months of the war may also have had something to do with the government's instructions to the censor on ways of 'minimizing harmful agitation and resentment among our people of Irish descent', L F Fitzhardinge, *William Morris Hughes: The Little Digger* (Sydney, Angus & Robertson, 1979), 60–61.

15 *Freeman's Journal*, 4 May 1916, 25; *Catholic Press*, 11 May 1916, 21. Even Archbishop Mannix initially described the rising as deplorable and its leaders as misguided (*Advocate*, 6 May 1916, 25). See Jeff Kildea, *Tearing the Fabric: Sectarianism in Australia 1910–1925* (Sydney: Citadel Books, 2002), 134–136; Peter Overlack, '"Easter 1916" in Dublin and the Australian press: background and response', *Journal of Australian Studies*, 21/54–55 (1997): 188–193; R P Davis, 'Tasmania and the Irish revolution, 1916–22', *Tasmanian Historical Research Association: Papers and Proceedings*, 21/2 (1974): 69–88.

16 The 'No' majority was only 72,476 out of a total of 2,247,590 formal votes. Three states recorded 'Yes' majorities (Victoria, Western Australia and Tasmania) and three 'No' (New South Wales, Queensland and South Australia); Ernest Scott, *Australia during the war*, vol. XI of *The official history of Australia in the war of 1914–18*, (Sydney: Angus & Robertson, 1936), 352.

margin.[17] After the result of the first referendum was announced, it was not long before the finger of blame was being pointed at the Irish Catholic community as being responsible for its defeat. A Protestant newspaper, the *Australian Christian Commonwealth* observed:

> Strong support throughout the Commonwealth came to the 'No' army from the Roman Catholics. ... It is common rumour that their priests, with few exceptions, were openly or secretly opposed to conscription.[18]

Prime Minister Hughes' added his voice, claiming that the Catholic Church was secretly against recruiting and that its influence killed conscription.[19] After the second referendum the Governor General, Sir Ronald Munro Ferguson, in his report to the colonial secretary wrote, 'The organised opposition was composed of the Labour Party and the Roman Catholics. This body, organised and capably led by Archbishop Mannix comprises the Irish element which would be hostile to any proposals of the Government'.[20]

This perception was to become the occasion of some of the most vitriolic attacks ever made on the Irish Catholic community in Australia. Charges of disloyalty, shirking and plotting to overthrow the Empire added a more sinister dimension to the customary sectarian taunts. The growing anti-Catholic animus was stirred up even more in January 1917, when Archbishop Mannix described the war as 'an ordinary trade war', reported in some newspapers as 'a sordid trade war'.[21] This and other public utterances by Mannix, critical of the government's war policy, elevated him to national status. He soon became the accepted spokesman of the Irish Australian community, but at the same time a lightning-rod attracting much of the rising anti-Catholic and anti-Irish bigotry which falsely claimed that Australia's Irish Catholics were shirkers, Sinn Feiners and pro-German.[22]

The armistice of 11 November 1918 brought an end to the war of the nations but not to Australia's sectarian war. Although a significant factor

---

17 The 'No' majority was 166,588 out of a total of 2,196,906 votes cast. This time Victoria joined the 'No' majority while Tasmania's 'Yes' majority was only 379 out of a total of 77,383 votes cast. (Scott, *Australia during the war,* 427).

18 *Australian Christian Commonwealth,* 3 Nov 1916, 3.

19 Fitzhardinge, *The Little Digger,* 276.

20 Quoted in D J Murphy, 'Religion, Race and Conscription in World War I', *Australian Journal of Politics and History,* 30 (1974): 155–163, 160.

21 Cyril Bryan, 'Archbishop Mannix: champion of democracy', *The Advocate Press,* Melbourne, 1918, 72.

22 Fitzhardinge, *The Little Digger,* 286.

souring interdenominational relations had been removed, the two issues that had divided the nation before the war remained unresolved: state aid for Catholic schools and Irish self-determination. The Irish War of Independence saw a renewal of sectarian tension. Beginning in 1919, it intensified in 1920, with Australian newspapers carrying lurid reports of atrocities on both sides, particularly following the introduction of the Black and Tans in March 1920. In Australia itself a series of events exacerbated chronic sectarian tensions: in May the government determined to deport a German-born Sydney priest, Father Charles Jerger, provoking Catholic protests around the country, including one at Moore Park in Sydney which attracted 150,000 people; in July Sister Liguori fled from her convent in Wagga Wagga and placed herself under the protection of the Orange lodge, igniting a bitter controversy that was played out in the courts, the NSW parliament and the press; in August the Royal Navy hijacked Archbishop Mannix from an ocean liner in order to prevent him landing in Ireland, provoking angry protests by Irish Catholics around the world and especially in Australia; in November Hugh Mahon, the Irish-Catholic Labor member for Kalgoorlie in the federal parliament, was expelled because of his criticism of British rule in Ireland.[23]

Sectarianism in Western Australia

That is an overview of Australian sectarianism told from a national perspective. But how much of it applied to Western Australia? I will seek to answer that question by looking at how the issues of state aid, Irish self-government and conscription played out in the west.

State aid

The history of education in Western Australia followed a similar pattern to that of the eastern colonies, though delayed. It was not until 1895 that state aid to non-government schools was abolished in favour of free, secular and compulsory education. Through each phase Catholics fought vigorously to maintain grants to their schools, often provoking a backlash from secularists and Protestants.

With the discovery of gold in the 1890s and the influx of miners, the colony expanded from 48,500 in 1890 to 180,000 by the end of the decade. Most of the influx were t'Othersiders imbued with the secular liberalism that had inspired the education reforms in their home states. One of the

---

23 Kildea, 'A veritable hurricane of sectarianism'.

principal advocates of the reforms was John Winthrop Hackett, editor of the *West Australian* newspaper, whose Irish Protestant background and Masonic connections had, according to historian Geoffrey Bolton, 'prejudiced him towards a measure that would embarrass Catholic schools'.[24] Bishop Gibney fought a rear-guard action to retain denominational funding but when the legislation passed he accepted it with resignation, disavowing the sort of bitter campaigning that Archbishop Vaughan had initiated in New South Wales.

So, at the start of the twentieth century the issue of state aid for Catholic schools was settled in the west as it was elsewhere. As in the east, an attempt to re-open the education question was made in the years leading up to the war by promoting the establishment of a Catholic Federation in Perth. But, despite the support of Archbishop Clune, it failed to materialise. This was partly because Catholic schools in Western Australia enjoyed concessions that were not available in the east. As a correspondent to the *WA Record* explained:

> We do not labour under the disabilities which harass the Eastern Catholics and hardly need the Federation ... [T]he times are not 'rotten' enough, to need the Federation remedy. We enjoy ... most of the rights which the Archbishops in the East and the Catholic Federation are endeavouring to wrest from the unwilling powers that should not be.[25]

But it was also the result of deliberate policy. As Archbishop Clune's biographer Chris Dowd observed:

> Clune was careful not to voice the schools' grievance too noisily, mindful of a possible backlash from militant Protestant and secular associations. He was guided by the principle he enunciated at the time of his consecration as bishop of Perth to do all in his power to avoid sectarian bitterness or social division.[26]

Thus, while Clune and other Catholic leaders often complained about the injustices suffered by Catholics in Western Australia, they did not embark on the type of aggressive political campaign that in the east had inflamed sectarian tensions.

---

24 Geoffrey Bolton, 'A Trinity man abroad: Sir Winthrop Hackett', *Studies in Western Australian History*, 20 (2000): 67–80, 73.

25 *W.A. Record*, 14 February 1914, 4.

26 Christopher Dowd, *Faith, Ireland and Empire: The Life of Patrick Joseph Clune CSSR 1864–1935* (Sydney: St Paul's Publications, 2014), 249.

Irish self-government

As noted, the issue of Irish home rule was a major point of sectarian division in the eastern states. In the west it does not seem to have been. A number of factors help to explain the difference. Firstly, the battle lines in the east were drawn early, in the nineteenth century, especially during visits by Irish nationalists. The western colony did not share that legacy. Until the opening of Fremantle as the gateway to the west in 1897 Irish envoys tended to bypass Western Australia.[27] Moreover, Western Australia was usually not represented at Irish-nationalist conferences in the east. Not until the 1900s did the west see organised Irish nationalism with the formation of the Celtic Club and branches of the United Irish League. Even so, there was a decided lack of radicalism in the Perth Irish community's response to Irish affairs. For example, a public meeting in the Perth Town Hall on 6 April 1900 called by Irish societies expressed appreciation of the visit of Queen Victoria to Ireland, hoping that it would soon lead to a beneficial settlement of Irish affairs.[28]

Despite a lack of radicalism, supporters of home rule did not shy from pressing their case in public, the parliament and the press. In 1903 more than 700 members of Irish societies marched through Perth to commemorate the centenary of the death of Robert Emmet.[29] In 1905 the Western Australian Legislative Assembly passed a resolution in support of Irish home rule.[30] In April 1912 a public meeting was held in Perth to celebrate the introduction of the third Home Rule Bill.[31] But these events passed-off peacefully.

The absence of rancour was due in part to the lukewarm reaction by the west's Protestants compared to the apocalyptic denunciations by their counterparts in the east.[32] Significantly, the *West Australian* under the anti-Catholic Hackett supported the Home Rule Bill, observing in 1912, 'it

---

27 Some, like John Dillon in 1889, gave a press conference at Albany as they passed through on their way to the eastern states, *Albany Mail*, 10 April 1889, 3.

28 *W. A. Record*, 14 April 1900, 15.

29 *West Australian*, 21 September 1903, 3.

30 W A Hansard 16 August 1905, 731–743.

31 *West Australian*, 17 April 1912, 8.

32 At an Orange meeting in Perth in July 1913, Rev. A S C James lamented, 'In Sydney particularly the Protestant thermometer was pretty high and he had sometimes wondered why it was not so high in Western Australia. He thought it was their fault and his fault, because they had not been earnest enough in the enunciation of their principles and in propagation of them', *West Australian*, 15 July 1913, 9.

is difficult for an Australian ... to find the underlying reasons of Ulster hostility to the Bill' and, in 1914 at the height of the home rule crisis in Britain, declaring 'The Home Rule Bill must pass'.[33] Furthermore, in the west there was no entanglement of the home rule and state aid issues, and, significantly, home rule was not a de facto party political issue as it was in the east. The 1905 home-rule resolution was passed by the WA Legislative Assembly with Labor and non-Labor members spread across the ayes and the noes.

Historian Ian Chambers has written that the Irish in Western Australia 'were not quick to organise Home Rule demonstrations.' But it is also true that opponents of home rule were not quick to organise anti-home-rule meetings.[34] So, overall, there was little heat in the issue.

Conscription

As regards conscription, the main opposition in the eastern states came from the industrial wing of the labour movement which sought to impose its will on Labor parliamentarians. Those who did not conform were expelled, including in New South Wales the federal leader Hughes and the state leader Holman. In Western Australia the industrial and political wings were combined in the one organisation and the movement was divided almost evenly, so that neither side could dictate to the other. In May 1916 the party congress at Kalgoorlie voted to leave it to the federal Labor government to determine if conscription was necessary. This left room during the first referendum campaign for conscriptionists and anti-conscriptionists to argue their cases within the movement.

In the east the conscription issue opened up a major fault line between Protestant empire loyalists who supported conscription and Catholics of Irish descent who mostly opposed it. In the west that fault line was not as pronounced, partly because Archbishop Clune advocated conscription and partly because the Irish Catholic community was not as strongly identified with radical Labor.

As historian Danny Cusack has pointed out, in the late 1890s and early 1900s prominent Irish Catholic politicians in Western Australia were drawn almost exclusively from the professional and farming classes—lawyers,

---

33 *West Australian*, 10 June 1912, 6; 26 March 1914, 6.
34 Ian Chambers, 'I'm an Australian and speak as such: The Perth Catholic Irish Community's Responses to Events in Ireland, 1900–1914', *Studies in Western Australian History*, 20 (2000): 117–134, 132.

businessmen and pastoralists. They were socially ambitious, therefore politically conservative and culturally assimilationist.[35] Significantly, there was no geographically-concentrated Irish Catholic proletariat.[36] Cusack further noted that 'There was nothing to compare with the affinity between Cardinal Moran and the early New South Wales labour movement ... nor to compare with the affinity, somewhat later, between Archbishop Mannix and the Labor Party in Victoria'.[37] By contrast, Bishop Matthew Gibney was essentially 'a conservative and a loyal Imperialist', a strong and steadfast supporter of John Forrest. Over a period of at least fifteen years he used his episcopal influence to rally Catholic support for Forrest: 'The Gibney-Forrest alliance served to undermine ... sectarianism by reassuring the Protestant establishment of the Catholic Church's loyalty whilst at the same time making the conservative parties more acceptable to the great mass of ordinary Catholics'.[38] Cusack noted that the close relationship with conservative politicians was continued during Clune's episcopacy.[39] He also contrasted 'the moderate and assimilationist nature of Irish Catholicism in Anglo-Protestant dominated Western Australia' with 'the more militant and nationalistic climate of Irish Catholic and Labor politics' that prevailed in the east.[40]

The first referendum in October 1916 was defeated when the Yes vote received 48.4 per cent of the vote. In Western Australia almost 70 per cent of voters approved conscription, the highest vote in the country, with all five federal electorates recording a Yes majority. After the vote was taken the anti-conscriptionists in the Labor organisations in the east undertook a heresy hunt expelling Labor MPs who had supported conscription. In the west attempts were made to avoid this fratricidal strife, but eventually the party split in April 1917. Of the state's eight federal Labor parliamentarians only two remained with the Labor Party, both Catholics (Senator Edward Needham and Hugh Mahon). Another Catholic, Senator Patrick Lynch, followed Hughes out of the party. At the second referendum in December

---

35 Cusack, 'With an Olive Branch and a Shillelagh', 361.
36 Cusack, 'With an Olive Branch and a Shillelagh', 358.
37 Cusack, 'With an Olive Branch and a Shillelagh', 361.
38 Cusack, 'With an Olive Branch and a Shillelagh', 362–363.
39 Cusack, 'With an Olive Branch and a Shillelagh', 367.
40 Danny Cusack, 'Contrasting Irish-Australian Responses to Empire Hugh Mahon MHR and Senator Paddy Lynch', *Australian Journal of Irish Studies*, 5 (2005): 19– 35, 28.

1917 the Yes vote fell to 46.2 per cent and that in Western Australia to 64.4 per cent, once again the highest affirmative vote by far.

As a result of the different make-up of the Catholic community in the west, its lower level of industrialism, the absence of aggressive enforcement of anti-conscription orthodoxy and the higher level of support for conscription, including among Catholics, conscription was not the sectarian issue it was in the east.

Conclusion

In the early 1900s Western Australia, like the rest of the nation, did experience the blight of sectarianism and often for the same reasons. Yet, the three issues that contributed most to rising sectarian tensions in the east in the 1910s did not have a similar impact in the west.

While Western Australia's Catholics, like their eastern counterparts, insisted on running their own schools, thus drawing some sectarian taunts, they did not embrace the Catholic Federation movement and its aggressive political campaigning on the issue which provoked the bitter Protestant backlash in New South Wales and Victoria.

While Western Australia's Catholics supported Irish home rule, Western Australia's Protestants did not vigorously oppose it as did their counterparts in the east, nor did the issue become entangled with other issues such as state aid or Labor politics.

While large numbers of Western Australia's Catholics opposed conscription, Catholicism and anti-conscription were not closely identified as they were in the east: Archbishop Clune strongly supported conscription, there was no geographically-concentrated Irish Catholic proletariat, there was broad community support for conscription.

From time to time in the west gangs of men with hurleys did break up Orange meetings and sectarian warriors like Winthrop Hackett did rant about the evils of Roman Catholicism. So, sectarianism did exist in the west in the first quarter of the twentieth century. But such events were isolated and not part of an unrelenting pattern as was the case in the east.

Newman's Female Friends: Celebrating John Henry Newman's Canonisation

Edmund Campion*

for The Grail

It's sometimes said that we historians read other people's mail. Certainly I've spent a lot of my life reading John Henry Newman's mail – the 32 volumes of his letters and diaries, which I began reading early in 1962, as a young curate in the parish of The Entrance, and I suppose I've never stopped. 'A man's life lies in his letters,' he wrote to his sister Jemima – if you want to know the man John Henry Newman, read his letters.

Reading the letters gives you a true picture of the great man, which lightens a too reverential approach to him. One discovers him writing his hymns while shaving in the morning, bursting out laughing in bed after reading Trollope's new novel and then waking in the middle of the night to laugh again; worrying over the butcher's bills; troubled with toothache; attending a children's party; writing nonsense verse to thank a girl who baked him a cake; putting in a shower bath and using it five times a week; joking with female parishioners for petitioning him to expand a sermon on the saints; and haunted by a nightmare that he was back in Oxford, about to preach the University Sermon with nothing prepared. Here is John Henry Newman in all his humanity. Of course the letters will push you back to read, or read again, his books. We all have our favourites among Newman's books but I'm not going to go there today.

What I want to do today, is to introduce you to a book that John Henry Newman did not write. Reading Newman's letters, one cannot help noticing how many women friends he had – women to whom he opened his heart and with whom he shared his most private thoughts, and who became his close friends. He once thought of writing about his women friends, calling them 'a galaxy'. Alas, Newman never wrote the book and we are left to guess which stars would shine in his galaxy.

Certainly, Lady Catherine Simeon, wife of a politician, would be there, for he shared with her his sharpest criticism of Henry Edward Manning, Archbishop of Westminster. Certainly too, William Froude's intelligent

---

*   Edmund Campion is a Sydney priest who taught church history at the Catholic Institute of Sydney. This paper was delivered to *The Grail* on 13 October 2019, on the occasion of John Henry Newman's canonisation.

wife Catherine, with whom Newman conducted a long theological correspondence. And I would like to think that he would find a place for Jane Todd, a seamstress who followed him from the Tractarian movement into the Church. She made underclothes for him as well as waistcoats and night caps and counselled him to wear horsehair innersoles in his shoes because the friction would keep his feet warm.

...

Let me introduce you to Mrs Frances Wooten. At Oxford she had been the wife of a Tractarian medical man, who was the doctor to many leaders of the movement. After his death, she became a Catholic and moved to Birmingham. There, the Oratorians were thinking of starting a small school. After his experience at his university in Dublin, Newman saw that a good school was needed to prepare boys for university life. A headmaster would be in charge of the academic side but – and here was the novelty in his thinking – the human and religious side of the boys' development would be in the hands of a woman, known as a Dame. Newman wanted Mrs Wooten for this post. He had a high opinion of her, saying that she was 'more like a saint than most people'. She soon won the approbation of the boys' parents, to whom she reported regularly: one mother asked that her son needed a glass of wine and a biscuit each night; another's sons required compresses for their stomach aches. Like most schools of that time, a cane was used as an instrument of discipline in the classroom; here, Mrs Wooten was known to be an intercessor: 'He's such a delicate boy,' she would say. She was happy in the school and donated more than ten thousand pounds to it besides deeding her property to the Oratory in return for an annuity. She agreed with Newman that junior seminaries were a mistake: true vocations to the priesthood or religious life were not destroyed by contact with the world. Mrs Wooten wrote to the Duchess of Norfolk, whose son was one of her charges, that Newman 'by simple gentle easy ways will form his boys for useful manhood.'

So the Oratory School was somewhat novel: a partnership between the headmaster and the Dame, under Newman's presidency. Another novelty was its lay involvement: its beginning was in response to a request from 32 prominent laymen (and their wives) for Newman to start a school. He always regarded it as a laymen's project: when problems arose, he waited for lay action to solve them. He had been used to laymen participating in his

Tractarian schemes. As a Catholic, he followed the same instinct – sharing his ministry with laymen like Hope-Scott and Bellasis, Acton and Simpson. You could not call Newman a clericalist.

An example of this came early. The headmaster, an Oratorian priest, disliked the sharing of authority and wanted to remove Mrs Wooten. Newman handed the problem to the parents, who unanimously wanted Newman and the Dame; so the priest resigned … and later left the Oratory. In the history of the school there is a tiny detail which reveals how closely Mrs Wooten shared Newman's vision. Like Newman, she had a devotion to the Roman Oratory's founder, St Philip Neri; many boys in her care took Philip for their Confirmation name. It's a telling detail.

Newman once said that the success of the school was due to Mrs Wooten's 'great care taken of the persons of the boys, of soul and body' and few parents would have disputed this. The school started with nine boys and in Newman's lifetime never exceeded 80 boys. A small school allows maximum pastoral care, which is a central part of the Dame's charge. For its first 17 years Frances Wooten was the life of the school. At her death, her doctor, not a Catholic, said he had never met anyone like her – her one aim was to serve God and she had no fear of death. The Oratorians buried her in their own cemetery, at Rednal in the countryside, the only woman to be so honoured. If he had written the book, I'm sure Newman would have included her in his galaxy.

…

Mrs Wooten died early in 1876, leaving Newman with a quandary – who could replace her? A decision was urgent because the boys would soon be coming back to school after the Christmas holidays. So he was relieved when the writer Emily Bowles volunteered. He accepted but said she could leave if the post didn't suit her. In fact, she stayed for five years, although her first generation of boys found her stern and tough after Mrs Wooten – of course!

Emily Bowles had known Newman since she was a young woman. Her brother had introduced her to the Tracts and the Tractarians' poetry. Impressed with Newman's poems, she persuaded her mother to take her to Littlemore to hear him preach. His voice brought her to tears, it was so unearthly; at the church luncheon afterwards, however, she was brought down with a thud when he came round with the serving-dish and asked her, 'Will you have some cold chicken?'

She became a Catholic when she was 25 and three years later joined Cornelia Connelly, the first recruit in her new religious sisterhood. She lasted a dozen years but fell out with Cornelia, leaving the convent after a visit from Newman, who sided with her in her quarrel with the founder. Emily thought of joining other congregations, such as the Dominicans, but Cornelia advised her to work for God as a laywoman

Emily came from a well-to-do family and bought a house in London as a base for work with the poor and hospital and prison visits. Newman sent her money, gently urging her to spend some of it on herself, on such things as cabs and umbrellas and boots ... for herself. Their correspondence blossomed. He sometimes visited her in London or she came to Birmingham, staying at the Plough and Harrow, a hotel across the road from the Oratory. In a letter to another friend Newman said Emily was 'a very great friend of mine – very good, very clever and very active.'

Sometimes Newman would send her to women who were thinking of becoming Catholics or were having religious difficulties. One such was Geraldine Fitzgerald, daughter of an Irish Ascendancy family who discovered the A*pologia pro vita sua* in a cousin's library, which set her (as many, many more) on the path to Rome. Newman alerted Emily to Geraldine's situation, although the young Irish woman ignored his advice to go to the Jesuits rather than the London Oratorians. Her family made her conversion uncomfortable but when Newman came to lunch he charmed them with his simplicity of manner and his capacity for a joke. They did not turn her out, as she expected. Giving up a madcap plan to become a nun, she remained unmarried and spent much of her life, like so many woman in Newman's circle, writing novels. He kept their books on a shelf at Rednal, the Oratorians' holiday home, and sometimes wrote critiques for their authors.

Emily Bowles was primarily a writer – her description for Newman of a London dinner party, where she met Thackeray is vivid. She wrote articles for a Catholic illustrated magazine, *The Lamp,* short stories and (unlike her three-decker contemporaries) short novels. His letter on one of her novels would make any writer glow: 'It is brilliant, interesting and graphic – few Tales, that I have read, equal it. I do hope you will go on writing, that is, if you can get paid for it. There is just enough Catholicism in it – not too much.' It is noticeable that in Emily's novels her heroines do not become nuns.

Newman allowed Emily to goad him on his silence about many religious questions of the day. He knew, however, how out of favour he was in certain Catholic circles. So he wrote back to her honestly and revealingly, letters that show the true inner Newman as he is squeezed by Roman centralism and local clericalism. A good example is his letter in May 1863, of which he told her, 'I never wrote such a letter to any one yet.' It's a very long letter, which is quoted by everyone who writes about him in the Vatican I decade.

Allow me to share a few sentences:

> This age of the Church is peculiar—in former times, primitive and medieval, there was not the extreme centralization which now is in use. If a private theologian said any thing free, another answered him. If the controversy grew, then it went to a Bishop, a theological faculty, or to some foreign University. The Holy See was but the court of ultimate appeal. Now, if I, as a private priest, put any thing into print, Propaganda [Rome's department for non-Catholic countries] answers me at once. How can I fight with such a chain on my arm? It is like the Persians driven to fight under the lash. There was true private judgment in the primitive and medieval schools—there are no schools now, no private judgment (in the religious sense of the phrase) no freedom, that is, of opinion. That is, no exercise of the intellect. No, the system goes on by the tradition of the intellect of former times. This is a way of things which, in God's own time, will work its own cure, of necessity.

...

Now I want to introduce you to Maria Rosina Giberne, who was to have a big part in the Newman story. Tom Mozley, husband of Newman's sister Harriett, described Maria: 'Tall, strong of build, majestic, with aquiline nose, well-formed mouth, dark penetrating eyes, and a luxuriance of glossy black hair, she would command attention anywhere.' She certainly commanded men's attention, notably John's brother Frank, who proposed to her several times. Nothing doing. She became engaged to an Army officer who went out to India, died there and left her his fortune.

Maria was a friend of the Newman sisters. She was there when the youngest, Mary, aged 19, died suddenly, an event which scarred John Henry and which he commemorated in the last lines of *Lead, kindly light*:

'And with the morn those Angel faces smile,

Which I have loved long since, and lost awhile.'

Mary's death became a bond between Newman and Maria Giberne, who was a year younger than he.

Of Huguenot background, like John Henry's mother, she was an evangelical when they met but soon was swept up by the Tractarian tide. All her life she was an enthusiast of one kind or another. As a Tractarian she slept on the floor, getting up to say Matins at 3.00 am. Attempting a kiddies' book, she went on her knees to write the book. Two months after Newman joined the Church of Rome she followed him.

For some years she lived in papal Rome, maintaining a studio there. She was there when Newman and Ambrose St John spent a short year at Propaganda Fide College, learning their way into Catholic culture. She painted them at their books under a picture of the Blessed Virgin Mary, beaky Newman staring soulfully at his fair Saxon companion. It was a painting that Newman obtained to put outside the door of his room at the Oratory, where it still is today.

Back in England, Newman was persuaded to give some non-ecumenical lectures that landed him in public disgrace. He attacked a runaway friar, Giovanni Achilli, who had scattered his desires among women around the Mediterranean and come to England to lecture on the evils of Catholicism. Alas for Newman, English libel laws threatened him and a trial was pending. Maria, fluent in French and Italian, and with a crucifix and New Testament in her handbag, came to his aid. She would collect witnesses against Achilli and keep them occupied in Paris, buying one lame witness an elevated shoe and another two cigars a day – buy him more, urged Newman, and take him to the theatre, to equestrian displays, to sideshows, to the zoo... It came to no good: Newman was found guilty. Yet her five months looking after his witnesses proved Maria Giberne's loyalty to him. She began to speak of her 'spiritual' (that is, non-carnal) love for John Henry Newman, so when one of the lay brothers created a scandal by announcing that he had 'spiritual love' for Mrs Wooten, Newman grumbled that he had got the phrase from Maria. When she came visiting while he was away, he warned that she might be collecting souvenirs of him for later use.

Nevertheless, Newman and the Oratorian community put up with her, knowing that she had a good heart. They treated her almost as one of the family, commissioning her for religious paintings, wrote to her when she was overseas to share news of the house, and sent things she needed. They were almoners of her charity.

149

Still, they were surprised when they got a letter from her one day from Rome to say that she had had what might be called a visitation by the Blessed Virgin Mary, telling her to be a nun. The Pope told her to enter the Visitation order. She came back to England and did the rounds of the convents there – Newman sent her a very stern finger-wagging letter about religious obedience after she had spoken of 'flooring' the Superior of a convent she might join. Hers was a long pilgrimage until late 1863, when she found a safe harbour in the Visitation convent at Autun in France.

From the time she entered the convent until her death in 1885, Newman's letters to Maria (now Sister Mary Pia), give us a window into their friendship. They range from a sharing of his difficulties in meditating to answering her questions about biblical interpretation and the meaning of grammatical terms. He worries about his health and is anxious that weak ankles will give him a fall crossing the road. He tells her he wears woolen underclothes to counter rheumatism and wonders whether her spectacles are strong enough. There is news about her friends in England and increasingly news of deaths. He goes into excited details about a scheme to create an Oratory at Oxford; but then his enemies in the Church stop him from going there. When an ecumenical council is announced, he tells her, 'This general Council is a great idea'; but he will be disappointed there too. Oxford comes back into his life when he is made the first honorary fellow of his old college, Trinity. 'Trinity has never been unkind to me,' he had written in the *Apologia*. 'There used to be much snap-dragon on the walls opposite my freshman's rooms there, and I had for years taken it as the emblem of my own perpetual residence even unto death in my University.' He shares his happiness about the Trinity fellowship with Maria. Now there is a new Pope, Leo XIII, who sends Newman a signed holy card; and then news breaks that the new Pope will accede to the English laity's petition that he make Newman a Cardinal. There are misunderstandings and delay, but at last Newman got his red hat, on 15 May 1879.

On the way home from the ceremonies in Rome, he was intent on visiting his old friend Maria – 'I must go to Miss Giberne at Autun' – but he was felled by pneumonia and the doctor ordered him straight home. What a disappointment for her! In London, the new Cardinal was lionized and later Sir John Millais would paint his portrait in full cardinalitial fig; but his letters to Autun did not change their tone of true friendship. 'You are not an ostritch', he tells Maria, aged 80 with defective teeth. He warns her not to swallow unchewed meat which 'is as dangerous to the stomach as brick and stone, or a bunch of keys'. For years he has lived mainly on soup and milk; he recommends well boiled pease pudding (dried split peas boiled to a pulp) and omelettes without lumpy white bits. A postscript enquires about her spectacles. When she dies, suddenly, aged 83, he does not grieve for her. He tells someone that her long years in the convent were her Purgatory – now she is in Heaven.

...

There they are, three women whom Newman would certainly have included in his Galaxy book, if he had ever got round to writing it. Readers of his letters might find other female friends to include in the book: Maria Giberne's friend, the novelist Lady Georgiana Fullerton; or Fanny Taylor, first editor of *The Month*, who published his *Dream of Gerontius*; and surely Mother Margaret Hallahan and Mother Imelda Poole, Superiors of his favourite convent, the Dominicans at Stone.

His sisters would not feature in his Galaxy: much loved Mary died too young, and Jemima was distant, stand-offish, while Harriett broke off relations with her brother, in 1843, because she thought he was trying to talk her husband into becoming a Catholic (quite the reverse in fact – notice this was in 1843: Newman was still an Anglican).

But one might suggest that Harriett's daughter, Grace, could get a mention. She emigrated to Australia with her husband and went back to England for a visit in 1890. While she was there she wrote to her uncle, could she visit him? Newman wrote back, 'of course'; so she came to the Oratory, was taken upstairs and sat with him while he held her hand and talked about the family. Grace had a cold, which she gave to the Cardinal. It developed into pneumonia and two days later he was dead.

A quarter of a century ago, the writer Michael McGirr discovered Grace's great grand-daughter living in Melbourne. The family still had the book of his poems Newman had given Grace, as well as that last letter he ever wrote and other Newman letters. They told McGirr their jocose family tradition: 'We killed him, you know.' You could say that... and today he is being canonised, a Saint who depended on his female friends.

Julia Matilda Cater (Sister of Charity) Revisited

Maxwell J Coleman*, Margaret M K (Moira) O'Sullivan** and Sandra I Coleman***

On 8 August 1838 five volunteer Sisters of Charity left Dublin for London where on 23 August 1838, they set sail aboard the barque, *Francis Spaight*, for Sydney. The order was founded in Dublin in 1813 by Mary Aikenhead, the daughter of an apothecary and Catholic convert. The volunteers responded to Mary Aikenhead's request in 1835 from Bishop Polding to send sisters to assist with the spiritual and temporal needs of the predominantly Catholic female convicts and orphans in Sydney. This ultimately led to the establishment of St Vincent's Hospital in Sydney in 1857.

Four of the five sisters were Irish. They were Margaret Cahill (b 1793, Sr M John), Alicia De Lacy (b 1799, Sr M John Baptist), Elizabeth Williams (b 1800, Sr Francis Xavier) and Catherine O'Brien (b 1809, Sr M Francis De Sales). The fifth was English and was professed on 23 January 1833. Recent research has uncovered additional information about Julia Matilda Cater (b 1807, Sr Lawrence Magdalen Chantal).

It is the information about Julia that contradicts what the Sisters of Charity believed. Not only is Julia four years older than in the Sisters of Charity records, but also like Mary Aikenhead, she was not a cradle Catholic but originally belonged to the Established Church. The Church of England Baptismal records for St Pancras Old Church in London show Julia Cater's date of birth to be 11 June 1807 and the baptism to have taken place on 16 July 1807. Prior to this her year of birth was recorded in Sisters of Charity Archives as 1811. One wonders about a transcription error with the day 11 being substituted for the year 07. Her parents are recorded as John Augustus and Matilda Cater.

John Cater completed his Articles of Clerkship in his father's (Harry Cater) legal practice in 1794. He married Matilda Ayrton in July 1805 at St

* Maxwell J Coleman FRACS, FRCS Retired Surgeon, St Vincent's Hospital, Darlinghurst. Author of *The Doers. A Surgical History of St Vincent's Hospital, Sydney 1857–2007.*
** Margaret Mary Kathleen (Moira) O'Sullivan, RSC, PhD. Historian, Sisters of Charity, Edgecliff. Author of *'A Cause of Trouble?' Irish Nuns and English Clerics.*
*** Sandra I Coleman, Retired Nurse

George Church in Hanover Square, London. Matilda Cater died two months after her daughter Victoria's birth and her husband died the following year. Following so soon after childbirth one wonders if Matilda's death was causally related. She was buried at St Marylebone, Westminster on 21 December 1812. Her husband, John Augustus Cater was buried at the same place on 28 December 1813. John Cater's will mentioned financial support for his children till the age of 21 years. It is, however, difficult to read and any amount is not decipherable.

John Cater had six siblings: Henry Wells Cater (b 1774), Catherine E Cater (b 1776–1837), Harriet Cater (b 1777), Margaret Cater (b 1781), Samuel (b 1783), and Sophia Ann F Cater (b 1785). Only two of his siblings married. There was thus sufficient family to possibly care for their orphaned children.

It is easier to follow the lives of Julia Cater's two siblings. Dudley Frank Cater was born on 22 July 1808, baptised on 21 August 1808, and died in 1891. He married Sarah Bisdee on 11 May 1840 in the Parish Church of Hulton, County Somerset. His occupation was silversmith. Dudley and Sarah had no children. Dudley wrote quite harshly to Mary Aikenhead criticising her for not wanting Julia back when she returned to England in 1846.

Victoria Cater married the Reverend George Johnson, a Wesleyan missionary after they had moved to Canada where she died in 1893. An Obituary in *The Times* on 28 April, 1893 wrote:

> Mrs Johnson's maiden name was Cater, the old Cter (? Cater) family of Uffington, Berkshire, England. Her father was a member of an eminent London Legal firm and for some time an under Sheriff of the City of London. In early life she was a pupil of the eminent musician Count Mezinghi and was first to teach a classical style in music in New Brundswick. The deceased was a mother of George Johnson, the Dominion statistician, Ottawa.

This new data raises several important issues. Following the death of their parents, who raised Julia Cater and her siblings? Who was responsible for her conversion to Catholicism and when did it occur? The first census was in 1841 by which time Julia Cater had been converted, professed and was in Sydney. There is thus no census household data to analyse to determine whether Julia was taken in by an aunt or uncle. John and Matilda Cater's deaths at a young age may explain why Julia had difficulty in providing a dowry on entering the novitiate.

After baptism, there is no trace of Julia until she becomes a Sister of Charity. She features in Ullathorne's memoir, *From Cabin-boy to Archbishop*, on the visit to Australia, praised for her education and wit, but not praised unreservedly. She received significant tasks from Bishop Polding in Sydney, but then returned to London in 1846. Julia next appears in the 1851 census at the Benedictine Nunnery in King Street, Hammersmith as a teacher. This is consistent with the tradition among the Irish Sisters that Julia became a Benedictine oblate, that is, a lay person who lived according to Benedictine spirituality, a form of the Benedictine life.

This information came to light when Dr Coleman sought to find the date and place of death of Julia Cater which was missing from "A Cause of Trouble?" He was well assisted by his wife's facility with Ancestry.com. Even though Cater left Australia after eight years, her talents helped to establish the Sisters' works, especially education. The heat, lack of funds and the rawness of life in a penal colony could easily make it seem as if talents like hers could better be employed in a more settled situation. The belief among the Irish Sisters of Charity is that Julia ended her days as a governess in France. We could find no English record of her death.

Sources

London, England Baptisms, Marriages and Burials, 1538–1812.

London, England Deaths and Burials 1813–1980

England Census 1841–1901

England and Wales, Prerogative Court of Canterbury Wills, 1348–1858

At Sea with Bishop John Bede Polding: the Journals of Lewis Harding – 1835 (Liverpool to Sydney) & 1846 (Sydney to London)

Editor & transcriber: C F Fowler
Publisher: ATF Press, Adelaide, 2019
ISBN: 9781925872736
Paperback, 360 pages
Price: $47.95

Reviewed by T J Kavenagh*

Forty-five years ago I was trying to compile a list of all the Benedictine monks in nineteenth-century Sydney – ranging from the three bishops/archbishops down to the humblest boy-postulants. It was not very satisfactory, and there were more than a few mistakes. One particular annoyance was a certain 'Brother Lewis', who suddenly emerged out of nowhere on 8th October 1845 in the monastery chronicle at St. Mary's, and then seemingly disappeared again into silence. He wrote as follows: 'Br. Lewis who commences this day to edit this book is weak and sickly & recommends himself to the prayers of the reader.' In 1974, I had no idea who this weak, sickly 'Br. Lewis' was, but as we now know, he was the compiler of the two maritime journals so ably transcribed and edited by Colin Fowler, and published here for the first time.

As for the structure of this book, the bulk of its pages are obviously given over to the two shipboard diaries. The 1835 journal was reported to have been lost, but Fowler's curiosity and determination led to its rediscovery in the archives of Downside Abbey. Harding's second journal, that of 1846, seems to have been little known until recently, but it can now be found in the Sydney Archdiocesan Archives. Included in this journal are Harding's sketches. Immediately following the texts of the two journals, Fowler has obligingly assembled two appendices—Appendix I (1835 journal), Appendix II (1846 journal)—containing relevant contemporary documents.

---

* Brother Terence Kavenagh OSB, through his many articles in the Australian Benedictine journal *Tjurunga* from 1974 to 2005, is regarded as the 'doyen' among historians of Sydney's monks. His current research and publications focus on the history of his Sylvestrine congregation.

We now come to the 55-page 'Introduction'. This section of the book is a 'tour de force' and sometimes quite surprising. In the first section, 'Bishop', Polding is presented in the context of all his sea voyages not just those of 1835 and 1846. It is a sort of bird's-eye view and moves very quickly - lots of unfamiliar information but presented in an attractive and exciting way. This is equally the case with the third section, 'Voyages', less than three pages long, but wonderfully informative.

Because the centre of attention in this book has to be the journals, it seems inevitable that the key figure will actually be Lewis Harding, not Polding. Admittedly, one could argue that the journals' historical interest rests largely on the information it provides about John Bede Polding, especially in his more informal moments. However, the 1835 journal in particular is to be valued for the broader picture it presents, i.e. of the whole missionary group Polding had gathered around him. We know what their future was to be, in particular the inadequacies that were to be revealed in the years ahead. And this is part of the fascination of Harding's pages. But it is more than that too. This young man was himself a fascinating figure, who is still well worth 'meeting', and one grows in sympathy and admiration for him.

'The Diarist' (Harding) is the subject of the fourth of the introductory sections and the longest. There is much to cover here: birth and baptism into a Catholic convert family in 1807; maternal grandfather a baronet (and later a priest); same grandfather establishes a Catholic mission on main estate and hires young Irish Dominican, James Vincent Corcoran, as chaplain; after three years Corcoran volunteers to sail with Polding to Australia; Harding, a late addition to the passenger list, sails off with the official status of 'catechist'. Most of this section, however is about Norfolk Island, and how in 1838 Lewis is sent to the penal colony there, filling in until a priest chaplain might arrive. Remarkably, Harding lasted for four years, so he should not be underestimated.

Back in Sydney in 1842, references to Harding's ill-health increase. As we have seen, in his sole entry in the Benedictine Journal he described himself as 'Br. Lewis', so he was at least a Benedictine novice. On 16 February 1846 he and Archbishop Polding set sail for the U.K. via Cape Horn. Harding's health deteriorated even further during this voyage. Thereafter he was regarded as an invalid, and it was rooks and photography that saved his life —until the grand age of 86.

Finally, there should be some acknowledgement of just how onerous the task of transcribing and editing a journal, let alone two, really is. Pages 47 to 56 contain a fascinating and meticulous account of how it was done, as well as a very detailed description of the two manuscripts. The second enormous task that Fowler faced was the footnotes—how to identify or explain the many people, places, books and 'things' that the reader might want to know about. Some of these are quite recondite and were not at all easy to track down.

Colin Fowler's record of publications, three books that range from Descartes to Pyrmont parish and now round the Capes, plus a growing list of journal articles, all these attest to his enthusiasm, persistence and quite formidable research skills. These three elements, plus his lucid prose, are clearly in evidence in *At Sea with Bishop John Bede Polding*.

BOOK REVIEW

The Indomitable Mr Cotham: Missioner, Convict Chaplain and Monk

Author: Joanna Vials
Publisher: Gracewing UK 2019
ISBN: 978 085244 928 8
Paperback, 594 pages
Price: $55.95

Reviewed by Colin Fowler*

This is a monumental work, covering a single life in 45 chapters of almost 600 pages with ample referencing and commentary in multiple endnotes. The book is divided into two parts comparable in size, the first dealing with Cotham's 16 years on mission in Van Diemen's Land, the second on his 32 years of ministry back in England.

This is a most impressive biography based on meticulous research. Its subject could be considered an unlikely candidate for such detailed and sustained attention. James Ambrose Cotham, an English Benedictine monk, came to the notice of the author through her interest in the history of the once fashionable English spa-town of Cheltenham, where Cotham, as priest-

---

* Colin Fowler was parish priest of Pyrmont. His book *150 Years on Pyrmont Peninsula: The Catholic Community of Saint Bede 1867–2017*, was reviewed in *JACHS* 37 (2).

in-charge of the local Catholic mission, had initiated the building of a fine gothic church. Her initial research revealed Cotham as the 'missioner, convict chaplain and monk' of the sub-title.

The fourth chapter affords a glimpse of the impressive range of research found throughout the book – the 15 pages are followed by 3 pages of 41 footnotes containing references to six Hobart newspapers of 1835, correspondence from the archives of Downside and Douai Abbeys, citations from the multi-volume Historical Documents of Australia, a University of Tasmania thesis, a Newsletter of the Pugin Association, and secondary sources published in 1886, 1891, 1911, 1995, 2001, 2008.

Of interest to Australian readers will be the first part of the book dealing with Cotham's period in Van Diemen's Land, 1835-1851, perhaps particularly his involvement in the 1836 dismissal of the Irish Vicar-General, Philip Connolly, after 14 years as the only Catholic priest on the island. Vials presents, in an appendix, the full text of a letter of March 1836 from Cotham to Bishop Polding in Sydney. In the letter, which Vials describes as 'written with immature audacity' (p 543), the young monk reported negatively on Connolly's personal and ministerial behaviour and threatened to abandon the mission unless the Vicar-General was removed. Polding's immediate response was to sail to Hobart Town with his NSW Vicar-General, William Ullathorne. On arrival he publicly dismissed Connolly and appointed Ullathorne in his place. Vials acknowledges that on arriving in Hobart Cotham had immediately sided with Connolly's critics, led by a Stonyhurst schoolmate and including his own brother Laurence Cotham. Readers might wish to compare Vials' treatment of the controversy with that of the Doyen of historians of the Tasmanian Church, the late Fr Terry Southerwood, who sought to exonerate Connolly from the condemnation of the Benedictines —Polding, Ullathorne and Cotham—and from that of the historian Norbert Birt, 'a monk trapped in the confines of Downside's dusty archives'. Vials acknowledges Southerwood as 'a pioneer in his own right' (p xi) and includes a few of his many articles in her bibliography, but she does not cite his biography of Connolly, *Lonely Shepherd in Van Diemen's Isle*.[1]

One rare instance of a factual error occurs in reporting that during Cotham's one brief visit to Sydney in 1844 he met 'some of the later

---

1   W T Southerwood, *Lonely Shepherd in Van Diemen's Isle: Father Philip Conolly, Australia's first Vicar-General* (George Town, Tas: Stella Maris Books, 1988).

Benedictine arrivals in the Australian mission such as Vincent Dowling' (p 139). Dowling was a Dominican who had arrived in 1831.

In the foreword to the book, Abbot Geoffrey Scott of the Douay Benedictine community, to which James Ambrose Cotham belonged, comments that this book marks a shift in biographies of English Catholic clergy from studies of leaders to the 'lower echelons of the ordinary parish clergy'. The same cannot be said for Australia, where leading Benedictines, Archbishop Roger Vaughan and bishop-elect (évêque manqué) Austin Sheehy, still lack biographies.

This is the definitive biography of Cotham; there will not be another. It fully realises the dedication Vials has shown to her subject and her exceptional grasp of the sources.

BOOK REVIEW

A Cause of Trouble? Irish Nuns and English Clerics, 2nd edition

Author: M M K O'Sullivan (Moira RSC)
Publisher: Kindle Direct Publishing
ISBN: 9781986685405
Paperback, 268 pages

Reviewed by Irene Franklin[*]

Having read the book several days ago the main impression I have of its substance is that it contains a catalogue of differences between the first Catholic nuns to arrive in Australia, in 1838 (the Sisters of Charity from Ireland) and Archbishop Polding and other priests, particularly his right-hand man Abbot Gregory.

Polding was a Benedictine whose ambition it was to grow the Benedictine presence and therefore influence in the colony. He also firmly believed that all money from a Catholic source should be under his control no matter what the donors' intentions were. He greatly resented it if he was unable to wrangle away, for example, money raised for the building and setting up of St Vincent's Convent and Hospital.

The few dowries that were sent to Australia with nuns from Ireland were

---

[*] Irene Franklin is a member of the ACHS.

taken by Polding and added to diocesan funds. (Some were left in Ireland because the Mother House did not realise the dire straits of the nuns on arrival.)

A parishioner Mary Corcoran had a deed drawn up in which she "sold" two cottages for a nominal sum to two priests to be rented out with the money going to the support of the nuns, but the nuns never received any benefit. Similarly when property in Parramatta that the nuns had used was sold when they went to work in Sydney, the money again was not available to them. William Davis willed a house and invested £1500 for the nuns to yield an income, but again they received nothing.

One of the sisters, Sr Mary Baptist de Lacy, charged Polding with amalgamating the Sisters of Charity with the Sisters of the Good Shepherd, changing the rules and constitutions that had been approved by the Holy See and should not have been changed by any lesser authority. Polding had also had himself declared principal superior of the congregation against the constitution.

In order to attract nuns to do necessary work Polding had agreed that the Archdiocese would be responsible for their upkeep, but he did not keep his word. He disgracefully claimed to Propaganda Fide in Rome, the Society for the Propagation of the Faith in Lyon, and to Sydney Catholics that the Sisters of Charity were a financial burden on the Archdiocese.

When the Sisters of Charity began in Ireland their constitution was radically different from other orders because they were not to be an enclosed order. The clerics misunderstood this and how it impacted on the nuns' lives.

Fr John McEncroe, who was Irish and not a Benedictine, was very active in working to meet the needs of the Catholic Church in Sydney. That did not please Polding as he saw it working against his Benedictine hopes, so, with questionable judgement, he was obstructionist.

Polding's behaviour was a clear example of the clericalism that has infected the Church up to almost today. The unrealistic belief that being ordained made the priest infinitely superior to a normal human being resulted in hiding priests' misbehaviour to avoid scandal. The very act of hiding priests' misdemeanours is yet another scandal, as shown in the reaction to bishops hiding sexual abuse of children by priests. The intention of Pope John XXIII in calling the Second Vatican Council was to correct such attitudes and behaviour. His intentions have been disregarded and abuses have continued.

The book has a number of other interesting observations of personalities, behaviour, both singular and collective, but these can be discovered by those lay Catholics who sincerely want to find out what went on inside the religious and clerical sides of the Catholic Church.

BOOK REVIEW

The Doers: A Surgical History of St. Vincent's Hospital Sydney 1857–2007

Author: Maxwell J Coleman
Publisher: JAM Graphics, 2018
ISBN 9780646995205
363 pages
Price: $75

Reviewed by Anne Thoeming*

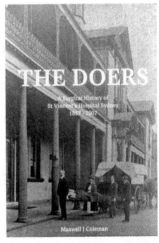

Perhaps marathon running and mountaineering should be pre-requisites for anyone writing a prosopography such as Maxwell J Coleman's *The Doers: A Surgical History of St. Vincent's Hospital Sydney 1857–2007*. Coleman—whose own entry is on page 272—completed such physical feats then turned his intellectual talents to crafting a corpus that is indispensable to Australian medical history. He has also presented historians with an intriguing classification dilemma: is the work a micro-biography of the men and few women surgeons who operated on the thousands of patients that passed through St. Vincent's Hospital in Sydney in a one hundred and fifty-year period; or is it an institutional history as seen through the engagement of its actors? It is probably a bit of both as Coleman has wrapped the institution around the people. Categorisations aside, the people in this extensive, painstakingly researched, carefully footnoted, and beautifully

*   Anne Thoeming is a PhD candidate at the University of Sydney, and an ACHS councillor.

presented work are witnesses to a powerful institutional history of the endeavour, love, and risky business of running a Catholic hospital.

Works such as these can pose a dilemma in terms of determining the content structure. In slicing this history into three parts: the first fifty years; the second fifty years; and the third which encompasses the development of the surgical specialities, there is an implicit acknowledgement of the overlapping roles of its subjects. Specialist surgeons worked in gynaecology and other speciality areas long before there was a department to host them, and Constance D'Arcy appears in part three when the gynaecology department was formed rather than in part two when she commenced work, but the community of readers interested in this history will be understanding. The stories of the four female and two hundred and twenty-eight male surgeons reflect the passion and dedication to their work and their commitment to St. Vincent's, as well as the gendered nature of surgical work, something which changed slowly and only in tiny increments. Coleman builds on John Hickie's exemplary examination of St Vincent's physicians, published in 2000, and carefully weaves together the threads of lives and stories which have made the institution. His historical narrative is a focussed one and the book's production has benefited from advances in digital technologies so that the legacy photographs are sharp and well contrasted. The two-column page makes for easy reading as does the diligent use of header bolding and text colour.

The Sisters of Charity arrived in Australian over 180 years ago with a mission to minister to female convicts and their children, but the vicissitudes of life in the new colonial settlement soon transformed their mission into one with a health care focus when the hospital was established, and the first patient arrived in 1857. The first fifty years of surgery as told in part one, is set against Sydney's historical development and the early reliance on British surgical training. The stories of these surgeons are generously told and include life-defining details, where known, about education, family life, politics, professional engagement. They are implicitly about class and privilege but also show how the newly arrived made their mark in an evolving society.

In an era of sepsis, hospital operating conditions were 'challenging' and the acceptance of antiseptic techniques was not universal. The first surgeon, the Anglican James Robertson, sometimes operated from the outdoor verandah where the light was better. The stories unfold from this beginning and Coleman's bibliography and online resource list of many valuable monographs ensures readers can easily explore additional background material relating to early funding conflicts, the role of the Sisters vis a vis that of the Catholic Church, relations with the University as well as other hospitals, and topical medical matters. Stories of medicine's evolution are woven through these individual women and men and the medical care they provided. The development of anaesthesia had an expansive effect on surgical practice as did the growth of speciality areas such as gynaecology and orthopaedics.

These individual lives vary in narrative length, but they are always interesting and provide insight in the development of Australian hospital surgery. Few, if any, of these surgeons worked exclusively at St Vincent's. These lives touched many others and the stories illustrate the transnational connections with Britain, Europe and later Asia and the transformational impact of the relations forged. Kevin O'Doherty's background is a riveting read of an Irish emancipationist who was arrested, imprisoned, sent to Australia in 1849, and eventually ended up as a surgeon at St Vincent's, although only for a brief period. His story contrasts with that of Robert Scott Skirving of privileged Scottish background who was renowned for his candour as well as his lengthy record of continuing service— some sixty-seven years. Coleman has sensibly included insights into the ordinariness of these people in surgical masks and has the fearless Scott Skirving describing the decorated Boer War doctor Sir William Williams as conceited, vain and 'rotten as a surgeon.' It is not clear why Herbert Moran is listed along with the first fifty-year cohort in part one rather than in part two when he commenced his medical career, but it is delightful to see him in near Alexander MacCormick of whom Moran was fond. Moran would have approved of his own placement slightly below MacCormick whom he described as a model teacher who tried to impart to his surgeons a reverence for the patient, saying 'the operation was less than the patient.'

Part three is a highly engaging overview of the historical development of surgical specialities, some quite detailed. These introductory snippets then background the evolution of these specialities at St. Vincent's and the surgeons working there. Many readers will quickly see the network of connections within this St. Vincent's family, whether it be through employment, association or family relationships. Good reads offer such rewarding experiences, and this reader delighted in being able to see Herbert Moran, Constance D'Arcy, Victor Kinsella, Harry Windsor and Walter Burfitt-Williams together in the one volume. Medical memoirs and institutional histories have been carefully mined for this exhaustive work, and the attentive reader will soon note the occasional entertaining re-appearance of earlier surgical characters in the plot lines of later lives.

Coleman's Epilogue is an insightful and generous tribute to the lives contributing to the life of this remarkable Catholic hospital, and he has provided a nicely crafted history of all that came to pass in its first one hundred and fifty surgical years. This volume is not readily available through non-institutional lending libraries but can be purchased from St. Vincent's Hospital in Sydney.

BOOK REVIEW

The Invention of Melbourne: A Baroque Archbishop and a Gothic Architect

Eds. Jaynie Anderson, Max Vodola and Shane Carmody

The Miegunyah Press, Carlton, 2019
ISBN: 9780522875638
Hardback, $54.99

Reviewed by Patrick Morgan*

Gold-rush Melbourne was largely free from sectarian tensions, which erupted later in the century. To bolster the denominational education system the Victorian Premier Sir John O'Shanassy doled out land grants for schools to the four main churches, giving his own tribe a prime site. Non-Catholic Melbourne was bemused when Bishop Goold built an enormous Gothic cathedral on land designated for educational purposes, with St Patrick's College squeezed into a far corner of the block meant for it. A decade earlier the pioneering priest Fr Geoghegan had established downtown the small St Francis Church, Irish baroque in outward structure, and with an overblown Italianate marble altar installed later. Melbourne thus had two contrasting sites of worship from the start.

* Patrick Morgan is author of a two volume history of the Melbourne Archdiocese, *Melbourne Before Mannix* and *The Mannix Era*: published by Connor Court.

This impressive and beautifully produced book is based on the Irish Archbishop Goold, the chief begetter of early Melbourne Catholicism, and on one of his collaborators, the English architect William Wardell, who designed the Gothic cathedral, the Italianate Government House and the Venetian style ES &A bank, considered by many the city's finest building. In past histories of Catholic Melbourne Goold's effort in establishing a thriving archdiocese, at a time when the population was rapidly expanding, has naturally received most attention. This book, a happy collaborative effort by a score of academic researchers, focuses for the first time on the field of church architecture, and on Goold's art and book collecting.

Medieval Revival styles in church building usually came to Australia not directly, but through Irish or English filters. But as a young man Goold, unlike his successors Carr and Mannix, trained for the priesthood in Italy, so his immersion in European religious culture was both immediate and long lasting. The key chapters in this book are on religious art; they explain the supposed antinomy between Baroque and Gothic suggested by the book's subtitle. Professor Jaynie Anderson unpacks this apparent conundrum when she writes: 'Although Goold's commissioning of Neo Gothic churches may initially appear inconsistent with his collection of late Baroque religious painting, consultation with early English sources on the Gothic Revival reveal similarities between the two styles, both being perceived as deeply religious and anti-classical'.

This book needs a brief discussion of the various Medieval Revival styles (Byzantine Basilica, Romanesque, Gothic, Baroque, Spanish Mission) and the relations between them; the large church of St Mary's West Melbourne, for example, combines a soaring French Gothic interior with Italianate marble decoration.

On his overseas trips Goold bought up Late Baroque paintings in job lots; one consignment shipped to Melbourne contained over 130 Old Masters. Many were previously thought to be copies, but research by local art experts has revealed some were important originals. The paintings were distributed to churches, religious houses and elsewhere, as aids to deepen religious faith. The German scholar Klaus Krüger provides a brilliantly clear exposition of how transcendental meaning can be effectively relayed to sublunary mortals through pictorial means.

A similar situation obtained with books. Wallace Kirsop and fellow researchers reveal that Goold amassed an extensive book collection, sourced from his overseas trips and from overseas catalogues. One highlight was his rare multi-volume collection of Piranesi's prints. He worked in collaboration with Sir Redmond Barry, who had similar interests and curiosities, as Barry was collecting on a massive scale for the State Library and Art Gallery. Unlike his paintings Goold kept his books in a secure private library, with limited use by colleagues. The authors conclude Goold acquired art and book collections equal to any in early Victoria. Both collections were, sadly, dispersed after his death. The researchers are compiling lists of items in his collections, and locating lost painings and editions where possible.

Early Melbourne was deemed a missionary archdiocese, so it has been assumed religious art was acquired for purposes of conversion. This was the case for priests going to Asia, Africa and the Americas, but as Melbourne was chock full of Irish Catholics, the main purpose here was retention of the faith, rather than acquiring it. Moreover Goold's collecting sprees suggest he enjoyed being a patron and connoisseur of the arts for their own sake, as much as being an aid to religious instruction.

The material in the book is wonderful but its overall framing has problems. Nobody, much less a few Catholics, invented Melbourne. On the first page the editors qualify their misleading title, admitting the book is limited to a study of two men who made a significant contribution to the 'architecture of our [Melbourne's] built environment'. Only post-modernists believe cultures are 'invented'. Worthwhile institutions and communities are painstakingly built over time by many actors, as Goold demonstrated; imagination, not invention, is one of the ingredients needed. The authors believe their mission is to 'radically reassess Goold'. Revisionist ventures of this kind tend to belittle the past, and to exaggerate the novelty of their own discoveries. We are told, strangely, that 'Goold's legacies were eclipsed in the late 1960s and early 1970s' by the Second Vatican Council. Revisionists seek out eclipses, where things change rapidly and drastically to their liking. This is an ahistorical perspective. During my lifetime we have had Popes Pius XII (conservative), John XXIII (liberal), Paul VI (moderate), John Paul II and Benedict XVI (traditionalists) and Francis (liberal). The church, like any healthy organism, balances itself by constantly taking on board differing insights and forming a new synthesis without sinking the ship and without jettisoning its past.

BOOK REVIEW

A New History of the Irish in Australia

Authors: Elizabeth Malcolm and Dianne Hall

Publisher: NewSouth Publishing, 2018
ISBN: 9781742235530
Paperback: 436 pages + *viii* pages.
Price: AUD$34.99, NZD$39.99

Reviewed by John Carmody*

Patrick O'Farrell began his *The Irish in Australia* (1987) with a question: 'The Irish in Australia is an impossible subject, too vast, too various, too complex, and certainly too elusive. Why attempt it when some degree of failure is assured?' My answer (though he gave another) is, 'When you are such an excellent and discerning historian and so fine a writer, your obligation is plain.' O' Farrell was a rare scholar, one of the 'old school' (Mark McKenna is another modern example), who believed that it is the primary task of the historian—after being as truthful and reliably-informed as possible—to tell a story: to the *entire* tribe (not just his academic colleagues), to help them understand their society and their part in it.

Of course, as more information comes to light—which it unremittingly does when there are so many students at work (and it's 30 years since Professor O'Farrell's book was published)—it is necessary to re-think and then rewrite *all* history. Like life itself, it is not set in stone. Nonetheless, to follow O'Farrell is a formidable challenge, even for people who see the world differently. Inevitably, therefore this new book by Drs Malcolm and Hall is different from his. To begin with, it is (paradoxically) almost entirely secular in its focus and it is nowhere as elegantly written. It has ten chapters, together with an Introduction and a (contemporary) Epilogue, group into three themes: Race, Stereotypes and Politics. O'Farrell's concerns were—intellectually, culturally and emotionally—distinctly different.

Unsurprisingly, because the authors are based in Victoria, their book

---

* John Carmody is President of the ACHS.

gives an unbalanced attention to Melbourne and, at times seems not to understand NSW ideally; then—for all that it opens with a paragraph on the St Patrick's Day March in 2018 in Brisbane—Queensland seems very much an afterthought. Given that there was a very significant Irish immigration to that state *and* that the ALP (with its Irish genes) was essentially born in regional Queensland, that is a regrettable absence from a book which purports to have a national purview.

Nevertheless, what the carefully researched book does offer is as engrossing as it is disturbing—even enraging. In that respect, 'The Irish race' (Chapter 1) is the one which will generate most readers' anger towards the splenetic bigotry and frank hostility which the dominant Protestant British part of society unremittingly directed at the Irish. The authors begin with examples from that British home-soil, citing the Scots anatomist, Robert Knox, who in 1850 wrote in *The Races of Men* that the 'Irish Race must be forced from the soil; by fair means if possible; still they must leave. England's safety requires it'; and the Anglican clergyman and novelist, Charles Kingsley, who 'was deeply unsettled by the sight of what he called "white chimpanzees"' when he visited Ireland in 1860. Colonial cartoonists, some of whose work Malcolm and Hall reproduce, habitually depicted the Irish with simian faces; they also quote the prejudice of Arthur Topp (leader-writer of *The Argus*)—'the Irish were a race of morally, socially and intellectually inferior people'—and the opinion of the Geelong doctor and Parliamentarian, Alexander Thompson, of the southern Irish as 'utterly useless; in point of intellect they are inferior to our own aborigines.' Modern readers might well remind themselves that Australia's first peoples still endure that sort of jejune contumely.

Their chapter on 'The Irish and indigenous Australians' considers the 'positive relationships that exited between Indigenous and Irish peoples, based at least in part on a recognition of shared injustice, dispossession and colonial oppression'; the fact that 'during the 20th century, Catholics became more actively involved in indigenous missions, with the laity, female religious and European male orders taking the lead'; and the public dispute, in 1892, between the Port Hedland squatter, Charles Harper, and Matthew Gibney (the Irish-born bishop of Perth) in which Gibney mentioned 'the white settlers whose deliberate murders in no single instance met with the punishment that invariably overtook the blackfellow convicted of a similar crime against the invaders of his country'. Otherwise, priests seem mentioned largely in references to the incessant grizzles of "Establishment" figures that the Irish were unduly susceptible to the bigoted, narrow-minded and seditious propaganda of their pastors.

This new history of the Irish in British Australia is an uncomfortable read – some might ask what has changed in this querulous society – but, like the putative virtues of bitter medicines, it has the potential to do us all good.

BOOK REVIEW

Angels, Incense and Revolution: Catholic Schooldays of the 1960s

Author: Wanda Skowronska
Publisher: Connor Court Publishing Pty Limited, 2019
ISBN: 9781925501919
Paperback: 226 pages
Price: $29.95

Reviewed by Catherine Thom[*]

It may seem odd to begin a review of a book with the final chapter. However, I do this because it seems to capture a strong emphasis of the author's reflections on Catholic Education in the 1960s. In Skowronska's words 'the post war generation... benefitted immensely from the richness, sense of mission and Christ-like compassion of the parochial school system'. She adds, 'in the 1950s and 1960s reason, mystery, true silence, reflection and good fundamental catechesis were pervasive, and fundamental to our spiritual formation.' (203) She does accept that, 'some will disagree with my version of events' and she welcomes their stories but she holds firm to her 'unending gratitude to the [sisters], priests and brothers who gave us so much as intrepid teachers, generous missionaries, witnesses and thinkers.' (205)

As Maureen O'Connor, a former Brigidine claims, this book 'is a must read for all Brigidines. A fabulous journey back into the past...' But it is more than this, and for more people than the Brigidines. Many Catholic students of the 60s and 70s, both boys and girls, would have memories similar to those enunciated in this small volume. Not all might be so positive

* Catherine Thom has been an educator since the 1960s and remains so today with a passion for History, especially that which involves our beleaguered Church.

but it is encouraging to know that there might be in 'post lapsed catholic land' many people who concur with Wanda Skowronska's memories of her childhood school experiences. The work recalls the pain and dislocation of the migrant experience; it also shows the creativity and companionship that enabled these refugees to survive and flourish.

Humour abounds in this reflection in the constant references to the *Church Triumphant* which is how Wanda felt about the security and hope engendered by her teachers in the Church of her day. She also inserts rhetorical questions throughout such as 'what could go wrong' with such an institution that we were surrounded by during our years of Catholic education. Throughout there are expressions of reverence, awe, and being totally absorbed in the rituals of the early sacramental experience of confession and holy Communion such as, 'it was not just a question of saying the words, it was the deep absorption of that spiritual territory which became the foundation of the Catholic legacy we were inheriting.' (52) Fleetingly she regrets that she does not have photos of such occasions but she is consoled by the fact that, 'moments and scenes of it are engraved in my memory.' (53) Speaking with friends from these times she makes the general statement, 'Catholic children, however young, could rarely forget this spiritual milestone.' (53)

After a family breakup she and her mother moved to 'Paddo' where there was a surgery for her mother's medical practice. Her father and grandmother moved to Darlinghurst so Wanda, the 'reffo kid', had the advantage of two families in the East of the city where she was to be enthralled by a new life built on 'characters' such as the Cat Lady and B Miles. Her father took her to places that required money and her mother took her to 'free' libraries and museums and for walks in the park.

Poor editing is visible throughout the text with typographical errors (cf. 1 and 63), many awkward expressions and inaccurate names for specifically 'catholic' items ('chalice' for 'ciborium'; 'novice' for 'postulant'; 'nun' instead of 'sister'). A number of photos which are intrinsic to the tale of the 1960s are not acknowledged either in the covering statement or with individual photos. I wonder if permission is needed for the commercial ads used?

Having said this, it remains true that the overall impression of this book of mature reflections on early school days is sincere and heartfelt. Many readers, this one included, have fond memories of these days and, as other commentators have said, Skowronska's recollections carry none of the hurt and bitterness that so often accompanies memories of this period of Catholic education. In successfully capturing this system of education, the author is to be congratulated for helping us relive what many might call days of blissful childhood in schools which enabled their students to make 'a smooth transition to the Catholic world of work.' (145)

BOOK REVIEW

Celebrating Freedom of Speech: Fiftieth Anniversary of the 1968 papal ban on birth control

Editor: Val Noone

Publisher: Mary Doyle and Val Noone, Fitzroy, Victoria, 2019

ISBN: 9780646807225

Price: $15.00

Paperback: 48 pages

Reviewed by Helen Scanlon*

This volume arose out of a one day gathering in Melbourne in October 2018 held to mark the 50th anniversary of *Humanae Vitae,* the encyclical of Pope Paul VI on contraception. The first paper in the volume is by Val Noone, *The 1968 papal birth control ban: its impact on church employees.* This is an overview from a personal perspective of the reception of the encyclical by both clergy and laity in the period following the announcement on 29 July 1968 and records the actions and responses of many journals, newspapers and groups throughout Australia and the world. Noone has been able to include photos of sections of various newspapers—*The Australian, The Age, The Advocate,* and *The Catholic Worker.* For me it was a reminder of perhaps the most dramatic and vision-expanding period of my life for like all thoughtful Catholics I had followed Vatican II and glimpsed a vision of a church prepared to go forward with a renewed openness. *Humanae Vitae* with its dogmatic insistence on authority signalled that the church had not been changed.

I was prepared to state my opposition to the teaching in the encyclical and

---

* Helen Scanlon is ACHS Secretary

because my name and photo had been used in reporting protests by the laity, I was told by a friend that my local parish priest had stated that if I came for communion he would publicly refuse me. Three of my children were then attending the parish school. I transferred them to a state school in the next parish lest they be penalised and I too found a welcome in the Jesuit parish nearby.

Noone includes in this publication a reprint of a tribute to Nicholas Crotty he wrote for *The Age* at the time of Crotty's death in 1998.

The second major paper presented on the day is a long and very comprehensive history of the Church in relation to attitudes to sex. *In Memoriam: Nicholas (Michael) Crotty, Peter Phelan and free Speech in 1968* by Robert Crotty, Emeritus Professor in the School of Education, University of South Australia and brother to Nicholas. Crotty explains the Greek philosophy of the Stoics, adopted by the Church, which claimed that the only ethical sexual actions were those intending procreation. He looks at the early hermits, the teaching of Augustine, a Stoic, and the development of the idea of 'natural law'. Thomas Aquinas also condemned contraception.

Crotty outlines the scientific developments throughout the 18th and 19th centuries. In 1905 a Catholic conference in Belgium was held which condemned any form of birth control. In 1930 the Anglican Lambeth Conference allowed contraception with certain provisos, and the subsequent *Casti Connubii* encyclical of Pope Pius XI was issued restating the natural law argument but adding the scriptural story of Onan as reinforcement. Many theologians began to question the arguments stated and particularly after the birth control pill became available it became difficult to justify the ban.

During Vatican II a papal commission was set up and after many meetings and changes in membership the final decision was a vote for allowing the use of the pill: 9 for, 3 opposing and 3 abstaining and this report was sent to the Pope. A minority report was also sent by those opposing. The results of the commission were widely published and so it was a complete shock when Paul VI issued his encyclical.

Crotty then gives a personal account of the weeks and months that followed as his brother Nick and Peter Phelan negotiated their way from the priesthood. His conclusion is one of great pessimism for the church as it now exists.

The other inclusions in this important document are a tribute to Peter Phelan by a seminary friend Joe Broderick; a poem by Bruce Dawe, who was a family friend, called *At Mass for Peter Phelan*; a record of his time as de facto editor of *The Advocate* by Michael Costigan during this turbulent period; and a reprint of the paper given to the Australian Catholic Historical Society in July 2018 by Des Cahill, Emeritus professor of International Studies, RMIT University. Lastly there are some of the comments and statements made during the forum which concluded the day.

This publication is important as a public record of the turmoil in the church which came to a head in 1968 and which is ongoing.

BOOK REVIEW

The Extraordinary Case of Sister Liguori

Author: Maureen McKeown
Publisher: Leo Press, 2017
ISBN: 9780995577503
192 pages, paperback
Price: $23.25

Reviewed by Jeff Kildea[*]

'What goes around comes around', so the saying goes. And it aptly describes my being asked to write this review of Maureen McKeown's *The Extraordinary Case of Sister Liguori*. In 2005, at the Australian Catholic Historical Society's conference 'The Catholic Impact on Australia', I presented a paper entitled 'Where Crows Gather: The Sister Liguori Affair 1920–21'. The following year, the society published my paper in this journal. Then, in 2010, a woman in Ireland researching her family history came across the article and wrote to me, saying she was almost certain that Sr Liguori (Brigid Partridge) was her great aunt. That was my first contact with Maureen McKeown. I had always intended to write something more substantial on the Sr Liguori affair as it is a story worth telling, but other projects kept pushing it back. So, I was delighted when a couple of years

---

[*] Jeff Kildea is an Adjunct Professor in Irish Studies at the University of New South Wales and is the author of numerous books and articles on the Irish in Australia including *Tearing the Fabric: Sectarianism in Australia 1910–1925*.

later Maureen informed me she had decided to write a book about her great aunt's extraordinary life. Thereafter, we met in Sydney and I was impressed by her determination to uncover the facts. And here I am now, having read the book she eventually wrote, writing this review. But, why should I be surprised at this latest twist in the Liguori saga. After all, as I noted in my 2005 paper,[1] 'The story of Sr Liguori is a remarkable tale which, if written as a novel, would be considered too far divorced from reality to be acceptable as a serious work of fiction. Yet it is a true story, full of tragedy and farce'. Perhaps that is why Ms McKeown decided to write her book not strictly as history and not strictly as fiction, but as 'narrative non-fiction' a genre that uses the tools of dramatization but does not fictionalise.

Set in early twentieth-century Australia riven by sectarianism, it is the tale of a young Irish nun who in July 1920 flees her convent at Wagga Wagga, fearful she is about to be murdered by her Mother Superior, and places herself under the protection of the Orange Order. Arrested as a lunatic at the request of her bishop, Sr Liguori is declared sane by the Lunacy Court, which orders her release, whereupon Brigid Partridge, as she now prefers to be called, goes to live with a Congregational minister William Touchell and his wife. There are fisticuffs in parliament over the affair and Bridget sues her bishop for false imprisonment. If that is not enough she is also kidnapped off the streets of Kogarah by her brother who has been smuggled into Sydney by the Catholic Federation to persuade her to leave her Protestant gaolers or guardians, depending on your point of view. When a jury rejects Brigid's claim against the bishop the Catholics declare victory and the controversy dies down. Thereafter Brigid remains with the Touchells but ends her days in Rydalmere Psychiatric Hospital in 1966, ever-fearful that the Catholics are still trying to kidnap her.

McKeown's method using Brigid's first-person point of view enables her to lay bare personal emotions, capturing well the dread and utter helplessness that Brigid surely felt after she realised that convent life was not for her. Yet, when the book goes beyond speculating on individual emotions to narrating events it sometimes fails to grasp their wider historical import. This is not an uncommon problem for a non-historian writing narrative non-fiction. In the case of the Liguori affair, verbatim newspaper reports of the court case

---

1   Jeff Kildea, 'Where crows gather: the Sister Liguori affair 1920–21', *Journal of the Australian Catholic Historical Society* 27 (2006), 31–40.

provide copious material for both courtroom dialogue and as a source of facts relating to various events. But the reports do not provide the all-important background of those events, which the author must discover elsewhere. An example is McKeown's treatment of the role played by members of the Orange Order, who give Brigid refuge and support her in her determination not to return to the convent. Framed as an act of pure humanitarian kindness it neglects to show the full context in which that support was offered. And in doing so it misjudges the true nature of Brigid's predicament, one we have seen in other cases, e.g. in 2005 with Terri Schiavo over her 'right to die' and in 2000 with Elián González over his repatriation to Cuba. It is a situation in which activists on both sides of an ideological divide pull at the hapless victim like children fighting over a rag doll, each side proclaiming its motivation as purely the individual's best interests. It is no wonder Brigid started to come apart at the seams, for 1920 was arguably the worst year in Australia's history of sectarian conflict and she had unwittingly found herself in the middle of what the then Attorney-General Edward McTiernan described as a 'veritable hurricane of sectarian strife'.

While *The Extraordinary Case of Sister Liguori* tells very well the poignant story of a young woman wronged by her church who had the courage to do something about it, the Sr Liguori affair was much more than that. Those seeking to delve deeper into the controversy, to try to understand how and why Brigid Partridge came to be the centre of public attention for months on end in the press, the parliament and at public meetings, may find it less satisfying.

Hidden in the Shadow of Love: The story of Mother Theresa McLaughlin and Our Lady's Nurses for the Poor

Author: Jocelyn Hedley
Publisher: St Paul's Publications, Strathfield, NSW, 2019
ISBN: 9781925494372
Paperback: 237 pages, 20 photographs, 24 pages of source material.
Price: $24.95

Reviewed by Anne Power*

This story draws a mixed response from this reader. When it is soundly based upon the Medical Journal of the Nurses from 1913 onward, it is moving. The accounts of people cared for by the Brown Nurses (as they were known) are detailed about how the nurses walked to their patients and how they looked after patients' needs. At other times, when little is recorded about the actions of Theresa Mclaughlin (known to her family and companion nurses as Cissie), the writing resorts to sentiment. I'd encourage readers to continue as the events of Cissie's life, as she follows in the footsteps of founder Eileen O'Connor, whose cause for beatification is open, are remarkable.

At the side of this story of Cissie is the story of the expulsion and subsequent reinstating of Father McGrath, co-founder of Our Lady's Nurses for the Poor. There was a vision of Our Lady in 1915, shared by the nurses, whose confidence in their mission was strengthened. There were also the war years and the terrible 'Spanish Flu' which raged internationally and took so many lives. Again the Nurses' Medical Journal records individual cases,

---

* Anne Power is a music curriculum expert at Western Sydney University and an ACHS councillor.

eventually leading to the death of one of their own number who contracted the disease. Not long after Eileen O'Connor died.

With determination Cissie wrote to the Health Department and Randwick Council to ask that Eileen's body be buried with them, citing Mary MacKillop as an example. The Council gave permission but Archbishop Kelly felt it would be better if Eileen were buried in the cemetery. Five years later, Cissie wrote to Archbishop Kelly, asking to have the Blessed Sacrament reserved in their home. Once again, the request was denied as they were not an approved religious community. Consequently, Cissie wrote to her friend, the Vicar Apostolic of Papua Alain De Boismenu, for guidance about how they should proceed. He advised a request to the Apostolic Delegate by small steps: first a letter recommending the Nurses' work to the Archbishop; next an endorsement from the Archbishop; and finally, providing both documents to the Apostolic Delegate to take to Rome. This letter sequence brought Rome's approval for the Blessed Sacrament to be reserved in the Nurses' home.

Four years later (and 23 years after the founding of the Nurses), Cissie wrote again about burying Eileen O'Connor at their home; and the Archbishop agreed. When her casket was opened, Eileen's body was intact. Around the Nurses, the world went to war again. Cissie wrote to the Cardinal, the Apostolic Delegate and various clerics in the Archdiocese towards achieving religious order status. A spiritual director was assigned. The first step was to be accorded approval as a pious association. The Medical Journal of 1951 records that 1008 sick people were visited, meals provided and food parcels distributed by their company of 12 women. In 1953, they became the Diocesan Congregation of the Sisters of Our Lady ministering to the Infirm Poor. That same year, The Eucharistic Congress was held with a procession through the city streets and the nuns were led by Australia's newest religious Congregation.

The Congregation spread to Queensland at the request of Archbishop Duhig and in Sydney, built a new Novitiate, opened by Bishop Freeman in 1961. In 1965 Cissie died, having achieved a firm foundation for the work of the Congregation to carry on.

Book Review

Story of Our Country: Labor's Vision for Australia

Author: Adrian Pabst,
Publisher: Redland Bay, Qld: Kapunda Press, 2019
ISBN: 9781925826593
Paperback $32.95

Reviewed by Michael Easson*

Story of Our Country is an important book on the Australian Labor legacy and modern challenges. This review considers the challenge set out by the author and the gap between task and accomplishment.

The writer, Adrian Pabst, a UK academic commissioned by the PM Glynn Institute, a public policy research centre of the Australian Catholic University, clearly has worked hard in understanding the ALP and local nuances. The book displays his wide reading and engagement with dozens of Australians in thinking through what is good and bad in contemporary Labor.

He calls for a revival of values and connections with movements and compatible traditions, particularly Catholic and christian ideas of justice and moral integrity.

Pabst describes and elucidates Labor's rich paradoxical heritage—progressive and conservative, radical and traditional—in attempting to marry values of equality, diversity and redistributive justice.

The book is divided into an Introduction, Conclusion, and four separate Chapters on: The Present–the ALP's Positioning; The Past–A Short History of Labor's Ethical Purpose; Philosophy–Labor's traditions and Dispositions; and Politics and Policy–Renewing Party and Country.

Influenced by the Blue Labour stream of the UK labour movement, Pabst is inspired by Lord Maurice Glasman and creative, moderate thinkers like Jon Cruddas (an anti-Corbyn Labour MP). The "blue" is an allusion to the blue-collar traditional base of the movement—thrifty, family oriented, often Christian-inspired and tradition-respectful, earthy decency. The nice types you find in George Orwell's books, like *The Road to Wigan Pier*. Blue Labour's website proclaims: 'Our politics is a challenge to the liberal consensus of the capitalist order, it does not

* Michael Easson was Secretary of the Labor Council of New South Wales, 1989–1994.

belong to the revolutionary left. Its inheritance is the labour tradition.' Blue Labour shares with elements of the left, a revulsion about the alleged cosy corporatism of Blair Labour, the evils of globalism, as well as opposition to intolerant liberal humanism.

Before the 2019 Australian election, Pabst was writing in *The New Statesman* (London) about the appealing features of the Australian Labor model, which he foresaw as certain to win the forthcoming Australian election. This book, therefore, is partly a reckoning with illusions and delusion with aspects of a much hoped for Australian example. Pabst sees Australian ideals of the 'fair go' and 'mateship' as ethically inspired. He argues that:

The emphasis on rewarding work, which provides not just an income but also a sense of self-worth and meaning, is an example of how economic and socio-cultural concerns overlap and converge with ethical considerations. Linking them together is a certain conception of justice centred on the common good, which can be defined as an ordering of relationships in a way that holds in balance individual fulfilment with mutual flourishing, based on the dignity and equality of all people.

This is a fine statement about immanence in our daily world. But what is this in opposition to?

Pabst complains of the slide in recent decades into 'cartel capitalism, bureaucratic overreach, unfettered globalisation and rampant individualism.' The adjectives here are all pejorative and self-defining. Too often in Labor politics books, 'liberalism' is unmoored or unfettered, and 'individualism' is rampant or selfish, as if neat and tidy descriptions of such vices complete the morality play.

Threaded through the book are valuable references to historic Protestant and Catholic influences that shaped the ALP. The papal encyclical *Rerum Novarum* (1891) and local Catholic political activity is an obvious starting point. There is a history of some Labor figures seeing Christianity and labourism as intertwined. W G Spence, the founder and organiser of the Australian Workers Union was a lay-preacher. Indeed, Victor Daley, poet and dreamer wrote a poem that began: 'My Name is Labor, but they call me Christ.'

Pabst unearths information about The Rev. Lance Shilton's regret in a statement in the mid-1970s about the neglect by Protestant churchman compared to the Roman Catholics, of engagement with the unions and labour movement generally. He was then Dean of St. Andrew's Cathedral in Sydney. There is also reference to the Rev. Alan Walker's consideration of pre-selection as an ALP candidate for a seat under the guidance of Gough Whitlam. Walker was then a Methodist minister and soon a driving force in the merger of churches into the Uniting Church of Australia. These references are revealing and indicative of authoritative scholarship about source material

Pabst writes beautifully and persuasively throughout much of the book. He suggests that

the ethos of the ALP can best be understood as a paradoxical combination of radical and small-c conservative values in a Burkean sense: tackling injustice in the economy and renewing political institutions, while also conserving tradition and society.

The balance of individual rights and mutual obligations, secular and religious values, is part of the contemporary mix. There is much to be said for William Lane's argument in *The Workingman's Paradise* that: 'To understand Socialism is to endeavour to lead a better life.'

An issue not clearly addressed in the book, besides the consideration of Labor's imperfections, is why does it usually lose elections.

By describing the big-C Conservative enemy as tied to nineteenth century ideas of unregulated (or weakly-restrained) capitalism, as fear mongers on race and immigration, as uninspiring champions of dull white picket fence conformism, Labor can bask in the seemingly warm inner glow of moral superiority.

But Gina Rinehart/Kerry Packer unrestrained capitalist ideology is a distance from the politics of Menzies, Howard, and ScoMo.

Part of Labor's success has been in influencing its adversaries to be more moderate, compassionate and supportive of some important planks of social protection.

Ironically, the lack of a coherent account 'compassionate Australian Liberalism' is missing in Australian political writing. (Perhaps David Kemp, in the forthcoming, final two volumes of his history of Australian liberalism might be equal to that challenge.) There is a gap in the market for a Liberal book like Pabst's.

In the Pabst book, however, there is only a brief mention of families and what might be called the politics of families. This points to a vital feature of aspirational politics. Former Deputy Leader of the ALP, Tanya Plibersek said after the last Australian election that she did not understand what was meant by 'aspirational'. She was suggesting it is an easy cliché to bounce around the political park, but that the word does not tell us much. Except, it does in this importance sense: no successful political party in Australia will ever owe its success to 'possessive individualism' or free-range selfishness. In this country the Conservative appeal is not to (or just to) 'individualists' but to people wanting the best for their families. They see themselves in a wider context, not just as self-regarding automatons. They are families and parts of networked communities. Although she blundered in articulation of the point, there is insight in Margaret Thatcher's argument that: 'There is no such thing as society. There are individual men and women and there are *families.*' She was portrayed as a champion of 'rampant' individualism in that formulation, but I believe her point was that society can be an amorphous concept, whereas families and real people matter.

In some ways, the Australian achievement is a continuation of Australian exceptionalism, including the creation of a relatively prosperous and successful nation. In 2019, and in recent elections held among OECD members, Australian politics presents as the most boring, least antagonistic. This is something we should be proud of.

A further issue for Pabst and what might be broadly called the Blue Labour view, is ambivalence to the modern world. This has many manifestations, including contempt for the so-called neo-liberalism of the Blair, Brown, Hawke and Keating governments. Instead of seeing those administrations as commendable examples of social democratic reform, there is confusion about their place in the Labor heritage, and whether they have a place at all.

In other writings, Pabst is super-critical of neo-liberalism in its 'untrammelled' aspects. Australian Labor, under Whitlam and Hawke and Keating, were tariff reformers and modernisers. There is not so much criticism in this book of Australian Labor (compared to what might be said about UK Labour, even before the sainted red grandpa, Jeremy Corbyn took over), but there are hints of the ALP losing its way under 'neo-liberal' pressures. I am not sure, however, what this means.

There is a further ambivalence about the people Labor needs to appeal to. There seems to be an image of 'the workers' as a lot of blue-collar wage-earners out there somewhere who need to be won back as they emerge from the factory gates. That world vanished decades ago. Modern workers have moved to either the gig economy or self-employment. On the one hand there are precariously employed pizza deliverers, Pakistani Uber drivers and musos, and on the other, tradies, fast chicken franchisees and suburban reiki therapists. Is Labor speaking to them? I do not believe so.

Of relevance is Larry Bartels' book *Unequal Democracy: The Political Economy of the New Gilded Age* (2017, second edition). Although about the US, it is helpful in explaining why Labor lost and why people adhere to certain political views. The gist is that people are often guided, in voting, neither by rational economic calculation nor by cultural issues, but by 'unenlightened self-interest'. Bartels found that level of income had little to do whether someone favoured cutting the tax rate for the highest income band. Instead, voters were more likely to support cutting the rate if they felt their own tax burden was heavy. Bartels also found that inheritance tax was persistently and deeply unpopular among all income groups and even among people with egalitarian values who wanted more government spending.

How to best appeal to real people requires understanding them. How to shift opinions requires much more. This dilemma is indeed paradoxical to those who think in a linear or one-dimensional way. Each of us are made up of combinations of complex feelings, instincts, belief systems, and behaviours. Traditions, heritage, people we engage with, all matter in shaping our thinking. Characteristics like loyalty, solidarity, respect for the ethos of a movement, a church or an organisation, as well as active understanding through engagement in the stuff of daily life is part of the story. So too, in the calculation, rough and ready, of what is good for my family and my world.

Pabst has written a superb book that should provoke Labor to freshly assess its past and more easily engage with the challenges of tomorrow. The paradoxes he refers to, the ambivalence also of some of what he discusses, is present in his own writing. Perhaps that is one reason his phrasing and writing sometimes soars so high.

Hatch Match & Dispatch, A Catholic Guide to the Sacraments

Author: Richard Leonard, SJ
Publisher: Paulist Press, New Jersey
ISBN: 9780809106509
Hardcover: 179 pages
Price: $26.25

By Helen Scanlon*

Richard Leonard writes as he speaks, with an easy conversational style and yet he is able to give a careful history of each of the seven sacraments, and their development over the past two thousand years. He quotes scripture passages, the writings of popes, and many council edicts, setting each in historical context. The text is lightened by his personal anecdotes, because he is writing for a broad readership. For those well versed in church history there is still much that is new and for those who want the most recent teachings of the church, or an update of remembered catechetics from school this book has much to offer. In the section on Holy Orders he discusses clericalism and both the ordination of married men and that of women, and in the Marriage chapter he does not ignore same sex marriage and annulment. I recommend this book.

* Helen Scanlon is ACHS Secretary

Memories of Fr Paul Stenhouse (1935–2019)

Robert James Stove*

'Roooooooooob!'. There could be no mistaking that unique light-baritone speaking voice which so often greeted me, when I answered a call from a Sydney number. That greeting was Fr Stenhouse's vocal signature, just as John Bercow's command in the House of Commons – 'Or*derrrrrrrrrrrrr*!' – was *his* vocal signature. I now grieve at the realisation that never again in this life will that 'Roooooooooob!' float down the phone.

Considering that Fr Stenhouse and I (to me he was always 'Father' or 'Fr Stenhouse,' never 'Fr Paul', let alone 'Paul') wrote for several of the same late-1980s publications, I am surprised that our paths took so long to cross. That they did cross, I owe mostly to an expatriate friend we had in common: the late, great Alister Kershaw, whom during 1990 I met at his Loire Valley home. Alister lavished such hearty praise on Fr Stenhouse as to pique my interest, and I filed this enthusiasm in my memory-bank; but I somehow failed to meet Fr Stenhouse for another two years.

Over the next decade I turned into a regular *Annals* reader and then an occasional *Annals* writer, having already become an *Annals* recipient. (A useful research project for some bright graduate: to find a single Australian, living or dead, who actually paid full price for receiving *Annals* year after year. I know of no such Australian, though I know of several Australians – including non-Catholics – who were getting *Annals* gratis from the 1950s onwards.) That which Fr Stenhouse did very largely single-handed in keeping *Annals* going, would in the USA, France, or any Latin American country have required several dozen staffers.

On the extremely rare occasions when I had encountered an author whom even Fr Stenhouse had never heard of, I must admit to rather preening myself on this short-term, factitious attainment. Nineteen times out of 20, the intellectual debt operated in entirely the other direction: Fr Stenhouse had unearthed, for my and others' benefit, an obscure scribe from his prodigious library. How else but via *Annals* would I ever have stumbled across Christopher Hollis's *The American Heresy*? Or James Gairdner's

---

* Robert James Stove is the author of *César Franck: His Life and Times*.

accounts of the Lollards? Or Sir Arnold Lunn's rebuttal of H.C. Lea on the Spanish Inquisition? Or anything by Gabriel Marcel? Or anything by William Cobbett (perhaps Fr Stenhouse's greatest literary hero)? Or most of Chesterton? Or most of Belloc? Or most of Ronald Knox? The list could continue for pages.

Marking Fr Stenhouse's conversation—how desperately I miss our thrice-yearly late-breakfast get-togethers at Circular Quay—was a sportive delight in human foibles. During one such rendezvous, he suddenly admitted to never having mastered German. I replied that I found this failure hard to credit, given his extreme fluency in Arabic, Aramaic, and Hebrew as well as in the Romance languages. Yet still he insisted that German had always defeated him. As he explained the situation, though, it grew obvious that he found a certain philosophical merit in his linguistic shortcoming.

He embarked on the sad tale of a female student from his Sydney University youth, circa 1959. This student one day alarmingly announced that she had begun studying German, so as to read Hegel in the original. On and on she toiled at her Teutonic grammatical apparatus; over and over she perused the *ipsissima verba* of Hegelian dialectic. In the end she reached (Fr Stenhouse sadly assured me) so esoteric a stage of enlightenment that she *had* to defend Hegel, through fear of being otherwise forced to admit that she would have remained happier for never having learnt a single German word. That notion she could not bear to contemplate. Prussian statist metaphysics trapped her as surely as regicide trapped Macbeth; and, like Macbeth, she had plunged 'in so far that should I wade no more / Returning were as tedious as go o'er.'

It was typical of Fr Stenhouse that my eventual submission to Rome (2002) did not make the slightest outward difference in our dealings. He knew where my religious loyalties lay, perhaps before I fully knew myself. Both before and after my conversion he displayed astounding financial generosity to me. When I once queried how *Annals* would survive if he showed (as he probably did show) similar financial generosity to other and more frequent *Annals* contributors, he calmly replied: '*Rerum Novarum* is still binding.'

I never presumed to ask Fr Stenhouse about the sexual abuse crisis which engulfed the Church during his last years. His innate cheerfulness of temperament and extreme busyness of schedule helped, I am convinced, to keep him from succumbing to despair.

Even more crucial to his endurance, I think, was that gift so rare among

Australians as to seem almost weird: a gift for *institutional* loyalty. The commonest intellectual vice among Australians is the precise opposite: an absurd over-confidence about achieving the political millennium through some individual or other. Fr Stenhouse allowed himself no such rash trust in merely secular messiahs. In the very marrow of his bones, he accepted the truth of Matthew 16:18. He thereby judged each passing doctrine – each political movement, each cultural vogue, each intellectual fad – according to its compatibility or incompatibility with the Catholic Church. On whose side, ultimately, was it? The side of Saints Thomas More, John Fisher, Edmund Campion, Margaret Clitherow, and Oliver Plunkett? Or the side of Henry VIII, Elizabeth I, William Cecil, Richard Topcliffe, and Titus Oates? Such clarity of mind, and the courage which it instils, Fr Stenhouse found to be as natural as breathing.

Meanwhile, the following passage from Sydney Smith (an *Annals* favourite) can stand as Fr Stenhouse's epitaph:

> *The meaning of an extraordinary man is that he is*
> ***eight men**, not one man; that he has as much wit as*
> *if he had no sense, and as much sense as if he had*
> *no wit ... But when wit is combined with sense and*
> *information; when it is softened by benevolence and*
> *restrained by strong principle; when it is in the hands*
> *of a man who can use it and despise it, who can be*
> *witty, and something much better than witty, who*
> *loves honour, justice, decency, good-nature, morality,*
> *and religion ten thousand times better than wit; why,*
>
> *wit is then a beautiful part of our nature.*

+++++++++++++++++++++++

Fr Paul Stenhouse: Scholar, writer, hero for God

Wanda Skowronska[*]

In the months and years to come, much will be written about Fr Stenhouse (1935–2019) as a historian, linguist, scholar of Hebrew and Samaritan texts, writer and priest. He will be particularly remembered for his editorship of *Annals*, that unique journal of culture and religion which he edited from 1966 onwards, making it the longest surviving journal in Australian history.

My 15 year involvement with *Annals* is threaded with many memories. One of my first articles was about Bonegilla, a migrant camp in northern Victoria. Unusually, Fr Stenhouse knew where it was, its place in Australian history and in a very short time, I experienced that sense of someone 'getting it', not being fazed by Polish, Hungarian and Ukrainian names and keenly grasping cultural contexts.

When Fr Stenhouse found out that I was a psychologist, I recall him asking me 'So why are you so sane?' I felt nonplussed and thought this was my cue to walk around the room like Inspector Clouseau in witty reply. Instead I answered that if you had parents who had been shot, tortured, had experienced gulags and camps, you became inclined to hard realities and increasingly allergic to ideology and illusions. He seemed to like that reply. I only found out at his funeral that he did not like psychologists, so in retrospect I realised I had passed a kind of test. Fr Stenhouse asked me to write articles on psychology, hoping they might help others. After I did an article on psychopaths a lady contacted me to inform me that she now definitely knew that her deceased husband was a psychopath!

As well as writing on psychology, I covered significant historical events such as the canonisation of St Mary of the Cross in Rome in 2010. I had no difficulty getting up at 4am on canonisation day as I stayed in a guest house, near St Peter's Square, run by a gypsy couple who argued loudly every night. After singing Waltzing Matilda with Australian pilgrims outside the window of Pope Benedict XVI and after the Mass, I was excited that I would

[*]   Wanda Skowronska's *Angels, Incense and Revolution: Catholic Schooldays of the 1960s* is reviewed in the current issue. She is writing a book on Fr Paul Stenhouse.

get a great papal photo. Closer and closer the Popemobile came ... and of all things, my Olympus camera jammed! My heart sank as the Pope sailed by and yes, it went 'click' once his back was in full view! On my return, I declared to Fr Stenhouse I would just stick to writing, no photos. To my surprise, he told me that there had been many frontal Papal pictures, now was the time for one of his back–and he printed it. He could pour balm onto photographic wounds.

I recall once entering his office, finding him poring over a manuscript in Arabic with his finger going rapidly from right to left. But such was his kindness, he put the manuscript aside to answer some questions. He had this ability to move from the world of eagles to those of sparrows and larks. He wore his erudition humbly, sharing it without fanfare with all who came his way.

He would often get phone calls, speaking in whatever language was required. He had written much of his doctorate in Dubrovnik (then Communist Yugoslavia), and had studied awhile at the Topkapi Palace in Istanbul, the administrative headquarters of the Ottoman sultans. He would tell his *Annals* writers that he was off to Albania, Malaysia, Estonia, Mexico, Timbuktu, Uzbekistan or to some dicey part of the Middle East, often ending up in Rome, no doubt informing the Pope of the persecuted church, as Australian director of Aid to the Church in Need for over 20 years, an organisation close to his heart.

In his research, from iconography to terrorism, Fr Stenhouse was a kind of intrepid, scholarly Indiana Jones, forging ahead always for Christ, making friends in different parts of the world. Once I emailed him with questions and he replied saying he was in Kashmir trying to decipher some inscriptions but he would get back to me when he could! During the war in Lebanon (1975 onwards), I was told by his friend Chris Lim, that Fr Stenhouse collected medications from Australian pharmaceutical companies but could not send them to Lebanon through the usual channels. So he flew to Malta, hired a boat (with crew) and sailed into Lebanon, and in this enterprising way, was able to get the medications to the needy. Another time I asked why he was going to Tartu in Estonia, and I should have anticipated his reply – he was to give a paper on Semitic studies there.

He transmitted the Gospels unceasingly – quoting the original passages in Greek, Latin and Hebrew. And if anyone had a dodgy interpretation of the

Koran, heaven help them—he could translate and explain relevant passages in Arabic accurately and reduce his opponents to silence.

He made friends with many Christians—among them Ukrainians, Poles, Malaysians, Lebanese, Syrians, Italians (and yes, he spoke fluent Italian), Chinese, Vietnamese among others. When the Armenian Patriarch, his Beatitude Nerses Peter XIX Tarmouni came to Australia in 2001, to celebrate the 1700th anniversary of the conversion of Armenia to Catholicism, he joined the long, colourful, procession into St Mary's Cathedral and said Mass alongside his Armenian brother priests surrounding the Patriarch. As one in the pews, I merely read the prayers in English translation. I also recall going to St George Coptic Orthodox church in Kensington and finding a pile of *Annals* on a stand. I remarked on this fact and was told, 'Oh Fr Paul, he was here just last week—yes, we know him well.'

A lady from Trinidad informed me recently that Fr Stenhouse used to say the annual Mass for the Trinidad-Tobago society in Sydney, attempting to play a Tobagan musical instrument in the festivities afterwards. He also journeyed to Damascus in 2011 to meet with the mufti of Syria, Muhammad Badr Din Hassoun, speaking Arabic with him for several hours. He questioned him on the Sunni Muslim attitude to the recent war. This conversation confirmed for Fr Stenhouse that the war was not from within the country but stoked by outside influences. He told me that he had comforted the Mufti in the recent loss of his son. His account reached the *Australian* as a valuable piece of investigative journalism.

Alongside the relentless investigation, the obliteration of illusions, scholarly defence of the faith and pioneering 'St Paul' like journeys, there was a 'gentleness born of wisdom' (James 3:13) permeating just about all Fr Stenhouse did. No doubt he would want us to diffuse these fruits of the spirit in our turbulent times – to be reasoning, questioning, sceptical and relentless pursuers of truth, all the while being peacemakers – as he was all his life.

Errol James Lea-Scarlett

John J Kenny*

Errol Lea-Scarlett studied organ for about 20 years. During that time, he became the second of two skilful young men who successively substituted for Connie Cloran at St Brigid's Marrickville when that remarkable titular organist was starting and raising her young family. This led on to two periods (1964 to 1972, then 1975 to 1978) when he held the appointment of organist at St Mary's Cathedral.

He had graduated from Sydney University with training in History, English Literature, Latin and Philosophy. After eight years as a public servant, he commenced a career in teaching, working in turn at Westmead, St John's Lakemba, St Augustine's Brookvale and Riverview College, the last of which sponsored his formal training at UNSW as a professional archivist, to the long-term benefit of the college. Meanwhile, he had been active in the study and practice of genealogy, the musicology of colonial Australia and local history.

His major contribution to writings about the craft of genealogy is *Roots and Branches, Ancestry for Australians* (1979). He had already contributed strongly to the work of the Society of Australian Genealogists (SAG), which made him a fellow and life member. 'Robert Dalley-Scarlett (1887–1959): musician—historian—bibliophile' (1962), concerning his uncle Bob, is one of the papers he presented to the SAG, subsequently published in its journal *Descent*.

Eight of Lea-Scarlett's 19 entries in the *Australian Dictionary of Biography* relate to musicians, but other contributions include Mei Quong Tart, merchant and philanthropist, whose spouse was Margaret Scarlett.

He contributed the chapter on music, choir and organ in *St Mary's Cathedral Sydney 1821–1971* edited by Patrick O'Farrell (1971). In the previous year, his article 'Music-making in early Sydney' was published in *Miscellanea musicologica: Adelaide Studies in Musicology* 5 (1970), 26–57. Later, he would present 'A cathedral reaches out—the impact of St. Mary's music on Sydney life' in *Musicology Australia* 5/1 (1979), 173–190. During the years when the liturgical Guild of St Pius X flourished in Sydney, Lea-

* John J Kenny is a former public service lawyer who sang in the St Mary's Cathedral Choir in 1967–71.

Scarlett contributed articles to its journal *Hosanna* and co-authored a short tract *Church Music Today* (1973).

Lea-Scarlett's published texts in the field of local history include books on Queanbeyan (1968), Gundaroo (1972), parish histories for St Felix parish, Bankstown (1982) and Hurstville (1985), and *Riverview: aspects of the story of Saint Ignatius' College and its peninsula, 1836-1988* (1989). In 1983, the Hurstville Historical Society published his history of Catholics in St George. He co-authored a book of historic photographs of Canberra and Queanbeyan in 1986. The Queanbeyan City Council's museum holds his local research notes and his participation in oral history work in the Monaro is evident in the National Library of Australia. Unpublished works may also be found in the NSW State Library.

His article 'The Fitzpatrick Family' appeared in *JACHS* 2/1 (1966). His address to the society's Christmas luncheon in December 2004, entitled 'Earthquake, wind and fire: the writing of parish history', was published in *JACHS* in 2005.

Lea-Scarlett died after a long illness on 30 December 2019, aged 87. His body will be interred at Waltham Abbey, Essex, England.

OBITUARY

Dr Rosa MacGinley pbvm

Sophie McGrath[*]

Erudite pioneer in the area of the history of women religious, member of the pioneering Religious Research Centre and a Co-Founder of the Golding Centre for Women's History, Theology and Spirituality at the Australian Catholic University.

Sr Rosa died suddenly on the 11th November 2018 at the Presentation Convent, Herston, Brisbane. Rosa, officially, Mary Rose, was the third child of a close-knit family of four, two boys and two girls, and grew up on a sheep property thirty-two kilometres from Emerald in north-western Queensland. The MacGinley family was one in which a love of learning was nourished—their home was well stocked with bookshelves containing

* Dr Sophie McGrath rsm is the Director of the Golding Centre for Women's History, Theology and Spirituality, Australian Catholic University.

many literary classics especially of an historical nature. Rosa recalled that her father usually read for three or four hours a day throughout his life and it was in this environment that the seeds were sown for her love of literature and history.

Rosa enjoyed her carefree life on the property. While the MacGinley boys attended the small boarding school in Emerald provided by the Presentation Sisters the early education of the two girls was by correspondence under the guidance of their mother, a talented ex-student of the Sisters of Mercy, Rockhampton. According to Rosa school work usually occupied the morning which left ample time for such activities as the riding of her beloved horse. Every few days Rosa and her sister Margaret would ride their horses to collect the mail at the small railway siding of Gindi. The MacGinley family was strongly Catholic with the rosary being part of the family's daily routine and each Sunday they travelled the 32 kilometres of unsealed road to participate in the Mass at Emerald.

After achieving excellent results in the public Queensland Scholarship Examination, Rosa was enrolled at the Presentation Sisters' St Rita's College, Clayfield. Here she excelled, regularly winning prizes in the annual Catholic Readers and Writers essay competition. She passed the Junior and Senior examinations with the highest honours and was awarded an open scholarship to the University of Queensland. However, Rosa felt drawn to the religious life and on 23rd April 1951 entered the Congregation of the Sisters of the Presentation at Longreach. Here she spent two years during which time the Novitiate was moved to Manly (Brisbane). Here she completed her final year as a novice before being professed as a Presentation Sister in 1954.

Convent Life and Higher Education

Rosa's first appointment was to St Ursula's College, Yeppoon, a developing boarding and day school. This was a time when the 'hard sciences' of chemistry and physics were being introduced into secondary girls' schools. Rosa responded by studying these subjects herself and introducing them into the curriculum at St Ursula's. After fourteen years at St Ursula's, Rosa was appointed to St Rita's College, Clayfield where she taught for five years. Many years later, it was Maree Ganley, an ex-student of St Rita's College, Clayfield, and a mature-aged student at ACU, who led the charge for Rosa to be recognised as a significant contributor to education in Australia which resulted in Rosa being awarded in 2012 an Order of Australia Medal for outstanding service in the field of education.

At Clayfield Rosa undertook significant research at the University of Queensland. Her broad ranging MA thesis was titled: 'A Study of Irish Migration to, and settlement of Queensland, 1885–1912'. This led to her doctoral thesis titled: 'Catholicism in Queensland, 1910–1935: A Social History'. Subsequently, Rosa was appointed Superior at the Manly Convent as well as Director of the Junior Professed Sisters. After the first year she was sent to Rome to participate in the ARC program for religious women, which focused on Scripture and Theology. On her return Rosa continued working with those in formation in the Novitiate as well as with the Junior Professed. It was also during this time that Rosa, drawing upon her academic research, produced the significant publications: *Roads to Sion: Presentation Sisters in Australia 1866–1980* and *A Place of Springs: The Story of the Queensland Presentation Sisters, 1900–1960.*

The Post-Vatican II Era

Following Vatican II Council in the 1960's, Pope Paul VI, aware of the importance of historical research and the developing social sciences, urged that these areas of research be drawn upon to contribute to the future development of religious congregations involved in the various ministries of the Church. In Australia this led to the Bishops establishing the National Catholic Research Council. This in turn led to the major superiors of religious institutions in Australia commissioning a National Research Project on Religious Life in Australia. The academics appointed to be responsible for this project were Dr Carmel Leavey OP, Dr Rosa MacGinley PBVM and Dr Rosalie O'Neill RSJ.

Following the successful completion of this significant research project, Dr Carmel Leavey, aware of the ongoing need for such studies, took the initiative to negotiate with Congregational Leaders for these three key religious women academics to form the Institute of Religious Studies (IRS) to be at the service of the Church and the wider community. IRS was frequently contacted by researchers from various universities, including many secular ones, concerned with such significant areas of Australian life as Education, Health Care and Child Care and the many aspects of Social Welfare.

During her time with the Institute of Religious Studies, Rosa taught Church History at the Catholic Theological Union (CTU) at Hunters Hill, which was part of the Sydney College of Divinity (SCD). At that time Dr Sophie McGrath rsm was teaching the course Women's History Across the Ages at CTU and on many occasions consulted with Rosa. Marist Brother, Dr John Luttrell, who was teaching Church History at St Paul's Seminary Kensington, invited Sophie to teach the Women's History course at St Paul's Seminary Kensington, which was also part of SCD—it was common for the various member Colleges and Institutes of SCD to share courses and personnel.

As a result of this invitation, Sophie became aware of the Australian Bishops' major project on 'The Participation of Women in the Australian Catholic Church' when Dr Michael Costigan, Secretary to the Australian Bishops' Commission, enrolled to audit the course on Women's History. This led to Sophie later being requested to write the contextual history paper to accompany the final Report published as *Woman and Man: One in Christ Jesus*.

Genesis of the Golding Centre

Sophie suggested to Rosa that they submit a proposal to the Bishops' Research Committee for the establishment of a Centre for Women's History in association with an institution which had an ongoing life of its own such as the newly established Australian Catholic University (ACU). Rosa strongly agreed. In the proposal it was pointed out that mainstream history was mainly researched by men and mainly concerned with men and that it was this inadequate history which was drawn upon to inform social and political policies as well as various theologies and spiritualities.

Through Rosa's Presentation contacts we were able to involve Kim Power, a Melbourne lay woman, as a possible founding member of such a Centre. Kim had recently published her MA thesis which focused on St Augustine in relation to women. Lay woman Dr Anne O'Brien, lecturer in history at the University of NSW, supported the submission and with Sophie spoke to it at the Sydney formal hearings concerning the Project. Many others also registered their support.

The submission received support from the then Vice-Chancellor Professor Peter Sheehan, providing 'Theology and Spiritualty' were added to the title.

Pro-Vice-Chancellor Research W. Grichting, was most supportive and, as he was retiring, was anxious to get the project in place before he moved on. His successor, Professor John Coll, strongly supported the fledgling project giving the Founding Team every opportunity to flourish.

It was during this time that Rosa was completing her history focusing on 'Institutes of Women Religious in Australia', which was significantly encouraged by historian Fr Edmund Campion (Catholic Institute of Sydney). This was a wide ranging and demanding project that drew upon Rosa's background in Canon Law and involved work in the numerous relevant archives around Australia. This pioneering work was finally published by Crossing Press in 2002 in a book tilted *A Dynamic of Hope: Women Religious in Australia 1848–2000*. She was later to write several commissioned histories for Congregations of Religious in Australia—all thoroughly researched.

Shortly after the commencement of the Golding Centre as a Research Project in 2000, Rosa was requested by the Presentation Sisters to write a history of St Rita's College, Clayfield. She responded that she personally would not do it but would supervise a Masters Student at ACU in association with the Golding Centre to undertake this research. Anna Barbaro, a talented lay Catholic teacher, responded to the invitation and worked on the Master's thesis, which was duly published as a history of Sr Rita's but Anna was keen to develop it into a doctoral thesis. Alas, as is often the case with women students, Anna married and it was not until two children later and after Rosa had retired that Anna undertook this doctoral project finally titled: 'The Origins of the Convent High School in Europe and Its Implantation and Evolution in the Antipodes—A Case Study: St Rita's College Brisbane (1926–2008)'.

Following her work with Anna, Rosa supervised doctoral student Heather O'Connor, a retired teacher and political activist for women's rights. Heather had lived her early life in Ballarat and was greatly interested in undertaking a thesis on Catholic regional education focusing specifically on the Loreto and Mercy Sisters in Ballarat. In due course it passed the three examiners, including one from the Women's College, Oxford University, with high praise. The last doctoral thesis Rosa supervised was that of Teresa (Tess) Flaherty, a Sister of Mercy from Adelaide. Tess's research focussed on the Sisters of Mercy in Papua New Guinea where she had spent many years in various capacities including teaching at the University of PNG. Her work has been published and she continues to be in touch with and serve the Papua New Guinea community.

Even after her retirement Rosa was continually being approached by various people engaged in research projects—women and men, lay and religious—seeking her advice and often requesting her to critically assess their work. For a number of years after her retirement Rosa travelled to Sydney for the Golding Centre's annual Colloquia and always responded to the biannual Newsletter. While originally in a unit in a Retirement Village, in 2014 Rosa requested to move to the Presentation Convent at Herston. In these latter years she suffered from bouts of poor health and but, as stated in the Eulogy delivered on the occasion of her requiem Mass, 'she maintained a deep faith and was always the most generous, gracious women, abundantly gifted with the gifts and fruits of the Spirit.'

The news of Rosa's passing reverberated around Historical communities. While based in Sydney Sr Rosa was an active member of the Australian Catholic Historical Society and was Vice-President and Journal Editor. The ACHS James MacGinley Award for papers by emerging scholars was established by a benefaction of the MacGinley family and was named to honour of their father James. Rosa was also a foundation and active member of the Brisbane Catholic Historical Society.

Rosa had always been interested in the MacGinley family history and produced a 'booklet', as she modestly termed it, titled *From Donegal to the Darling Downs—the Story of Roger MacGinley and his wife Ellen Cannon.* Roger MacGinley migrated from County Donegal to Queensland in 1887.

Vale Rosa! Thank you for your rich contribution to the history of women in Australia. May there be successors to you benefiting from your pioneering work! You leave us with many challenges!

CPSIA information can be obtained
at www.ICGtesting.com
Printed in the USA
JSHW032200030520
5465JS00005B/104